Escape has always figured largely in Rosemary Bailey's life. Born in Yorkshire in 1953, the eldest of five children, she grew up with her Baptist minister father's sermons ringing in her ears. Eventually she escaped to a life of sex, drugs and rock 'n' roll, acquiring a southern accent and a degree in English and Philosophy at Bristol University along the way. Unwilling to take a proper job, she lived on a farm commune in Somerset before moving to London to become a journalist.

Rosemary met the biographer Barry Miles and escaped to New York for several years, living in a Greenwich Village apartment with a view of the Empire State Building if you leaned far enough out of the window. Back in the UK, she edited and wrote many travel guides, including the *National Geographic Traveler Guide to France*. Although her writing took her to Africa and the Far East, the Philippines, Hong Kong and Indonesia, France remained the dream.

In 1992, her brother Simon, a Yorkshire vicar, revealed that he was HIV positive. Rosemary wrote a book about his experience, the acclaimed *Scarlet Ribbons: A Priest with Aids*, published in 1997.

LIFE IN A POSTCARD

ESCAPE TO THE
FRENCH PYRENEES

Rosemary Bailey

BANTAM BOOKS

LONDON · NEW YORK · TORONTO · SYDNEY · AUCKLAND

LIFE IN A POSTCARD
A BANTAM BOOK : 0553 81341 2

First publication in Great Britain

PRINTING HISTORY
Bantam Books edition published 2002

3 5 7 9 10 8 6 4 2

Extracts taken from:
Catalan France by Basil Collier (J M Dent & Sons Ltd, 1939),
The Romantic Roussillon by Isabel Savory (T Fisher Unwin Ltd, 1919),
The Pyrenees Crown by Hilaire Belloc, (Methuen & Co, 1928)
reproduced by kind permission of Peters Fraser & Dunlop.

Set in 11/12pt Sabon by
Phoenix Typesetting, Ilkley, West Yorkshire.

Bantam Books are published by Transworld Publishers,
61–63 Uxbridge Road, London W5 5SA,
a division of The Random House Group Ltd,
in Australia by Random House Australia (Pty) Ltd,
20 Alfred Street, Milsons Point, Sydney, NSW 2061, Australia,
in New Zealand by Random House New Zealand Ltd,
18 Poland Road, Glenfield, Auckland 10, New Zealand
and in South Africa by Random House (Pty) Ltd,
Endulini, 5a Jubilee Road, Parktown 2193, South Africa.

Printed and bound in Great Britain by
Clays Ltd, St Ives plc.

For Miles and Theo

Acknowledgements

When I first began writing this book, I tried to think of it as weaving a tapestry. I had a great basket of many threads, some bright and golden, many dark. But as I sat surrounded by years of journals, photo albums, notebooks, and the stones of the monastery itself I began to feel like Rumpelstiltskin's princess and it seemed I would never finish. So then I thought of it as a patchwork quilt. I could sew different pieces of patchwork and then put them together. It has turned out to be a complicated quilt, and the pattern that has emerged has sometimes surprised me as well as others who know the story.

Friends and family have supported me in so many ways. For always believing it was possible I would like to thank Peter Ayley; Penelope Austin; Caroline Bailey; Irene Bailey; Frances Bentley; Peter Boyden; Kate Carr; Sara Davies; Leslie Dick; Robin Eggar; Jaqui Eggar; Michael Henshaw; Nicholas Inman; Kathy John; Hugh Johnson; Kate Hickmott; Suzie Mackenzie; Ilona Medved-Lost; Jackie, Pierce, Jack and Martha O'Carroll; Paulette Puig; Martha Shulman; Roger Williams and Peter Wollen.

My thanks to all who appear in this book and everyone else I have interviewed and talked to; Jacqueline Bergès; Kathy, Monique, Olivier and Pierre Betoin; Patrick Blot; André Bousquet; Lydie Bousquet; Skall Braun; Ludewijk Breel; José Caballero; Thérèse Caron; Martha Casulleras; Charles and Hélène Coll; Liliane Csuka; Piet Dankert; Marie-Jo Delattre; Michel Delaunay; Francis Desmet; Guillaume and Clemence Desmet; Isabelle and Nenes Didier; Helen Dixon; Robert Eek; Arthur Feeijoo; Veronique Flas-Desmet; Catherine Friloux; Alain, Clément and Pierre Froideveaux; Michele Galibern-Soler; Patrice Gintrand; Marie Goarin; Pascal Gomez; Marianne Goris; Louisette Grau; Michel Hadji; Albert Heijdens; Philip Hooper; Klara Kempenaar; Carole Laplace; Jean Llaury; Patrick Mereau; Monique Didier-Mereau; René and Yvonne Mestres; Rose Murray; Corinne Nanette; Danielle Oliva; Monique Padroza; Didier Payré; Arnaud Perpigna; Andre Perpigna; Michel Perpigna; Hans Peters; Helena Peters; Père Oleguer Porcel, Abbot of St Michel-de-Cuxa; Yvette Querol; Jacqueline Ramada; Abigail, Gwen and Robert Royston; Alain and Marie-Christine Ruel; George, Sylvie, Garance and Maxime Sarda; Henri Sentenac; Alain Siré; Martha and Sarah Stevns; Eileen Strange; Paul Tempelman; Paul Timberlake; Polly Timberlake; Lettie Uiterwijk; Gerard van Westerloo; Margriet Wijffels and Clara Villanueva.

My thanks are due to all the citizens of Mosset. I hope this book is an honest portrayal of a remarkable community.

I am indebted to the following books for information and inspiration; Thomas Culpeper: *Complete Herbal and English Physician*, Dorothy Hall: *The Book of Herbs*, Alain Corbin: *Village Bells*, Peter Levi: *The Frontiers of Paradise*, Patrick Leigh Fermor: *A Time to Keep Silence*, Dom Gregory Dix: *The Shape of the Liturgy*, Kathleen Norris: *The Cloister Walk*, Geoffrey Moorhouse: *Sun Dancing*, Jean Gimpel: *The Cathedral Builders*, Wolfgang Braunfels: *Monasteries of Western Europe. The Architecture of the Orders*, Jean-Jacques Ruffiandis: *Mosset: Vieille Cité*, Jean Bousquet: *Mosset: Le vingtième siècle d'un village pyrénéen*, and Michel Perpigna: *Mosset et le pessebre*.

I have been most fortunate in my editors. Thank-you to Joanna Goldsworthy for commissioning the book, and for her engaged and experienced editing, and to Sadie Mayne, for steering me through the final stages with great skill and patience. Thanks to Rina Fenby for correcting my haphazard French.

Thanks to my agents, Helen Allen, Georgia Garrett and Andrew Wylie, and to John Dunbar for the cover picture.

Thank-you to my husband, Barry Miles, who has, with his usual grace and style, succeeded in being both subject and scrupulous editor at the same time.

And thank-you to Theo who has waited with great patience for me to finish writing the book and permitted me to write about him. I hope his memories will be as good as mine.

Contents

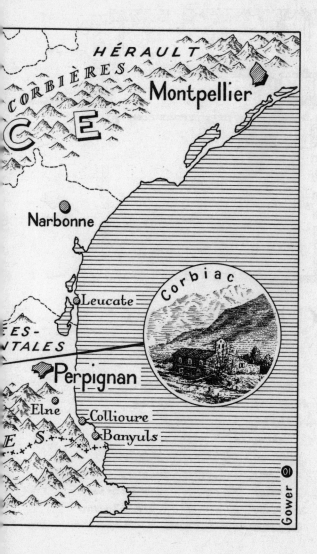

HÉRAULT

CORBIÈRES

CORBIÈRES

C   E

Montpellier

Narbonne

Corbiac

Leucate

ES-
NTALES

Perpignan

Elne

Collioure

Banyuls

E   S

Gower

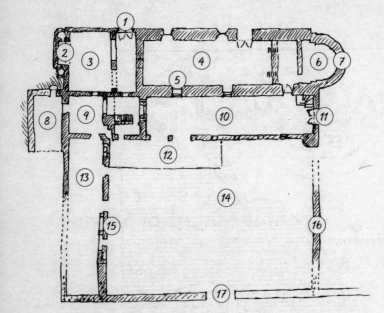

CORBIAC

1

A day in the hours of a monk

I wake to the sun striking gold on a stone wall. If I lean out of the window I can see Mount Canigou newly iced with snow. The rays of sun from the east illuminate the peak like a strong spotlight and light up the upper half of the valley. Below, all is still in deep-green shadow. When I look out of the other window, which faces west, I see that the sun has gilded the hilltops there too, peaks that rise up from the Mediterranean and stretch the length of the Pyrenees to the Atlantic coast. For a moment the whole monastery is bathed in the glow of the sun and I can almost feel the tilt of the earth as it greets the light. It is as if I am standing on a high mountain and not barefoot in my red dressing gown in the bedroom.

It is wonderful to live in a building with windows all round, to see both sunrise and sunset, to be constantly aware of the passage of the sun and moon. It was the way the monastery was built for the sun that first kindled my interest in the monks who once lived here. How cleverly they planned it. In winter when the sun is low it

13

beams through the cloister arches and the upper-floor windows and heats the rooms. The high summer sun passes overhead, leaving the rooms as cool as the stones of which they are built. But the chapel with its high windows on the north side of the monastery remains bitterly cold in the winter months, and I imagine the monks chanting the nightly vigil in the chill, candlelit darkness.

We have restored enough of the building so that again it feels like a monastery; we have rebuilt stone arches, rendered walls in ochre lime mortar, pleasingly rough to the touch, and laid handmade terracotta tiles on floors of solid rock that were buried under centuries of cow shit and cement. It is as if we have recaptured some of the spirit of the place, and it is since we have started to live in the renovated west end that I have most felt the presence of the monks, been able to imagine their daily rhythm of work and prayer, more palpable among cool restored arches than picturesque ruins.

The battered but beautiful thirteenth-century Romanesque chapel was abandoned by the monks at the Revolution and has been used as a barn and cowshed ever since. Once after going in for firewood stored there we forgot to turn off the light and it shone all night, the only light in the darkness of the valley, just as it would have done seven centuries ago when the chapel was built and there was a hermit in residence to keep a candle burning day and night. He would have been alone here, looking up at the mountains, watching the clouds scudding past and hearing the wind in the trees. The first monastery was built at some time in the sixteenth century, so for at least two centuries the monks chanted their daily offices in the barrel-vaulted chapel, cooked their simple meals in the great arched fireplace of the old kitchen and paced the cloister in silent meditation.

After the Revolution the farmers filled in the arches of

14

the cloisters, blocked the windows and widened the stone archways for cows, goats and sheep. Sometimes there is still an animal whiff about the place, though now the air smells of linseed oil and turpentine since only yesterday I treated the final patch of terracotta tiles we brought from Spain; on my knees rubbing the oil into the porous clay, admiring the variegated colours from ochre to orange. The Catalan artisan, Christian, who laid the tiles told me he had seen the very same ones in a thirteenth-century church in Arles-sur-Tech, a village in the next valley. I like to think the monks would have oiled their tiles too. Perhaps they had a field of flax from which to make their own linen, and pressed the seeds for linseed oil.

From the open stairwell I can see three stone Romanesque arches below, leading off the hallway, two of them newly restored. One curved stone has the faded remains of a fresco, a few arabesque strokes of pinkish lettering, their meaning no longer discernible. This arch leads down into our new kitchen, once, we figured, the abbot's quarters because the rotten old beams were embellished with carving. The kitchen too is terracotta tiled, with off-the-peg beechwood cupboards and work-tops, built in but dwarfed into submission by the sheer height of the room, the exposed stones and the arches.

There are so many arches – perhaps the one architectural component that now I could not live without. They have an organic sensuality which makes the regular angles and straight lines of ordinary doors seem lifeless and dull. The whole building is comprised of curves and round Romanesque arches, with only one inexplicable pointed Gothic arch in the south side of the church. It is only in northern Europe that the architecture needs the sharply articulated angles and needle points of Gothic to give it definition in the grey light. In the south the sunlight is so bright that the forms can be less precise, more rounded, more natural somehow. I admire the triumphs of Gothic architecture but with diminishing affection. Romanesque increasingly seems more human, easier to inhabit. Just like living in a southern climate; not for nothing was the Mediterranean the birthplace of Western civilization.

The arched glass door from the kitchen leads outside to a corner of the original cloister where there is a deep stone sink, probably the lavatorium, where the monks would ritually wash hands and head before processing into the church for the morning prayers. In this corner we have created a courtyard, with a bamboo trellis for shade strung between the wooden beams installed to strengthen the ruined walls each side. Below is a wooden table, chairs, pots of geraniums and yellow roses. We would like to add a vine and, round the walls, benches made from the huge oak planks, long slices of an entire tree, that supported the animal mangers in the chapel, oak which has hardened like iron and is smoothed from the constant action of animal necks.

Another of the arches leads from the hallway to the sitting room, a big tiled room that was once the monastery kitchen. It has a vast fireplace; perhaps ten people could stand in it. Instead of a fire of logs, we have installed a sturdy black cast-iron stove whose embers are often still warm from the night before. On the wall each side of the fireplace are bread ovens, terracotta tiled half domes inside, with stone apertures about the size of a large book, through which the loaves were slid with a long-handled paddle. We have lit them from within to display our treasures: small phials of Roman glass, iridescent with age, a head of a small terracotta statue, an Egyptian *shabti* tomb figure of turquoise stone, whorled shells and crystals, contemporary ceramic pots with cracked and golden glazes, made by a local potter.

The room is divided from the front door by two more arches, of narrow red bricks this time, a style that can still be seen in the Roman aqueduct at nearby Ansignan, still in use after two thousand years, channelling water to the fields and vineyards as it has always done. We fancy that Corbiac may once have been the site of a Roman villa, and have found fragments of Roman column to support the theory.

The furniture is minimal, rather than minimalist, since all the money has gone on stones. But there are a sofa and chairs of beaten-up brown leather bought from a second-hand shop, and colourful woven kelims on the floor. One we bought in the market in Prades, our nearest town, haggling in customary fashion for a carpet. It is patched and faded but handsome, and somehow all these old faded things fit together. The young trader, who bought the rug in Afghanistan, said the best way to clean it was to hang it out in the Tramontane, the great wind from the Pyrenees that howls down the valley on a regular basis. 'Let the wind do the carpet spanking,' he said.

With candles lit and the flickering light of the fire dancing shadows on the walls I sometimes think of the monks here, in their white habits, sitting around the hearth, warming their inks, soaking beans for tomorrow's lunch, and then processing into the chapel for the daily offices, to sing matins and lauds in the early hours, vespers and compline to end the day.

More and more I think of them, trying to isolate the elements of this extraordinary place that would have been the same then. There are indeed many. The mountains, the weather, the winds, the seasonal cycle of planting the crops, picking cherries and nuts, the wood-gathering and preparing for winter. Looking after the building itself, whitewashing walls, sweeping the stone floors, cleaning out wood ash, scouring dishes and making bread. I try to imagine a day in the life of one of the monks of Corbiac.

*

A Day in the Hours of a Monk, AD 1590

I wake to the ringing of the Abbot's bell. It is 2 a.m., the eighth hour since sunset. Time for vigils; the Night Watch. I rise from my straw mattress, sign myself with the cross and put the scapular over the habit I was wearing as I slept and the soft boots of rabbit fur we are permitted for the night offices. It is so cold in the chapel. And we must make no sound with our footsteps during these hours of the Greater Silence of the night. I sit on my bed with the cowl over my head until the Abbot comes, gently summoning the brothers from sleep with the ringing of his bell. All are assembled now, waiting in silence in the shadows of the cloister, shivering a little. The Tramontane is blowing down the valley, and the trees are moaning in response, but here within the stone arches we are sheltered. The wind has cleared the air; the stars are like diamonds and an ivory crescent moon is rising over the treetops. I can hear an owl, and the faint sound of bleating sheep. The shepherds also like to rise at this hour so they can guide their flocks to pasture to catch the morning dew.

With the bell still ringing we process in single file through the oak door with its skilfully wrought ironwork, hammered out here in the great forges of the Castellane river. We pause to dip a finger into the holy water in the stone stoup and cross ourselves. The floor is newly swept – I did it myself as part of my weekly duties, and I can smell the fresh bay leaves I scattered to scent the air. On the altar are the white linen cloths we look after so carefully, and which I smoothed using the heated glass ball kept specially for the purpose. The single candle of precious beeswax is lit, its flame flickering on the red and gold pattern of the frescos on the wall and the painted wooden statue of the Virgin and Child on the altar.

We recite the psalms and the lessons for matins, the night office, beginning in the early hours of the morning, the great vigil when all the world seems dark. '*Domine labia mea aperies*,' we begin as we always do, 'Lord, open my lips!' At first we are so cold it is difficult to concentrate; the brother who is in charge of the lantern tonight has to shine it gently in front of several eyes that are closing with sleep. Then the rhythm of the chanting takes over, and I forget myself in the repetitions of the familiar texts. The words lose their meaning and only the sound rises to God, as natural as the waves on the beach.

It is two hours or more before we have sung all the psalms prescribed, but it is as if time has stood still, as if we could have been there for centuries or merely minutes. For a while we enter together what our founder St Augustine called 'The now that does not pass away'. Then as we sing the *Te Deum*, 'The heaven and earth are full of thy glory', there is a first glimmer of light – dawn is breaking – there is a sense of climax, and our energy is renewed.

I feel hunger. We have been fasting in preparation for the great feast of 15 August, the Assumption of the Blessed Virgin, Notre Dame de Corbiac, with just one meal a day, no meat, and only bread and raw vegetables on Friday. But we have another office to sing before we can break our fast. We are permitted to walk around the cloister to restore our circulation before Lauds, the morning worship, and I can see the first rays of the sun coming over the hill to the east, shining already on the mountain called Canigou. They say that sometimes for the most holy souls on Easter day it is possible to see the sun dance at sunrise, but it hasn't happened to me yet. I banish thoughts of the beans I saw simmering on the fire in the kitchen yesterday.

The sun is shafting through the high windows as we return again to the chapel to sing lauds, the dawn morning worship. The demons of the night have fled; we are safe again. 'The sun has risen,' we intone as the light surrounds us, and our chanting is renewed.

The work day begins with Prime, the prayers we say together in the Chapter House. Here we listen to a chapter of St Benedict's Rule for the proper organizations of monasteries, and we are permitted to speak in order to confess our failings. One of the brethren is chastised for breaking the rule of Silence, and the Abbot gently explains why it is important to our vocation. He tells us that Benedict's Latin word for silence is *taciturnitas*, which means quiet or speechless, a quality attributed to a river and the stars. We must welcome wordlessness as a way to closer communion with God.

The fast we have just observed has perhaps stimulated an unseemly interest in food, and another brother enquires whether it is permitted to eat goose; is it meat or not? The cantor explains, after consulting one of the precious manuscripts of vellum, bound in tooled leather and closed with a clasp of bronze, that he keeps locked in the armorium, a great wooden chest, that this is a debate that has been going on for centuries. Since we are rarely permitted to eat meat, the question of whether fowl is meat or not is of great moment. The barnacle goose in particular some consider to be a fish, because it nests so close to the sea, and it can thus be eaten during Lent.

Terce is observed mid-morning; it is called one of the Little Hours of prayer, a brief moment of worship that always helps to keep me going a little longer. Then we celebrate the mass, with the Abbot presiding at the altar. All the candles are lit, a forest of lights illuminating the dim interior of the chapel, glinting off the crucifix, the chalice and the reliquaries, small boxes of wood holding the precious bones of St Donat and St Honeste, verified by the Archbishop and carefully wrapped in marbled paper and tied with red ribbon.

The light seems to shine from the chalice itself as I

drink, and that is the moment I most cherish, remembering the sacrifice of the Lord's blood, resolving to try harder to devote my own life to worship Him and the world He has made.

When we return to the cloister it is hot. It is the Hour of sext, and the Midi sun is high in the sky. All is quiet – the birds have ceased singing – only the buzzing of the bees and flies can be heard. The Angelus bell is rung from the great *clocher* of the monastery, its sound pealing across the fields. Everyone in the fields waits for the Angelus, a signal to stop, rest, say the noonday prayers, and eat the midday repast in the shade of the trees.

Before entering the refectory we ritually wash our hands and tonsured pates at the deep stone sink on the west corner of the cloister. My head feels smooth again because we were all shaved yesterday, one after another, in preparation for the feast. My habit and scapular are freshly washed.

In the kitchen the beans have been taken from the fire, the pots washed as St Benedict recommended. The new loaves have been taken from the ovens each side of the fireplace, the stone floor swept, and fresh rushes laid down. We wait for Father Bartolomeu, the Abbot, to enter the refectory, and wash his hands in the ewer of water held for him at the door. Each place is laid with plate, bread and a small cup of wine, covered with a little sprig of box to keep off the flies and, beside it, a twig of vine dipped in glue as a fly trap. We have taken only bread and water so far today, and the newly harvested beans are served, with a dish of onions and cabbages from the *potager*, the vegetable garden, mixed with wild green leaves of nettle and sorrel. Tomorrow, for the Feast of Our Lady, we will eat trout from the fishpond, lavender-scented honey from the beehives, fresh goat's cheese wrapped in bay leaves and figs from the orchard.

The food is blessed, we take our napkins from our

bread and the reading begins. Today's text is the 'Lives of the Popes', specially chosen as a suitable hardship for the fast. It is dull and the reader stumbles often. We eat in silence, signing to each other for our needs. I make the sign for more bread, using the first fingers and thumbs of both hands to make a circle, like a small bun.

St Benedict recommends five hours of manual labour a day. This is fulfilled by the brothers with work in the kitchen – preparing meals, washing the cooking vessels – and chopping wood to feed the fire and the bread ovens. We scythe hay for the goats and cows, thresh and grind the wheat and make bread for the poor of the village. We must also tend the animals – the sheep grazing the pasture beside the river, and, of course, the donkeys. We are called *Les frères des ânes*, the donkey brothers. When the Brothers must go abroad in the Lord's work, rescuing poor Christian folk from the Moorish infidel, they always travel by donkey, and it is important the animals are well fed, and not lame.

I have responsibility for the herb garden, where we grow herbs and medicinal plants, for cooking and treating ailments. One of our most important duties is to care for the sick and needy and there are many in need in the village of Mosset. The lavender is ready to cut, so the flowers can be pressed for oil. It has so many uses: for bites and stings, rheumatism, and burns, as well as relieving tension and insomnia. The yellow flowers of St John's Wort, good for wounds and bruises, and used to dispel melancholy, are already steeping in oil in the sun. I nibble a few feathery leaves of chervil which we can add to the salad tomorrow; it is excellent for cleansing the blood. A little comfrey will ease brother Antoine's bronchitis. The hyssop is thriving. Pliny said that 'bruises disappear under applications of hyssop', and we use it to prevent the spread of infection. The juniper too is good when the plague comes: we burn it to cleanse the air in

22

the sickroom. The rosemary hedge around the garden is growing tall; we burn sprigs sometimes as incense and prescribe rosemary tea for all manner of complaints as well as for stimulating the memory. They say that the bush will grow for thirty-three years, until it reaches the height Christ was when he was crucified, and then it dies. I weed carefully around the rue, since the leaves sometimes give blisters, but it is so good for the eyesight, and we sprinkle it, 'the herb of grace', before exorcisms.

The Feast of the Assumption of Our Lady is the day when we will pray for the healing power of these herbs in the months to come. It is also the time to bless the orchards, animals and fields around us. The next thirty days are Our Lady's Thirty days, the most blessed time of year, when all food is especially nourishing, all water healthy and invigorating. They say that a swim on the Feast of the Assumption or in the following thirty days will keep you healthy for the whole of the next year. Perhaps the Abbot will permit a swim in the river tomorrow. It is hot already and here in the cloister garden I need the big flat hat. Mount Canigou is clearly visible, and I recall as I work the psalm 'I will lift up mine eyes unto the hills from whence cometh my help'.

By mid-afternoon the day is fading. We pray at this hour for a holy death. The Abbot says we must have death at all times before our eyes. He says that knowledge of death helps us to live fully. It is as if one's whole life is played out every day as the sun rises and sets.

I return to the monastery in time for Vespers and the lighting of the lamps. All have put away their tools, and taken off their aprons, ready for the solemn celebration of vespers as the sun sets before the darkness descends. The wind has ceased now and it is quiet, serene. The trees are silhouettes in the dusk, and the first evening star appears. After vespers we walk in the cloister garden, where, with the warmth of the soil and the splashing of

the fountain, the scent rises from the herbs we have carefully tended. There is the fragrance of lavender, rosemary,
and thyme, recommended for infections of the throat, and
good in a pillow for dispelling nightmares. As I brush past
I can smell the vervain, a magical plant that keeps witches
at bay, and is excellent for headaches when it is made into
tea. I pause in my meditation to rub the leaves of santolina
between my fingers, releasing the pungent medicinal smell
that repels insects when the leaves are strewn on the floor.

As the night silence descends, all we can hear are the
crickets and frogs. Moths are fluttering to the lamps and a
bat swoops low. We return to the cloister, where the stones
still feel warm from the sun, and sup briefly, a meagre
ration of cheese and bread and a little wine. It is time for
the three short psalms of compline to end the day, and then
sleep. As darkness falls, the circle of the day is completed.

'A peaceful night and a perfect end grant us,' we pray,
and then exhort each other, 'Be vigilant,' as the night and
its demons descend around us. The Abbot sprinkles holy
water over us, and I am comforted. 'He has commanded
the angels to guard you in all your ways so that you would
not even dash your foot against a stone.'

Tomorrow we will rise again and follow the same
pattern and I am grateful for such order, such peace. The
tendency to be weary, melancholic, in despair, the sin of
accidie that besets all monks from time to time, is best
held at bay by the simple repetitions of the Hours of
prayer and worship. You can follow the path even
without knowing its end.

*

Now in the month of May at the beginning of the third
millennium we are planning to use the chapel again. After
two hundred years there will be music and singing once
more, with a concert in honour of Martha's birthday. A

24

soprano and a mezzosoprano, accompanied by a pianist, will perform a selection of classical music and songs to an audience of eighty of Martha's friends and ours. The pieces – by Bach, Mendelssohn, Strauss, Debussy, Berlioz, Satie – are Martha's favourites and the walls of the chapel have been hung with paintings and sculptures by friends, mainly local artists, most of whom she has previously exhibited in her own gallery in Suffolk.

All the ancient dust has been swept out, and plaster scraped away to reveal the painted crosses and patterned frescos hidden for centuries. Thirty years of straw have been shovelled out and reused as mulch for the new olive hedge.

The chapel is still in serious need of restoration – we need a roof fund, perhaps with one of those thermometers they put outside ailing churches in England; we need to fix the great gaping crack in one corner that scars the wall from vault to floor; we need to reopen blocked-up windows and we must restore the precious frescos. But for now the walls have been painted white, curtains obscure the rubble over the crypt, and clever lighting illuminates the fresco in the apse, the rounded east end of the chapel where the altar once stood.

Delighted to find a kindred soul in this obscure mountain village, we have become close friends with Martha since we met here over ten years ago. This is perhaps not surprising, on reflection, since we were both seeking the same things: beauty, tranquillity, mountains, a different space. Martha's fridge broke down yesterday, the day she arrived from England, where she lives most of the time, and the day before her birthday party. The obliging *marchand* in Prades who supplies our gas stoves, washing machines and wood stoves tried to deliver it here instead of her house. We both agree that we are flattered to be mistaken for each other. Despite the fact that she is Swiss and I am English, to people here we are both foreign women of a certain age, independent, bossy, bespectacled, with only one child apiece, and a peculiar penchant for buying dilapidated old mills and monasteries.

Before the concert we plan a reception in our garden. We have never had so many people here before but everything has been so well organized I haven't even needed to make a list. Glasses have been bought and borrowed, the fridge is jammed with Blanquette de Limoux, our local champagne, and our ten-year-old son Theo has carefully drawn signs for *les toilettes*.

Outside in the garden, now the wind has dropped the air is still, a few clouds hover over the mountain peaks in the distance and blur the blue sky, but it is warm. Thrushes and blackbirds are singing, a cuckoo calls, and swallows are diving. The grass has been trimmed and geraniums have been placed judiciously to mask the remaining piles of rubble. Under the shade of the big pine tree a table is laid with a white linen embroidered cloth and a big terracotta bowl of cherries. Miraculously the cherries on our trees have ripened just in time and Miles, my husband, and Theo have been picking them assiduously. An hour suffices to fill a basket with dark-red sweet cherries, and still leaves plenty of time for Theo to climb to the top branches, stuff his mouth with ripe fruit and practise cherry-stone spitting as well. If the branches are too high to reach they pull them down with the hook of the wooden bishop's crook that my brother Simon, who died five years ago now, left to Theo in his will.

Jacqueline has just delivered a tray of fresh goat's cheeses; white, crumbly, mild, they are perfect with cherries. Jacqueline is short, stocky, dark-haired, warmly friendly, ready to chat when she is selling her cheese in the village square. She keeps goats on a farm just above the village on the way up to the Col de Jau, the mountain pass that separates this valley in Roussillon, French Catalonia, from the Languedoc, the Aude department

26

and France proper. She is not from here, not Catalan; she is from the Languedoc, she says. To the local Catalans it is still another foreign world over there; one of the village gateways is still called the Porte de France.

We pick herbs from the garden to decorate the plates of cheese – sprays of spiky rosemary, soft grey leaves of sage, sprigs of thyme with minute blue flowers. After four years of planting tiny cuttings the herbs have grown tall, and I love to weed among them, rubbing the leaves between my fingers to release their fragrance. The cloister garden is still theoretical, since only two sides of the ruined walls remain standing, and it is divided into two terraces due to the incline on which the monastery is built. But now we can walk around it like the monks, or snooze among the bees and lavender in more secular style. One day we will move the old stone stoup, once used for holy water, and make a fountain in the middle of the cloister. For now there is a swing and a sandpit.

I go to pick scented yellow broom and white valerian to decorate the house. It is only later I discover the colours of white and gold are right for Ascension Day, the ritual colours for the end of May. Now I wonder if the colours worn by the priests at all the seasons of the church – the red for Pentecost, the gold for Christmas, the purple for Lent – were dictated by seasonal flowers.

The pine trees murmuring in the gentle breeze give us shade and accommodate a natural orchestra of thrushes, finches and sparrows, so many they weigh down the branches. A row of cypresses now stand sentinel at the end of the lower terrace where steps lead down to the field and river below. Cypresses, a recent innovation in this area, were at first scorned by the locals. What use were they after all? You can't eat them, and they provide no shade. But they add definition to the landscape, punctuating the horizontal lines of the abandoned terraces that rib the hillsides of the valley.

The peach trees that used to surround the monastery were all cut down last year. The EEC and cheap Spanish peaches made them uneconomic and the chemicals they had to be sprayed with poisoned the land. Next autumn we will plant lavender instead, and already I imagine the chapel surrounded by rows of purple scented lavender, and a lifetime's supply of lavender oil. Hans is busy cutting the grass around the peach-tree stumps to provide car parking for the concert guests, a lifetime of Martha's friends arriving from all over the world. Hans is a Dutchman who was a careers adviser in Holland until two years ago, when he advised himself to move to Mosset and run a donkey-trekking outfit instead. He loves this new outdoor life, his ruddy face tanned brown and his plumpness turned to muscle. He prides himself on his work-scarred hands, his new peasant persona, and cherishes being part of the village community. Propping up the bar, beer in hand, as if he has been there for decades, Hans mercilessly practises his French on anyone who will listen. He waves cheerfully at every neighbour who drives past the field as he chops logs and cuts the grass. The villagers note with respect how hard he works.

Albert, another Dutchman, as urbane as Hans is earthy, with a wonderful beak nose and thick curly hair, in rose-pink shirt and purple shorts, is adjusting the lighting for the frescos in the chapel. He is exhibiting several of his paintings and a large zinc screen, swirling abstracts of deep blue and orange oils inscribed with fragments of hieroglyphic writing. Albert was a theatre director in Amsterdam, until he lost his hearing and turned successful sculptor instead. He lives here in the summer months with his partner Robert, a retired teacher, currently remaking himself as a Dutch Charles Trenet, crooning sentimental French *chansons*. Albert is happily celebrating his second grandchild; he was married and had a son before he met Robert. I relish the fact that we

28

have not one but two gay grandfathers in this remote little village. The other, a retired Englishman who runs a bed-and-breakfast and sings in a local choir, has helped to clean the chapel, with the aid of his super-powerful vacuum cleaner.

I want to strew the church floor with bay leaves, lavender and rosemary as the monks would have done, but Albert demurs and I content myself with great baskets of lavender, the armfuls I have cut and dried every year, and lighting incense to mask the whiff of cow that we can still smell when the doors and windows of the chapel have been closed too long.

Bob and Gwen arrive with two huge canvases strapped to the roof of their green Citroën. Bob, big, muscular, with close-shaved head and football shorts, helps Gwen – who is tiny, dark and intense – hang her huge dramatic paintings: abstract expressionistic slashes of orange, yellow, black and vibrant green. They are British artists who have lived here in Mosset for ten years, opening their studios to show their work and kick-starting what is rapidly turning into an artists' community. Bob drills a hole in the wall in order to attach a great slab of soot-blackened stone, rescued from a hearth, echoed in the photographic collage he hangs next to it. It is typical of his work, which mixes found objects – burnt wood, stones, fragments of metal and glass – with an imaginary landscape of photographs and fierce heavily worked oils.

So many people have contributed to the chapel clean-up: the holes in the floor have been filled with cement, the walls whitewashed, and a huge wooden beam that supported the hayloft has been wrenched from the wall. Hans has tackled the centuries of dust, emerging from time to time looking like a chimney sweep, with trickles of sweat making runnels through the thick grey dust that coated him from head to toe.

Yesterday the mayor of Mosset himself arrived, with

the loan of a baby-grand piano wrapped in blankets on a flatbed trailer. The pianist is practising now, the piano tuner listening attentively, and music fills the building. The acoustics meet with approval. The singers are waiting to practise, too. They are women, women singing here for the first time perhaps.

This is our life in a postcard, in a monastery that lies at the centre of the Castellane valley in the foothills of the Pyrenees. It was only when we spotted the card in the rack in the village *épicerie* during our first summer here that we discovered the monastery is the favourite subject for local postcards. I like giving instructions for visitors and deliveries. 'It is the chapel with the Romanesque bell tower, on the left, past the *ferme auberge*.'

2

Monastery for sale

We had always wanted to buy something unusual, and looked at the oddest places before we found Corbiac. The South of France had long been my dream, ever since staying on a rose farm near Vence, where we woke surrounded by flowers and flocks of white doves on the lawn. I was ravished by tales of making love in mountains of rose petals. We revelled in the terracotta-roofed villages, sunshine glinting off the sea, fields of aromatic lavender and gathering bunches of wild mountain thyme from the hillsides. We visited houses in the Luberon, magnificently restored farmhouses with stone floors and cool dim kitchens, and picnicked high in the mountains, feasting on perfect peaches, ripe red tomatoes, fragrant orange melons. I had found a life so much more warm, sensual and colourful than my cold Northern English upbringing and I was hooked.

Our first attempt to turn the dream into reality, however, was typically ludicrous. When a Parisian friend told us about a house in Corsica he was thinking of buying with his lawyer, we saw our chance, counted up our building society accounts and decided that the Corsican nationalists, with their nasty habit of blowing up cars and buildings as a protest against French rule, were probably not so bad really.

We arranged to meet our French friend out there, flew to Ajaccio and took a train right across the mountainous heart of the island. Corsica is very wild and very beautiful and we were totally smitten. Napoleon said he could smell the herb-scented *maquis* of his native island from several miles out to sea, and I could understand why. Walking in the wild hills of Cap de Corse, through fields full of spring flowers and herbs, among clouds of multicoloured butter-flies, I truly thought myself in paradise. The beaches were deserted and I swam in sea that was crystal clear, perhaps still the cleanest in the Mediterranean. Visiting a place with a view to buying property is a fine way to learn about it, I decided: everything becomes invested with so much more significance and the pleasures are enhanced by the thought of establishing a permanent grasp.

In the event, our flaky Parisian friend never even turned up and our level of communication with the Corsican lawyer was pretty limited. The house in question turned out to be four ruined walls, rent with huge cracks, on a precipice overlooking the bay of Bastia in the north of Corsica. The view was spectacular, but the house barely existed. The fact that it was called Hangman's House did not increase our confidence. It was being sold by the lawyer's uncle, the Comte de Corse. When we enquired about the threat from the Corsican Nationalists, he simply said, 'Is no problem. We kill them.' Agile goats picked their way over the craggy rocks on the hillside and scattered below were the rusting skeletons of cars that had not made it round the hairpin bends. I fantasized about establishing a herb farm, calculating the cost of packets of herbs in London. We considered how we would rebuild the house, but even to us it was pretty clear that the whole idea was completely insane.

We moved to New York for several years while Miles wrote a biography of poet Allen Ginsberg and, apart from brief sojourns in the Hamptons and a trip to New Mexico, where I became enamoured of adobe houses and we considered buying a ruined house in a desert ghost town, my exotic rural fantasies were put on hold. Miles in any case was perfectly happy with city life; indeed, he would most of all prefer to live in a hotel in New York. Even then my favourite places in the urban sophistication of Manhattan were the farmers' markets full of fresh rural produce, stalls piled high with pumpkins and apples, and the Cloisters, part of the Metropolitan Museum of Art in Fort Tryon Park at the northern tip of Manhattan. I sometimes escaped the bustle of the city to the scented medieval herb garden of the museum high above the Hudson river, and fantasized about one day creating my own.

When we returned to England my dreams of cottages, cats and babies resurfaced. Despite Miles's reluctance my fantasies prevailed. He has always found that the best way to deal with all my proposals is to say yes: it avoids argument and they rarely come to anything anyway. In this case, however, his method backfired. I suppose he is also a victim of feminism in his commitment to equality and personal freedom. He has always encouraged me to go my own way.

We began looking at rural properties in England, starting with an unconverted stone barn in Herefordshire. It was literally on the Welsh border, in the Black Mountains, and even then I loved the idea of living on a frontier, that I would be in England overlooking a Welsh hill. Two countries for the price of one, in a way, and all the intriguing elements of the conjunction of the two. The barn could have been splendidly converted but the farmer wanted more than we could afford to spend, since it was going to take twice as much again to render it habitable, and we reluctantly abandoned that idea.

We scanned property pages and particulars and considered all sorts of bizarre follies, making one gruelling round trip all the way to North Wales, to see a property on the Menai Straits, overlooking the vast sweep of sandy bay where the Sixties cult TV series *The Prisoner* was made. It was little more than a beach hut, with no services and really only two rooms. Still, Churchill had painted there and the owner had added a small tower with a flagpole. It was reached by walking across the sand, the same sand the property's toilets and drains emptied onto. It was a silly amount of money and it was much too far from London, but the view was amazing and we lingered. My abiding memory of the trip is picnicking by Lake Bala and skimming stones across its smooth glassy waters.

We very nearly bought another house in Symonds Yat, high above the Wye river in the Black Mountains, on the border between Herefordshire and Wales. It was on a steep bank dropping down to the river below, accessible by a dirt road, with a great tall cypress tree in the garden, and woodland above it, where we merrily planned a sculpture park. I only realized later the bank was so steep that the woman selling the house was clearly terrified of her toddler falling down it and into the river, and she was desperate to sell. (I never thought about the fate of the children I was anxious to have.)

The price was reasonable, so we found a local lawyer and commissioned a survey, and drove back to London with our car loaded with pheasant and fresh eggs, which were so much cheaper than Marks & Spencer's we were convinced we would be able to live there on nothing at all. Then the vendors phoned very apologetically to say they had received a higher offer. Later they called us in a panic, because the deal had fallen through, but by then it was too late. We had seen Corbiac and the die was cast.

Another visit to St Tropez had revived our fantasy of living a Bohemian life in the South of France. We stayed in Ramatuelle, a picturesque and expensive hill village perched above St Tropez, with rich Swedish art dealers we had met in New York. We sat on their roof terrace with glasses of cool rosé, and looked dreamily over the red-tiled roofs to the deep-blue Mediterranean, and thought again, why not? Well, there were of course a lot of reasons. Money for starters. And the cat we had only recently acquired as part of my master plan, a sweet little black kitten that had strayed a few streets from Soho and climbed over our yard wall. Despite Miles's sensible reservations my sentimental nature had prevailed and Kitty was installed. We had no child at that point, though this too was on my agenda, along with the country cottage. Miles, it must be admitted, was considerably less keen on these developments.

The truth of the matter was that he had no desire at all to live in the country, and it was becoming increasingly difficult to harness our different ambitions. He once wrote an article about his country childhood for *Country Living* magazine which received an overwhelming response from people who harboured similar treacherous opinions and were delighted to find someone prepared to voice their loathing. He had grown up in the Cotswolds before it became fashionable and remembered the dampness and penetrating cold, the mud and blood that was the reality of country life. I had always lived in small towns and had country holidays, which gave me a sense of unsatisfied longing for the space and landscape I experienced in brief, tantalizing visits. Miles was rural working-class and could not wait to escape. I was suburban middle-class, and grew up with my father's sentimental attachment to the Lake District and the Yorkshire Dales, exemplified by the Woolworth's reproductions of Constable on my parents' walls, and walks on the Yorkshire moors where my father would suddenly stop to listen spellbound to an ascending skylark.

Family holidays were usually spent in the Lake District, attending an evangelical Christian convention in Keswick; two weeks each July, going to meetings in huge marquee tents smelling of wet grass, singing rousing hymns and choruses and giving our hearts to Jesus on a regular basis. We stayed in a camp overlooking Derwentwater, surrounded by craggy mountain peaks. Accommodation was mainly in ex-military bell tents, or wooden chalets with iron bunk beds. Washing facilities were in rudimentary huts with cold water in enamel basins; chilly early mornings were accompanied by persistent Lakeland rain drumming on the corrugated iron roof.

I think my desire for travel was ignited in drafty church halls watching missionary slides of Africa and Malaysia. My uncle was a Baptist missionary in Brazil and I remember as a small child seeing him off, waving as he climbed aboard an unimaginably huge train, thunderously puffing steam in Darlington station, *en route* for Portugal and a ship across the Atlantic. He came back with pictures of grass huts in the jungle, exotic natives, baptisms in the Amazon and a large furry brown tarantula in a jar of formaldehyde with which we used to scare our school friends. I declared my determination to go everywhere.

Although I had spent much of my journalistic career writing travel books and articles I was never much enamoured of the trainspotting school of travel journalism ('You haven't ever been to the camel market in Rajasthan? I'm going for the seventh time.' Or, 'There's a wonderful little man who sells antique sarongs in the Jogjakarta market just past the spice aisle, opposite the chicken-feet stall.' Or, 'Of course you've really got to eat sheep's eyeballs when they are offered in Baluchistan, otherwise they won't show you anything . . .').

I travelled to the Philippines and wrote about rice-growing, went to see tea plantations in Java, lavender production in Yugoslavia, reported on the transport system of Hong Kong and perfume-making in Grasse. After the first visits Miles and I paid to the South of France I was totally enamoured and focused on it thereafter, writing many guidebooks and articles.

Brief visits were too tantalizing. I always wanted to know what lay beneath the skin. I think in truth all I ever really wanted to do was find the perfect place and stay there. Miles was certainly convinced of the pleasures of the South of France, so somehow we persuaded ourselves that this would be a respectable compromise for us both.

I began sending for particulars from estate agents abroad. We loved Provence, but we knew it was too expensive. Several friends had bought houses in the Languedoc and this seemed a good place to look. In truth I had only a vague idea where it was, but Miles looked up the sunshine ratings: Perpignan had 322 days of sun a year compared with London's 47, so off we went. It was 1988, the height of a property boom in Britain, and an old friend turned property dealer began to salivate over the prices in the particulars we had received and he came along to give advice, encouraging us further in our over-ambitious dreams.

One of the estate agents we contacted said they knew of a Romanesque monastery surrounded by peach orchards, which immediately had us drooling in anticipation. There never were any particulars for Corbiac, and it is hard to imagine how the reality of the place would have been rendered in estate agent's hyperbole:

FOR SALE. Large frescoed Romanesque chapel with monastic cloister wing attached, surrounded by its own peach orchard. Converted section with one large mezzanine above, kitchen and bathroom. Adjoining section with large living room/kitchen, two bedrooms and bathroom. Further range with original monastic fireplace, arched room, two further rooms in need of restoration. Two and a half hectares of land, adjoined on two sides by rivers, mainly used for peaches. Remains of cloister garden. Water and electricity supplied. Nearest village about 2 km.; town with supermarkets and all services about 10 mins. drive. An hour's drive to the Mediterranean. Magnificent mountain views.

It sounded completely mad. Just the thing we were looking for.

We booked ourselves into the Grand Spa hotel in Molitg-les-Bains, about three kilometres from the monastery. The hotel turned out to be a surprisingly lavish 1920s confection in pink marble in a deep gorge, surrounded by palm trees with huge gardens and thermal lake below. The spa baths were built entirely of marble; everything was carved marble – the baths, the basins, even the lavatories – pure white, pale green, pinky-red or black veined with orange.

As we sat for a drink under the palms on the terrace, the place assumed a Buñuel quality. It was the time of the Prades Pablo Casals music festival, and out of the hotel lobby a complete symphony orchestra appeared, dressed in penguin suits and long black gowns, carrying bassoon and cello cases. Meanwhile the spa guests, including children, wandered slowly by in white towelling bath robes, heading for the baths or the sinister-sounding 'plankton level' where they would be coated in green mud from head to toe.

We waited in anticipation for the next day and our appointment with the estate agents. As it turned out, they were the Estate Agents from Hell, but we didn't know that

38

then and Madame compensated for her husband's brusque manner with her charming English accent and seductive descriptions of glorious weather, mountains full of wild orchids and all the little restaurants they knew.

We got up early and drove up to see the property, following the winding road with its blind hairpin bends a further three kilometres towards the village of Mosset. We glimpsed the chapel and its bell tower from a turn in the road, but drove past it without realizing this was what we were looking for. Behind a sea of peach trees in full leaf, heavy with fruit, was a sturdy and solid Romanesque chapel of ochre-coloured stone, with a curved apse, a roof of scalloped grey slates and a bell tower, against a backdrop of hillside covered in trees and pasture. It looked exquisite in its setting, with the peak of Canigou rising behind it, and swallows circling in the cloudless blue sky above. There was no sound other than birdsong and the clicking of cicadas. The chapel stood there quietly as it had done for centuries, ready to withstand yet another onslaught on its integrity. We didn't know it then but we had fallen hook, line and sinker for the favourite tourist-office image of the Roussillon, a Romanesque chapel with snow-capped mountains behind. As often as not the picture also features pink peach blossom, but that was yet to come.

We were early and the estate agents had yet to arrive, so we ventured around the building, trying to make sense of it. Much of it was obscured with a thick curtain of ivy, embedded in the cracks between the stones and twisted round every iron bar. It was hard to discern much detail, but in one wall we could see a lovely pointed Gothic window beneath the leaves, and dogtooth stonework under the roofline round the apse, the curved east end of the chapel. There was a small white marble statue of a saint in a niche above the stone arch of the east door, adjoining the chapel. The door itself was ancient, deeply grained and weathered oak held together with bands of forged iron and studs. To the south side of the church we could discern the remains of the monastery cloister, a row of seven arches, all but two crudely blocked with stones and mortar.

The two open arches were obscured by mulberry trees on a raised stone terrace, and their French windows were shuttered. We tried to peer through them but could see nothing. It was very hot and the canopy of mulberry leaves created a cool, dim space. I sat down on one of the stone steps and felt at home. Miles had explored further, and was trying to date it all, exclaiming over the cut stones lying in heaps of rubble, and even what looked like part of a Roman column. I was already planning where I would put my table under the trees, and where to plant the herb garden. The property dealer was rubbing his hands in glee, comparing prices of rural property in the Cotswolds. 'You couldn't get a decent-sized three-bedroom house with a garden for this price!'

It was difficult to make sense of the building because half of it was in ruins and the rest had clearly been considerably altered. The chapel was obviously the oldest part, to which a monastery had been added. The cloister was on the south side, in accordance with the traditional monastery layout, built as a lean-to against the chapel, and there was a second floor above the arches, which must have been the monks' dormitory. The monastery had been extended to the west, but these rooms were all ruinous and the floors had rotted away. Most of the windows had been blocked up, so the rooms were in darkness. A cigarette lighter briefly revealed a huge inglenook fireplace with bread ovens on either side, presumably the monks' kitchen. Although the place was enormous it was hardly des. res.

Miles and I sat together on the stone wall at the bottom of the overgrown garden, the smooth granite under my fingers already warm from the sun, looked at the mountain in one direction and the green and fertile valley stretching away to the east. We could hear the rhythmic flow of the river below, though we could only glimpse silver flashes of water through all the trees and vegetation along its banks. Small blue butterflies fluttered over the waist-high stalks of fennel, which filled the garden and scented the air as we brushed past.

We watched tiny lizards darting inquisitively in and out of the stone of the wall, their colour changing through a chameleon spectrum of grey and green depending on the stone or grass on which they paused. In the field below, rabbits nibbled cautiously and swallows swooped in a constant ballet overhead.

It was a *coup de foudre*, love at first sight. It answered every one of my fantasies at a stroke: mountains and sunshine, flowers and herbs, old stones and space. Miles was already seeing it fully restored in his mind; his very own Romanesque chapel. We wondered fleetingly about the monks who built it, enjoying the idea of the place as a centre of peace and retreat. We both wanted this place but I don't think either of us confronted the reality of how we were going to live in it.

When the estate agents arrived and opened the wooden doors with a giant iron key, we found the interior was as disgusting as the exterior was beguiling. The smell of cows still lingered. Most of the ground floor was dark and windowless, and the rooms we saw above the cloister, having been used by itinerant labourers, were in a pitiful state, completely filthy, with crumbling walls, rotten beams, grease-encrusted stoves and a fireplace thick with soot that had spilled over the floor. There was an attic floor above, but a brief glimpse indicated sacking, dead rats, evidence of a leaking roof and little more.

Efforts had been made to restore the west end of the

cloister – which had been used by the previous proprietor as a holiday home – with French windows cemented in two of the reopened arches, but it was locked and we had no key. Perhaps the estate agents fobbed us off so we would not see how few actual functional rooms there were. We peered briefly into the chapel filled with tractors and antique agricultural equipment leaking oil, and noted with astonishment a large fresco on the ceiling of the apse. Our friend the property dealer decided it would be a perfect place for an indoor swimming pool. He was amazed that it was possible simply to turn up and buy a medieval building, surrounded by its own land, that was in no way protected as a historic monument.

Undeterred, we immediately said we wanted to buy it. People don't usually have surveys done in France; anyway, it was obvious there was a lot to be done. And, as it turned out, the Estate Agents from Hell would have made sure we didn't get to know anything too unpalatable. We learned later that they told a local builder assessing the work required on another house not to mention the death-watch beetle or the need to replace all the wood.

Having agreed to the sale, we were permitted a few days' grace to change our minds, but in principle the usual practice in France is to pay a 10 per cent non-refundable deposit immediately. When we turned up the next day to finalize the deal, the tenant farmers who grew the peaches rattled up in a dusty orange 2CV, anxious to know our plans for the land and whether they would be allowed to stay on. We had no idea then of the considerable rights they had anyway, but since we had given not a single thought as to what to do with the land, we said magnanimously that we would want them to carry on and take care of it for us. This seemed to have the required effect, and they retired wreathed in satisfied smiles. We had probably inadvertently committed ourselves to giving them rights over the land for several lifetimes to come, but there was no way we were going to become peach farmers as well as historic-building restorers overnight. One folly at a time. They were also pleased because I kept saying *si, si* ('yes' in Catalan), instead of *oui*, having just come back from a travel assignment in Italy. They seemed to think I was attempting Catalan, which in truth I had not even heard of up to this point.

We made our first tentative explorations of the village of Mosset, two kilometres further up the valley, stacked defensively on the hillside surrounded by its ramparts, the stone houses steeply terraced round the remains of the château, a gloomy wall of stone pierced by tiny windows. The roofs are terracotta tiles, the walls ochre render or stone and the shutters dark-brown wood. There is one house outside the village with Mediterranean blue shutters, but the local tradition is more Pyrenean than Mediterranean. The whole village looks more Spanish than French, its stark outline and craggy backdrop making it quite different from the whitewashed walls overhung with purple bougainvillaea of Provençal hill villages.

Although it was midsummer, the village was quiet, rather dingy, with many of the houses closed and shuttered. A couple of dogs were sniffing round the square in front of the church and there was the usual quotient of dog dirt in the streets. A few elderly men in flat caps and blue dungarees, sitting on the parapet overlooking the valley, stared at us as we walked past. An old lady in a pinafore passed with a basket of lettuce. The church had a pine tree growing out of its bell tower, and looked in need of restoration, just like ours. There was no café open, and only two shops: an *épicerie* and a *boulangerie*. Among the eggs, vegetables, cartons of Long Life milk, slippers and flower-sprigged pinafores for sale, the *épicerie* stocked postcards. It was then we found that

43

Corbiac was the subject of the local postcard, along with the statue of Notre Dame de Corbiac, the thirteenth-century Virgin and Child, once worshipped in the chapel. We began to realize what a significant part of local history the monastery was, and our sense of responsibility for our postcard property grew appreciably.

That night we were in a celebratory mood and, despite the road sign urging 'Silence, Prudence' on entering the spa village, we drank so much champagne that the property dealer ended up lying flat on the floor of the restaurant exuberantly waving a bottle. The spa-hotel staff were used to less boisterous invalids, enervated by frequent baths in the warm, soporific waters of the spa. They were bemused by our wild antics, which perhaps contributed to the calming menu on offer the following evening, an entirely white meal: a white almond soup, blanquette de veau (veal in a white sauce), and îles flottantes (white meringues). There were no other choices available. They did allow us to drink white wine with it.

We spent the next few days in a state of total euphoria driving round the winding mountain roads of the area, in the enormous Mercedes the property dealer had hired. Gradually we began to get our bearings. The monastery is two kilometres outside Mosset at the head of a pass in the Pyrenees. Mosset faces down the fertile Castellane valley to Canigou, at 9,131 feet (2,784m) the first high peak of the eastern Pyrenees as they rise from the Mediterranean. The nearest town is Prades, about seven kilometres away at the bottom of the valley, where a Route Nationale connects to Perpignan and the modern world. This is the département of Pyrénées Orientales in the French region of Languedoc-Roussillon, which spans the Mediterranean coast from west of Marseilles to the Spanish border. Below Prades the road snakes down to the flat plain of Perpignan, lush with serried fruit trees and vines in spring and autumn, dry and burnt in summer. About an hour away is the sea, with traditional white-washed fishing ports such as Collioure and Banyuls and the cleanly swept beaches of new resorts such as Argelès and Canet.

It was new territory for us, a land of mountains as well as sea, of rivers pouring fresh waters from the high plateaux, of vines and olives, of remote Romanesque chapels and hermitages, a land dominated by the peak of Canigou, the highest in Catalonia and the sacred symbol of the Catalans. It was already working its magic, drawing us as magnetically as it once attracted aircraft. Twice planes have crashed into the mountains, their navigation instruments confused by the magnetism of the iron ore deep in the mountainside.

We basked in the views of mountain peaks, the smell of herbs on the craggy hillsides, the little wayside stalls selling local honey, wine and *foie gras*. We soon discovered the region was an intriguing *mélange* of French and Catalan. Road signs were written in both languages, and the yellow- and red-striped Catalan flag was much in evidence. This was Catalan France, once part of Spain, and only French since it was ceded by Spain as part of the Treaty of the Pyrenees in 1659. It had its own distinct identity, a frontier land that had retained its own special character. It was always difficult to establish a mountain frontier, and both sides resisted embracing the national identity they were assigned. Even today the French Catalans maintain a cranky independence and passionate attachment to their Catalan roots.

We ate in restaurants with strange menus offering *alberginies farcides amb anxoves* (stuffed aubergine with anchovies), *anec amb peres* (duck with pears), *bacalla amb mel* (salt cod with honey), *guatlles amb salsa de Magrana* (quails in pomegranate sauce), *botifarra amb mongetes* (pork sausage with white beans) and resolved to investigate Catalan cuisine immediately. I seemed to have got my frontier after all.

I did at least insist that we looked at other properties the following day in order to make some kind of comparison, but in any case nothing we saw came close. One property was large and exquisitely restored, with glorious views from a wide stone terrace shaded by wisteria and jasmine and a lovely stone pool surrounded by trees. It was high in the mountains, up a dirt road that was at least half an hour from any tarmac, close to the wartime refugee routes between Spain and France. We were most disconcerted by the fact that the dog which greeted us had only three legs. The fourth had been bitten off by a wild boar.

Another charming house was in a little verdant valley with a river, spanned by a Roman bridge, running past a huge window. It was shaded and serene, surrounded by an ancient olive grove dotted with old millstones that would make perfect alfresco picnic tables. Even I figured out that in winter it would probably not get much sun, and the river, which looked so cool and refreshing in the heat of summer, might well have pounded right through the property in winter flood.

In truth, though, we didn't think about the winter very much, except to relish the idea of the small ski resort only twenty minutes' drive up the mountain from Mosset, and we never considered what would happen to the property under a winter sun, or lack of it. Fortunately it is well placed, unlike the house purchased by another English woman here, which is in a sunny valley during the summer months but in permanent shadow from the surrounding mountains all winter long.

We went on to St Tropez to stay with our chic Swedish friends again. When we told them, 'We've bought a monastery in the Pyrenees,' they were appalled. As we described the building and its remote situation they looked more and more dismayed, and advised us firmly to try to extricate ourselves from the purchase immediately. As we sat and ate lunch in Club 55, one of St Tropez's smartest beachfront restaurants, all manicured lawns and attentive flunkeys bearing iced drinks, Corbiac did seem rather unreal.

The vendor was a rich Italian who had spent only eight weeks there in the thirteen years or so he had owned it (along with the house on the opposite side of the river, which he had bought for his mistress – another saga). It transpired that he had mortgaged it six times, so all the various mortgagees had to be tracked down. One was so elusive that everything was held up for months. It turned out she was on a walking tour of China and could not be contacted. Or so we were told. It seemed such an absurd excuse for a delay it simply had to be true.

It took a further eight months before we actually owned the property. Never believe anyone who tells you buying property in France is simple. As the months passed, the negotiations became ever more arcane and mysterious. The Estate Agents from Hell hinted that we needed to move fast because someone else was interested in buying it. What they didn't say was that 'someone else' was actually the village itself, and much later it transpired that there had been a plan to establish at the monastery a tourist office for the valley. For a while I worried guiltily that we had inadvertently scuppered their tourism initiative; later, I understood village politics better. There was no way the three villages of the valley would ever have been able to agree on such an enterprising plan: each village pursued an independent, blinkered tourist policy.

In any case, we were already hooked. Or at least I was, and Miles's passion for Romanesque architecture had triumphed over practicality as he contemplated researching and restoring the lovely neglected old chapel. We had spent many travels searching out Romanesque architecture, the small frescoed chapels of Burgundy and the Loire, the great carved tympanum of Moissac near Toulouse, the secluded Romanesque abbeys of Provence, the Pisan Romanesque churches of Tuscany. Now we had our own.

Romanesque is the style called 'Norman' in Britain, because it was the Norman French who introduced the distinctive round arches. In Europe, the style is known as Romanesque after the Romans, because the wave of church-building that took place after the rise of monasticism in the eleventh century used the still-standing Roman arenas, aqueducts and triumphal arches as models. In particular they used the Roman basilica as the prototype church; its central nave raised above the side aisles to allow a row of windows above the arches – the clerestory – provided enough light, and its stone barrel-vault roof safeguarded against fire. This model was perfected until, with the development of the pointed arch, which could take greater loads, and the flying buttress, which ensured greater stability, the new soaring Gothic style emerged. Confusingly, the French use the word *roman* for Romanesque architecture and *romain* for Roman. In French, *romanesque* means sentimental.

Miles is a true Renaissance man, and along with his interest in punk and William Burroughs, the Beats and rock 'n' roll, has a passion for medieval architecture, which he had taught himself in the library of the Metropolitan Museum in New York. On one of our first dates I had suggested a country outing, and we ended up travelling to the end of a Tube line in London, to Ongar, to look at the only wooden-stave church in Britain, even then Miles's idea of a walk in the country. He had always been a member of the Society for the Protection of Ancient Buildings, and would read their monthly bulletin with scrupulous devotion, explaining to me the importance of lime mortar versus cement, to allow old stones to breathe; already he was anxious about the cement used over the last twenty years or so at Corbiac, which was leaching the salts out of the centuries-old stones and rotting them. The responsibility to look after the building was beginning to weigh upon us. And then there was the ongoing debate about how best to preserve a building: whether it should be returned to its original state or preserved with all the changes made to it, as evidence of its life – what Miles called 'the hardline Stalinist SPAB approach, to preserve the building exactly as you found it'. Should we open the blocked-up cloister arches again, or move the floor levels back to their original place? What about the bread oven added to the corner of the cloister in the nineteenth century? I had listened indulgently, never realizing how much of it all I would need to know. Somehow our disparate interests, mine for a life in the country and his concern for old buildings, had elided in this unlikely fashion.

Back in London Miles immersed himself in 'The Church Architecture of the Roussillon', a two-volume doctoral thesis he ordered from America, and rummaged about in the second-hand bookshops of Charing Cross Road. He discovered two old travel books to the region we seemed destined to live in. In Basil Collier's *Catalan France*, published just before the outbreak of war in 1939, we came across an entrancing description of our very own valley, the Castellane:

In spring the road along the valley of the Castellane is lined with wild columbine, snapdragon and convolvulus and anchusa; iris, eglantine and daisy; sun rose and veronica and pimpernel. Flowers which in England one cultivates with jealous patience in a garden grow here unregarded in the roadside waste.

49

The baths of Molitg are open in summer for the treatment of various skin diseases; very cheap accommodation is available, and the place has a pleasant rustic air. The road goes through Campôme, near which there is a farm-house with a private chapel. It leads to Mosset, a large boldly situated village which was once a stronghold of some importance. Its streets are narrow, steep, and rather dirty, but here and there, in a fragment of carving or a moulding round a door, are signs of former grandeur.

We recognized with a thrill Corbiac as the farmhouse with private chapel, and I at least anticipated the pleasant rustic air with unbounded enthusiasm. The dirty streets of Mosset were another matter.

Reading Collier's book we began to realize what an intriguing region the Roussillon was. The Treaty of the Pyrenees was signed in 1659, after many years of war between France and Spain, and this area bordering the French side of the Pyrenees proved a bone of contention between the French and Spanish negotiators. One tetchy official grumbled that the mountains weren't as straight as they looked on the crudely drawn contemporary maps. There were inconvenient rows of hills heading off in different directions, which defied geographical classification because there were no clearly defined watersheds. Even today these hills remain difficult to traverse.

Eventually the Spanish conceded half the Cerdagne to France, but the Spanish had the last laugh: one town, Llivia, managed to remain Spanish, because the treaty had conceded all the villages of the Cerdagne to France, but missed the fact that Llivia was technically a town. Even to this day, Llivia is a Spanish enclave surrounded entirely by French territory. It is not very easy to find, since the French still avoid signposting it.

Romantic Roussillon by Isabel Savory, published in

1919, was another revelation, the account of two women travelling together researching the Romanesque architecture and sculpture of the region, from tiny chapels perched high in the mountains to the famous cloisters of Elne and St Michel de Cuxa. I discovered, to my delight, that some of the original columns and capitals of the cloisters of Cuxa had been used as the basis of the Cloisters museum in New York. Miss Savory wrote flourishing descriptions, and her companion Miss Muriel Landseer Mackenzie, great-niece of Sir Edwin Landseer, did the drawings. They were intrepid, setting off on walks and climbs of twenty or thirty miles in a day, wearing rope-soled espadrilles and carrying their knapsacks of bread and cheese, seeking guidance from chance meetings with muleteers, shepherds or charcoal-burners. Describing their quest for remote monasteries Miss Savory wrote: 'In England one connects monks with sheltered valleys and fat, green lands; in front of us lay a country so emphatic a denial of these notions that it was almost staggering. On grey rocky heights backed by a snowy Canigou a grey old church weathered the seasons and kept faith with its builders; their choice of so bony and gaunt a country, offering the barest livelihood to man, was hard to understand. We should know the reason later.'

Would I ever get to know why the monks of Corbiac settled where they did, I wondered. I wanted to follow in the footsteps of these pioneering women, determined that I too should climb Canigou, though I favoured walking boots over espadrilles. Miss Savory goes on to point out how recent is the passion for mountain climbing. 'It would have scandalised the thirteenth century,' she says, describing the first ascent of Canigou by Pierre of Aragon, who set off in secret on his blasphemous expedition. An account of the ascent, preserved in the Vatican, by monk Fra Salimbene begins, 'Mons Canigosus. This mountain, never has man inhabited it and never has the son of man dared to climb it, so great is its height, so difficult and painful the ascent thereof.' Miss Savory observes drily, 'No ancient would have dreamed of doing such a thing; the Romans must have used the pass near the Tres Vents and known all about the ice and snow; but it would never have entered their heads to climb the peak, and I should think it would beat them to understand the passion for high places reached at great discomfort, for the sake of eating sandwiches 9,000 feet above sea level.' Miles, I suspected, was with the Romans on this one, and in any case such elevated picnics were still in the future.

3

When angels travel
the heavens smile

The following summer, 1989, we stayed at Corbiac for the first time for a month or so. It was difficult even to focus our eyes on the mountains. Long vistas are rare in London. Regent's Park or the length of Oxford Street was about it, and it had been years since we had stretched our eyes such a distance. Dominating our view was the ice-cream peak of Canigou; Hilaire Belloc called it 'the mountain which many who have never heard the name before have been looking for all their lives'. It is a constant motif here, the sacred mountain of the Catalans, a description which these days is rapidly at risk of becoming an estate agents' cliché.

It soon became apparent that a lot more than our eyes would be stretched – nerves, purses, muscles, parts we didn't even know we had. I was going to need all those unfashionable monastic virtues of patience, humility and thrift. There was a lot to do, even to make the living quarters habitable for a few weeks, and we stayed at the nearby *ferme auberge* for a few days while we set to cleaning. We arrived with the car loaded up with useful items I had been squirrelling away for years – pots and pans, dishes and linen. A few pieces of furniture remained from the days when the monastery was used as a farm accommodating one or more families, with servants and farm labourers, to look after the cows and goats, and tend the fields of corn, potatoes and beans and orchards of apples, pears and, later, peaches. There was a really big wooden table to seat ten, several wicker-bottom chairs, a kitchen dresser, some serviceable iron bedsteads, and a couple of wooden *armoires*, tall wooden cupboards. There was also a baby's wooden high chair, which I insisted on keeping, planning to clean it and repaint the peeling blue paint, hoping for a day when there would be another baby for Corbiac.

The peach farmers had cleared out the worst of the mess for us, in particular the old mattresses where rats had made nests, and they had left bowls of red rat poison everywhere. There were still plenty of mice, as well as giant spiders. We comforted ourselves with the thought that if the spiders were that big they were clearly keeping at bay other equally nasty prey.

There were several things we needed immediately, like a mattress and a fridge, although we hadn't a clue where to buy them. It was odd not even knowing the names of department stores or shops. With no Selfridges, no John Lewis, no Marks & Spencer, how was one supposed to know their relative reputations? It was like trying to select washing powder without knowing any brand names. In Britain I had strong preferences in choosing household goods. Here I had no idea which were reputable brands or household names, and had to start from scratch, from the images and the graphics on the packets.

A trip to Perpignan, about an hour's drive away,

yielded mattress and fridge, delivered by bemused truck drivers who couldn't believe they had got the address right when they arrived at the medieval chapel obscured with ivy and tall grass. We arranged the bedroom on the mezzanine floor of the west end of the cloister, where the previous owner had made a holiday flat, balancing our new mattress on an old iron bedframe, and hanging our clothes from hooks on the walls.

I scrubbed out the *armoire* in the kitchen, which we filled with our motley collection of pots, plates and pans, a new coffeepot, pepper grinder, and a few food basics such as rice and coffee, carefully secured with clothes pegs against the mice. The old white porcelain sink leaked and we didn't dare light the antique-looking gas heater, so we made do with a small camping gas burner for cooking and for hot water.

Our very first night we made a creditable barbecue of lamb with garlic and lemon, grilled peppers and courgettes, accompanied by couscous and finished with peaches from the farmers, all washed down with plenty of red wine. As night fell we saw a bushy-tailed red squirrel run along the branch of the pine tree and along the ruined wall, as if he owned the place. Bats swooped low across the garden, the cicadas chirruped, and we watched the stars come out one by one.

We didn't sleep very well. The old bed frame was uncomfortable and we were covered in mosquito bites. Every five minutes something hooted outside, the building creaked or there was a strange scrabbling in the rafters. There were no convenient light switches, so I needed a torch to go down to the bathroom, and when I switched it on it illuminated a giant red centipede scuttling down the wall. I spent the rest of the night miserably worrying about bugs and cursing the fact I had not thought to spray insect killer anywhere. I had heard there were scorpions, for a start.

Staying in a remote farmhouse in the Luberon belonging to Christine Picasso, in the days when our own house in the South of France was still a safe fantasy, I once encountered a scorpion sitting in the empty bath. I think I only identified it from the zodiac. I knew there was a traditional way to deal with scorpions but couldn't for the life of me remember what it was, so I screamed for Miles to come instead and he bashed it with a shoe. Later I remembered it was an incident in Paul Scott's novel *The Jewel in the Crown*, about India. You surround the scorpion with a ring of fire and because it can't escape it curls over on itself and stings itself to death. It probably wasn't a very practical solution for someone else's bathtub anyway.

First light was a relief and I got up to make tea, heating water in an old saucepan on the camping gas burner. It was early, the birds had begun singing their morning chorus, and the dawn was a dramatic spectacle of orange and purple over the hills. We ate bread and fruit for breakfast, and washed sitting in the white enamel hip bath, a half-sized bath with a seat, using jugs of warmed water for hair rinsing.

It was Tuesday, market day in Prades, so we went to shop. We strolled the streets and found that, like the Grand Hotel, even the pavements were made of the local pink marble. Perhaps we could use it too. One little green shuttered house had a plaque to the American monk Thomas Merton, whose book *The Seven Storey Mountain*, about his experience as a Trappist monk, was such a success when it was first published in 1948. He was born in Prades and spent his first years with a constant view of Canigou.

It was a typical small French town, with queues of people outside the *boulangeries* and several cafés flanking the market square, dominated by the square stone bell tower of the church and overlooked by the mountains.

Only the older folk speaking Catalan to the market traders reminded us that this was not typical bourgeois France but a frontier land. In the market there were live ducks, rabbits and chickens in cages, bagfuls of snails, stalls selling pottery and fabrics. We bought apricots, cherries, local goat's cheese, a variety of salad greens, bright red and yellow peppers, glossy purple aubergines and a pot of basil to put on the windowsill (said to keep away mosquitoes, but in any case an essential summer herb.) We bought delicious local green olives, anchovies from Collioure and pickled lemons – these a sign of how far south we had come – perfect for making Moroccan chicken when we got home again. For sale were the local blue trout from the deep, cold water of Lake Nohèdes in the next valley, still swimming around in a tank. You chose the ones you wanted and then they were cheerfully banged on the head with a wooden stick and popped into a plastic bag. You had to gut them yourself of course.

Our shopping list also included more prosaic cleaning materials – dustpan and brush, pegs, buckets and rubber gloves. Miles bought himself a vicious-looking machete and I purchased the first of many baskets. How quickly we reverted to our respective hunting-and-gathering roles.

We had our first proper lunch, bringing out the rickety old wooden table from the kitchen onto the terrace under the shade of the mulberry trees. Their branches created a dim canopy that was welcome in the intense sun of August, but obscured rather more of the view than we liked, so Miles chopped off a few with his new machete to improve our view of Canigou. I covered the table with the yellow Provençal cloth I had bought years ago and kept for this moment; our very own garden table. Outside against the stone wall of the house was an ancient rectangular sink, cut from the local marble, pale pink veined with grey and white, its shallow square bowl

57

cracked and pitted with holes. I dug out a colander from our boxes and washed lettuce and bright red tomatoes under the cold running water. We gutted the trout at the sink and grilled them on the makeshift barbecue we had found.

It was all so simple – an earthenware bowl filled with sliced tomatoes and strewn with Collioure anchovies, a plate of Roquefort and Cantal cheese and a fresh baguette. We opened a bottle of local rosé wine, putting it into a bucket of water to keep cool. The farmers had left us a huge trayful of peaches and I piled them extravagantly in the largest bowl I could find. There were both yellow and white varieties. The yellow was sweet and luscious, as only peaches fully ripened on the tree can be, but the *pêche blanche* was a revelation, with a honeyed sweetness like liquid sugar in the mouth.

Lacking hot water, I decided to bathe in the river, so I headed down the path and across the field below the monastery to the river bank, wearing my sarong and carrying the machete to hack away the undergrowth, feeling just like Robinson Crusoe. The air was so fresh, it felt like a new set of clothes every day. I found myself thinking the Castellane valley had to be one of the most beautiful places in the world; the flowers, the herbs, the smells, the mountains and rushing streams, birds and pine trees, all cradled in this valley which felt strangely secure. I dipped naked in a deep pool and then lay on a big flat stone to dry in a patch of sunlight that had penetrated the trees, and a dragonfly with iridescent blue wings perched on my knee.

Among our priorities was the hanging-up of the hammock, which we had suspended between a branch of the mulberry tree and the iron grille on the kitchen window. I dozed happily under the dappled shade of the mulberry leaves, listening to the sound of birds and the faint murmur of the river below, remembering the description of indolent Creole women in the Caribbean as hammock-dwellers. A hammock-dweller I would become.

I was determined to experience this rustic life to the full, so one day I went to help the peach farmers pick their crop, arriving at 9 a.m. to find all the pickers had already been there for two hours. By eleven or so it would be too hot to work, and time for the sacrosanct Midi lunch and siesta. Wooden ladders were propped against the trees and the farmers, Jacques and Thérèse, had two Spanish itinerant workers to help them. When the peaches were plucked from the branches they were right away loaded gently into rubber buckets and carried to Thérèse, who would grade them and lay them out in wooden *plaquettes*. Jacques carefully demonstrated which fruit were too *vert* to pick, and should be left on the tree a bit longer. He reckoned women's hands were better for picking because they were more gentle. Eventually I got the idea, mainly by touch rather than eye. Peaches must be one of the best fruit to pick – I once spent a day laboriously picking tiny blackcurrants, which are just about the opposite. Under the shade of the trees the scent of the peaches was sweet and fragrant. The firm skin felt so smooth I stroked one small perfect peach against my cheek. I asked Jacques if he enjoyed his peaches. He said he never ate them. At lunchtime Jacques picked figs from a gnarled old tree growing beside the field and recommended we ate them with Roquefort. Ripe black figs, salty Roquefort and sprigs of wild mint made a perfect picnic that day.

The farmers had been guarding the monastery assiduously for twenty years or so, and seemed amused and intrigued by these latest proprietors. They did everything they could to help when we arrived, cutting the grass in the garden, leaving us little gifts of eggs and fruit and home-made preserves, which appeared on the door-step long before we got up. It was a bit like medieval peasants leaving traditional gifts for the monastery of baskets of grapes or measures of corn. They invited us to their house several times for aperitifs and we struggled to communicate, sitting at their oilcloth-covered table, sampling Thérèse's home-made preserves and admiring the jigsaw puzzles of horses that adorned the walls; at the time we had no idea how privileged we were to be invited into someone's house. They were always offering advice, most of which we didn't understand. They were classic *paysans* and proud to be called such. '*Je suis paysan*,' said Jacques, indicating himself for extra emphasis, in case we hadn't quite got it. The word 'peasant' does not have at all the same pejorative connotations in French as in English; in France the *paysans* are considered the salt of the earth, guardians of rural life with considerable rights to the land, whether they own it themselves or not.

Jacques was compactly built and strong, like a little bull, with weather-tanned skin and glossy black hair. His wife Thérèse was a sturdy peasant woman, and as they had no children she worked as hard as Jacques on the land, swinging a pick on a stony field and hauling baskets of fruit or great bales of hay for the animals.

They spoke with a very strong Catalan accent, and indeed always spoke Catalan together, so communication was difficult, especially since their total lack of subtlety meant it was impossible to bluff. Jacques was either wreathed in beaming smiles or looked as if he meant to punch you. Every few minutes during a conversation with him he would stop, look at me anxiously and say, '*Comprenez, Madame Rosa Marie?*' I would then have to repeat what he had said to prove I understood. He had an engaging habit of visually demonstrating everything he wanted to explain. If he was offered a drink he declined on the grounds it might make him drunk, indicated by curling his finger in front of his nose. When they were given a letter for us by the postman because we still had

60

no mailbox, he imitated the *facteur*, and our need for a *boîte aux lettres* with a mime of walking down the street delivering letters. He offered to kill the dreaded ivy with a chemical product (still an all too common solution for any unwanted plants in these parts) and wriggled his whole body to imitate a withering plant.

Jacques had a very pragmatic approach to everything he did. Once, in the house on my own, I found a very large snake curled up on the wooden staircase. I simply shrieked and Jacques, who happened to be working in the field, came running. He took one look at the snake and chopped it in half with his spade. It writhed down the banisters in a terrifying death dance, and now I feel ashamed since it was only a grass snake.

Thérèse told me that the best way to overcome a fear of snakes is to kill one. She said it worked for her. But mostly I managed to eject them with the aid of a broom and a bucket, depending on the size of snake. And I learnt to stamp my feet as I walked through long grass, in order to warn snakes to get out of the way.

The only really dangerous snake anyway is the adder, or *vipère*, though the local peasants don't take any chances. I have yet to sample the legendary *eau de vipère* – made from a live viper pushed into a wine bottle and then drowned in eau-de-vie, its death throes adding to the flavour.

We had a great deal of rubbish to dispose of, and Jacques offered to help, by taking Miles (he called him Emil) to the town dump in his *camion*, a rusting corrugated-iron Citroën which looked more like a garden shed on wheels than a roadworthy vehicle. His idea of driving was to stay firmly in the middle of the road, swerving at the last minute if another car had the temerity to approach, knowing that drivers would do everything in their power to avoid colliding with a vehicle that did not look as if it could possibly sustain any more damage than it already had. Miles spoke virtually no French, and

61

in any case Jacques' accent made it especially difficult to communicate. So Miles took along his electronic translator, back then a bulky piece of hardware that probably had a vocabulary of only about two hundred words. Anyway, they seemed to manage, Jacques gesturing expansively and frequently taking his eyes off the road to peer with astonishment at the words flickering on the tiny display screen.

I think for them we were like creatures from another planet. The idea of England was unimaginable to them. They certainly had no desire to go anywhere else. Thérèse was born in the village, though Jacques was considered a foreigner, originating from Ria, all of ten kilometres away. As far as they were concerned their life here was entirely satisfactory: '*C'est mon habitude*,' it is what we are used to. It was hard to disagree. Even the notion of going to Perpignan, about three-quarters of an hour's drive away, filled Jacques with horror, '*Allez! Arrête! Allez! Arrête!*' he exclaimed, demonstrating an entire traffic jam, with cars overtaking, traffic lights, appropriate car noises and klaxons thrown in.

We asked them once if they ever took holidays and they explained that because of the work – the peaches, the chickens, the rabbits, the horses, the typical mixture of fruit-growing and *élevage* (raising livestock) with which they were engaged – they could only take occasional days off.

Their notion of a perfect holiday, they explained, was '*aller chercher des champignons!*' mushroom-hunting in the mountain forests on an autumn day – the *arrière-saison*, when the tourists have gone, the harvest is in, but the days remain long and golden. They would find *cèpes* and chanterelles and cook up their finds right there and then on a small spirit stove. It sounded just fine to me, and I wondered if Jacques would take me mushroom-hunting one day.

Sometimes they would stop work and talk, telling us what they knew about the building. Thérèse told us the story of the crow. *Corbeau* means crow in French so this is one theory of the origin of the name Corbiac. According to the legend the image of the Virgin Mary was discovered under a fig tree. Two shepherds observed an old crow cawing insistently in the tree, and there they found the statue. They took it to the nearest church, but a few days later the crow was back in the fig tree and so was the statue. Such a holy place clearly deserved a church. Such findings are in fact relatively common legends, and may indeed have happened quite often during the twelfth and thirteenth centuries when the Moors were at the gates and Christian images may have been buried for safe-keeping. However, one can't help but wonder at the convenience of finding such a holy signal in quite such a perfectly aspected location.

We went with Thérèse to see the statue of Notre Dame de Corbiac, donated to the church in Mosset by one of the farmers at Corbiac after the Revolution. Tucked away in a little side chapel, there she was, a lovely thirteenth-century Spanish wooden polychrome carving of Virgin and Child, rather small and crudely carved, and very touching. It was venerated by the monks of Corbiac for hundreds of years.

Miles and I were like children as we explored Corbiac all over again. The garden, if that was the right word for a cloister garth turned farmyard, was totally overgrown, with waist-high grass, weeds and giant fennel which gave off a fragrant scent of aniseed as you brushed through it. The land around was the premise of the farmers. The fields in front were neatly planted with rows of peaches, crudely fenced with wooden stakes and barbed wire. It was all watered by an ancient system of *arrosage*, with canals threaded along the hillsides, channelling river water to each field by a complex system of pipes and sluice gates. An esoteric system allots times and days to each farmer, and when their turn comes for the *arrosage* they lift the iron panels to divert the water to run round their fields.

Every few days the farmers turned up to release the water and suddenly it would come rushing through the channels onto the land. One day it overflowed and the water threatened to flood the house, and Miles had to go and work out how to block the sluice. Apart from the peaches there were two more fields, bordered by the river Castellane below, and a tributary, the Corbiac, flowing into it from the hill behind the monastery. Access to the rest of the land was difficult because of the brambles and weeds that encroached from every side. When we scrambled our way down to the field and the river the entire edifice with its stone ramparts and tower looked more like a feudal castle than a place of peaceful meditation. Perhaps these monks did not have such a quiet time of it after all.

Miles attacked the jungle of vegetation with his machete, hacking determinedly at the ivy, which had engulfed the building; some of the branches were as thick as my arm. He tore all the ivy from the walls of the church, concerned about the way the roots were digging their way into the mortar between the stones. Blissfully unaware of the damage it was doing, I had thought the ivy looked rather pretty and romantic.

Jacques was most impressed, I think, by the fact that this pale, slight, urban northerner was capable of any physical work at all. He decided to help and drove up in his vintage tractor which, like most of his equipment, looked about a hundred years old, and as if it had been used for almost every day of a hundred years. Jacques attached the tractor to the ivy trunk with strong rope. Between them Miles and Jacques pulled great growths of ivy from the walls, revealing a church window we had not even known was there. Jacques said Miles was better than a Frenchman, which at the time we took to be a great compliment. It was only later we realized that, since Jacques is Catalan, he has very little time for either the French or the English. Miles was concerned about the loose iron grille on the little Gothic window, all the original ironwork that remained despite Jacques' belligerent stewardship. So our next shopping trip had to include a bag of cement so Miles could secure the grille. He started to murmur about the need for his own cement mixer.

We sat on the terrace after lunch one day drinking coffee, the table covered in guides and history books and pamphlets about the Romanesque churches in the region, and tried to piece together the history of the building. There was once a Roman presence in the valley. One pasture is still known as the field of Scipio, perhaps requisitioned by the Roman army under Scipio Africanus (the general who ordered landings on the coast of Spain to cut off Hannibal's supply lines in 218 BC.) There may have been a Roman villa on the site of Corbiac, and then perhaps a château – there are enough reused stones to suggest an earlier building. Several other places in the Pyrenees (such as St Bertrand de Comminges) also demonstrate that earlier Roman building materials, stone columns and inscriptions have been ingeniously incorporated into later structures. Two small sections of column of our own we fondly believe to be Roman (and I still, probably sacrilegiously, think will make a very nice coffee-table base supporting a glass top). The etymology of the name may derive from the Roman name Corbiacus. Certainly the site is a fine place for a villa, just up from the baths in Molitg-les-Bains, nicely remote and quiet with good pasture and orchards around, and clear views of approaching Barbarian hordes.

There was also a medieval family of Corbiacs, of which

there were several illustrious members, including Arnaud de Corbiac, abbot of St Martin de Canigou in 1303, and Pierre de Corbiac, a celebrated troubador. The family died out in 1376, but probably had a château at Corbiac sometime before the chapel was built. Village legend still recounts the *droit de seigneur de Corbiac* to deflower the local virgins on their wedding night. The only other mention of the name Corbiac Miles discovered on the Internet, where there is a website for Château de Corbiac in the Bergerac region. One day we will go and buy their wine.

The first recorded mention in documents, however, is of the church in 1334, when one Bernard Pallo of Villefranche left a donation of candle wax, in those days a precious commodity. There would always have been a hermit or a priest to keep the candles burning in the chapel and recite the prayers in memory of the dead. It is said that in France there is always a chapel within a day's walk, necessary for transporting bodies to their final resting places. This must be true of Roussillon. Perched high on windswept plateaux and tucked away in dark forested valleys throughout Roussillon and Spanish Catalonia are many small Romanesque chapels of the same period. Simple stone structures, with rounded apses and bell towers, they look like a natural, necessary part of the landscape, they have been there so long. Not only did the worship within guarantee heavenly forgiveness but the buildings themselves provided places of sanctuary and order in hard times, which for most of the Middle Ages was most of the time. Corbiac is part of that tradition, its light a glimmering beacon in the dark valley.

We went to look at the chapel again, the metre-thick walls providing a cool retreat from the hot summer sun. As we stood, awed, in the grimy light of the nave, what seemed remarkable was how unchanged the chapel was, despite the appalling treatment it had suffered, with holes and doors piercing the original stone walls, huge quantities of cement, mangers for the animals and a wooden hayloft full of dusty straw and mice.

With the aid of a torch we could see the frescos better. Around the interior walls were painted several crosses, the Trinitarian cross of four equal arms painted in red in a circle and a huge, ambitious fresco decorated the interior dome of the apse, depicting the Adoration of the shepherds with the Annunciation to the left and the Holy Family to the right. The unknown artist added a jolly Corbiac crow to the family.

A shaft of sunlight came through the upper windows, dancing patterns on the walls. I remembered one of the photos my brother, Simon, an Anglican priest in Yorkshire, had framed on the wall of the rectory. He had caught glimmers of light on the walls of Durham cathedral, making shapes that resembled human forms, which he whimsically described as angels. He said he liked believing in angels, and suddenly I wanted to believe there were angels guarding this lovely chapel too.

When we went outside again, pausing to pick peaches from the nearest trees and sinking our teeth into their firm sweet flesh, juice running down our fingers, the heat struck like a hammer. We retreated again to the cool shade of the terrace, boiled water on our camping gas burner to make more coffee and nibbled Catalan almond biscuits from the *boulangerie*. We tried to picture the monastic buildings from the fragments that remained. They adjoined the south and west end of the church, in the traditional manner. There was still a row of seven cloister arches, built on solid rectangular pillars of huge cut stones, which originally had one room above, lit by five windows, where the monks slept. When the building was converted to a farm, the cloister arches were all filled in with a mixture of boulders and sometimes even cut stones from other wrecked parts of the building. The original floor was torn out and two new floors inserted and new windows were cut through the thick walls. This gave the farmers an attic, a floor to live on and a cow barn on the ground floor. Whenever a medieval arch was too narrow for animals to pass through easily they knocked out the sides to widen it.

At the east end an exterior bread oven was added, its cylindrical fat belly protruding from the corner of the building and topped with a round cap of terracotta tiles. Two walls showed remains of sundials, presumably used by the monks to tell the hours of the daily offices.

Another doorway and windows of cut stone had been inserted in the cloister arches on the west side, which were probably filled in during the sixteenth century when the building was fortified against the Huguenots. One lovely low arch frames a view up the valley. From the other side you look through the arch into the magical wilderness of the overgrown garden.

Some of the stones were not fitted together well, and Miles guessed that the monks probably built those themselves, attempting the manual work that was prescribed by St Benedict in the famous Rule, which, written in the sixth century, outlined how monasteries were to be organized and is still largely followed even today. Travelling journeymen masons would have cut the stones and left them laid out on the ground for the monks to put together themselves. This had erratic results, with some of the arches different sizes and some of the pillars slightly crooked. Like us, perhaps the monks were more cerebral than practical, more used to prayers than masonry work.

We discovered the monks' cemetery in the course of installing a new septic tank. Miles, less satisfied than I with the sanitary arrangements, had gone looking for the cesspit. A logical analysis of the pipes and their gradient led him to a likely spot, and an experimental dig or two identified what was little more than a large cement drum in the ground, completely clogged with roots from a nearby pine tree. We had already been warned of the dreadful smell that manifested itself after a week or two of occupation, and the previous owner apparently simply left again when it got too bad. A new septic tank featured high on the agenda.

The negotiation for the *fosse septique* was bizarre. Monsieur Basagagna, the *plombier*, was a typical Catalan in appearance – small, wiry and deeply tanned, wearing a tiny pair of shorts, and clearly not at all comfortable having to discuss business with a woman. Although my French was poor, it was better than Miles's, so I was always the one to negotiate. We looked up every word we could think of to do with plumbing and sewage and tried them all out. It was always easier to talk than listen and I chattered on about the roots of the pine tree and how to avoid them, but my pronunciation of *pin*, meaning pine, came out sounding like *pine*, meaning penis. It was only afterwards that I worked out why poor Monsieur Basagagna was looking more uncomfortable than ever.

Naturally we needed a new and very expensive *fosse septique*, and we were resigned to the fact that his estimate was bound to allow for our foreignness and total ignorance of plumbing. As usual Miles was thinking big, anticipating the day when we would have seven bedrooms, all with *en suite* bathrooms, and he ordered the biggest *fosse* available. The *ferme auberge*, which overlooks us from the other side of the road, later reported watching the giant tank being delivered. They were astonished because it was bigger than theirs, and they have rooms for sixteen guests. The installation of the *fosse* also necessitated intense negotiation with the farmers because it was necessary to run the drainage pipes across the peach fields. Special allowances had to be made to avoid the channels for the watering system, the *arrosage*, all of which cost us even more money.

When the discussions between plumber and peach farmer became particularly heated I succeeded in appealing to their sympathy by pointing out that it was very unreasonable for them to expect me, a woman and English at that, to try to negotiate between two Catalan men. It was the first of many encounters with Catalan men, with whom I attempted to deal from my feminist London/New York perspective with varying, sometimes disastrous, results. They found it difficult to do business with a woman, especially when there was a husband in the background, and I made no effort to compromise to their world, taking it for granted that I should be treated with as much respect as a man. I forgot that women only got the vote in France in 1945, later than most European countries, perhaps because it was still largely a rural population. As Miles put it, 'You have to set your clock back one hour and thirty years.'

In the end the septic tank was installed east of the church, and it was then we discovered that that was where the monks' cemetery had been. In the course of digging a very large hole the plumber discovered human bones. We weren't there at the time, and Jacques simply told the plumber to put the bones back, cover them up and not to tell anyone. Which was probably a fairly typical approach to archaeological discoveries in a place where change is considered the greatest threat of all and where the past is simply taken for granted, ploughed over every year as it has been for centuries.

4

A cavern of bandits
and thieves

Somehow through all the layers, all the overgrown ivy, all the displaced stones, the wrecked arches, smashed statues and ugly lavished cement, the monks of Corbiac slowly emerged, shadowy figures, true, but the only ones that could make sense of the building. It was difficult to discover much; from the complex palimpsest of the architecture that remained and the fragmentary scattered references in wills and legacies, we learned there had been some kind of monastic community early on.

The chapel was built during the 1280s, going by the dating of the stonework on the apse, but no information exists about who built it. At that time the village of Mosset was still on the other side of the river from Corbiac; it was not until the early fourteenth century that the village moved further up the valley to shelter against the walls of the Baron's château.

We scrambled across the river one day to see the ruins

of the original village church, St Julien le Vieux, even older than Corbiac, which is all that remains of the old village. It was in a sorry dilapidated state, its tumbled walls and arches overgrown with ivy and tenacious weeds, and a rusting old Citroën van had been abandoned next to it. Miles couldn't bear to see the ancient stones further eroded by the ivy roots, and started trying to tear them off. He has a sense of responsibility for old buildings that extends way beyond his own.

The property was owned by a local farmer and no-one seemed able to decide if the church ruins are therefore his property too. In any case he is totally unwilling to allow any archaeological digs and we can only speculate about its history from our vantage point on the other side of the river, with Miles making occasional forays to saw through the ivy again. Jacques suggested one day that there was once a secret passage, between the old church of St Julien and the monastery, but despite his vivid demonstration it is hard to believe a passage going under the river.

There is mention of a hermit at Corbiac, Guilemus Ernach, in 1364. He must have had some sort of accommodation, perhaps only a rough *borie* of piled stones, like the shepherds' huts still to be seen all over the Pyrenees. I like to think the austere stone vault to the west of the cloister might have been his retreat, complete with niches for saints and candles, for his bread and basic provisions. Hermits always had an important role to play: as well as keeping the candles burning for the dead, they rang the bells to scare away thunderstorms and other dangers, including witches. At the other end of the Pyrenees, in the Basque Country, is La Rhune, a mountain long believed to have been witches' territory; right up until the end of the eighteenth century the mayors of the surrounding villages were still paying a volunteer monk to live on top as a hermit for a term of four years, to keep the witches at bay.

There is a brief tantalizing reference to a brotherhood of Servites at Corbiac, an Italian order devoted to the sorrow of the Virgin Mary, and sworn to chastity, poverty and obedience in the Benedictine tradition. Going by the Romanesque style of the architecture, perhaps it was they who built the first monastery here, at some time in the fifteenth century. The name of the church, Notre Dame – our Lady – suggests a connection. But nothing is known about them and for a long time afterwards the monastery seemed to have been abandoned, although there were still records of funerals in the chapel itself and burials in the cemetery, with donations of money for candles and beeswax.

Then towards the end of the sixteenth century a small group of monks were invited by the Baron of Mosset to rebuild the ruined monastery and re-establish a community. They were Trinitarians, an order of Augustinian canons, who, like the Cistercians, wished to return to a stricter monastic rule. The Augustinians went back to the early church and the teachings of St Augustine of Hippo, basing their rule on a letter written by Augustine on the founding of a monastery. Augustine also emphasized the need for communal life, abstinence and poverty, but since his Rule gave little practical guidance the Augustinians still observed the same basic monastic organization and hours of worship as the Benedictines.

The Baron of Mosset and his mother, Doña Louise de Cruilles et de Cabrera, had decided to fund the foundation of a monastery at Corbiac, to ensure their own salvation and that of their forebears and descendants with the constant prayer and supplication of the monks. They gave to the order of the Trinitarians 'the chapel of Corbiac, with all its vestments, and altar ornaments, houses, *cloitres*, pastures, fields, vines, wood, gardens, rights, dependances, and legacies'.

According to the documents that still exist, in June

1575 Don Gerard de Cruilles et de Santa Pau, Baron of Mosset, handed over the keys of Corbiac to Jerome Garcia, Bishop of Aragon. He would have taken the heavy iron key to open the great oak doors with their elaborate ironwork, and entered the chapel. The floor was uneven, still bare rock in most parts, the cracks and holes infilled with cobbles. The floor would traditionally have been scattered with fresh rushes and newly gathered herbs, filling the air with the scent of bay and rosemary. Candles were lit and flickered on the freshly painted frescos of the Virgin and Child on the ceiling of the apse, the reds and golds glowing in the dim light. To the side of the altar was the new mausoleum of the baron, a tomb ready prepared for him and his descendants. The Bishop approached the altar, spread with a fresh white linen cloth, on which stood the statue of the Virgin Mary, the painted wooden carving of the Virgin and Child, which had been revered in the chapel since it was built. He named Pierre Oriola to be the first abbot of the monastery.

Over four hundred years later I attended a remarkably similar ceremony in the village of Dinnington in Yorkshire, when my brother Simon was made rector of his parish in Yorkshire. He too was handed the keys of the church, solemnly charged by the Bishop to care for his flock, and tolled the bells himself for the first time to signify his appointment. There is something strangely comforting in the light of so many centuries of dramatic change in the Church, not least the English Reformation and the wholesale dissolution of the monasteries, to find such a ceremony has endured through it all.

Throughout the Middle Ages, during the time the chapel was built and the monks later arrived, France and Spain were in a constant state of warfare, inquisition, famine and plague. Although the Castellane valley was remote from main events, it was always a place of passage, and the turbulent time made its impact on the village and the few priests or hermits entrusted with the worship at Corbiac. Although it was not yet then part of the French kingdom, the valley was very close to the Languedoc, which had been racked by the Crusade against the Cathars for much of the thirteenth century. Perhaps the proximity of such dangerous heresies stimulated the building of the chapel at Corbiac.

Between 1318 and 1325 was held the famous trial of the Cathar heretics in the tiny Ariège village of Montaillou, about fifty kilometres away over the mountain pass. News of the inquisition by the determined Bishop Fournier (who in 1334 became Pope, taking these invaluable trial records with him to be preserved in the Vatican, the basis of Emmanuel Le Roy Ladurie's classic account, *Montaillou*), the imprisonment of the entire village and condemnation and burning of many would no doubt have reached Mosset. The villagers perhaps sat by the fire, in wooden hovels shared with their animals, similar to those of Montaillou, and listened with shivers of horror to tales of the burnings. They would have heard the dramatic, appalling tale of the last stand of the Cathars at Montsegur, when 250 of the faithful were burned in a huge pyre – men, women, children and even invalids flung into the flames on their stretchers. And no doubt too they speculated about the possibility of the mysterious Cathar treasure that everyone said had been secreted away, deep in the vast caves of the Ariège, or even perhaps closer to home.

In the chapel of Corbiac is a huge hole beneath the apse, dug in the 1970s by treasure-hunters, and I wonder if it was the vague memory of Cathar gold, still undiscovered, that motivated them. One day that first summer we decided to investigate the hole. In the dingy darkness of the apse, Miles rubbed the thick dust on the floor with his foot. 'This is the springing of an arch', he said, 'and you can just make out the tops of stones. There must have been a crypt.' We figured the crypt must have been filled in when the farmers took over the building, and it seemed unlikely there would be anything there to see now. Then we noticed what looked like a step to the side of the buried arch, and Miles got a trowel and started to dig around the steps. As he dug, another step emerged and we began to wonder if there was an entire flight of steps descending. Feeling as if we had fallen into a Famous Five adventure, and lacking any other tools, I fetched a large spoon and set to digging and scraping too. We got very excited and completely filthy scrabbling away, until we had revealed three more steps under the dust and rubble. It was obviously hopeless, since the entire area needed to be completely dug out and investigated and we soon gave up. We still don't know what if anything is down there. Could there be tombs, relics, Cathar treasure?

Just as the land was breathing again after the Cathar Inquisition it was devastated by the Great Plague of 1347–1349, which killed at least 25 per cent of the population of Europe. It was widely believed at the time that fully two-thirds of the world's inhabitants had died. No doubt as people dragged their dead out onto the streets, and carted them off to the plague pit, it must have felt like that. Perhaps the bodies were not buried at Corbiac, but no doubt prayers were lifted up in desperation, if the priests themselves survived, if only to save the souls of the paid-up benefactors of the chapel.

In France the Hundred Years War spanned the fourteenth century and most of the Southwest. Meanwhile, in Spain the process of Inquisition and the battle against heresy that started with the Cathar crusade was perfected by the Holy Inquisition. Then came the Reformation, and throughout the sixteenth century France was racked by the Wars of Religion as Protestants and Catholics tore each other apart. The Huguenots, as the Protestants were called, wrecked entire cities in the south, tearing down and mutilating churches in Nîmes and Montpellier and murdering Catholics wholesale. In 1562 Protestant Toulouse legalized the slaughter of heretics, and mobs wrecked the statues, holy-water fonts and crucifixes of the Catholic churches. By 1570 there were 1,200 Protestant churches in France. But the Catholics fought back and in Paris in 1572 the struggle culminated in the wholesale slaughter of thousands of Huguenots in the St Bartholomew's Day Massacre. This was just three years before the Trinitarians arrived at Corbiac.

At the southwest corner of the cloister at Corbiac are the remains of a tower, part of the fortifications against the Huguenots who even threatened the gates of Mosset. In 1576 one Dominique Gil, a squire of Mosset, made a donation of 204 ducats of gold to the monastery for the newly installed monks to fortify the ramparts and the walls, 'so the religious could live peacefully and in security given the grave threat of the Huguenots who menaced the monastery so distant far from the kingdom of France'. Gil had a personal reason for the donation: it was in memory of his father, who had been murdered on the path near to Corbiac six years before.

Most of the tower is now gone but enough shaped corner stones remain to show how solid and menacing it must have been. We imagined rebuilding the tower one day. Who knows who we might need to defend ourselves against? Or perhaps we could put a satellite dish on top, or rent it out as a cell phone relay, as English churches are now doing with their spires to supplement their roof funds.

The sixteenth century was a hard time for all. The year 1565 was long remembered for the horrific cold. It snowed on St John's day, 24 June, even in the South. Descriptions of that winter in France are terrifying. The harvest was destroyed, the animals starved because the grain was eaten by the people, and fuel was scarce. Those without fuel stayed in bed, only getting up to eat every twenty-four hours. Water not set close to the fire froze, wine froze in the vats, iron pots suspended over the fire had icicles hanging from them, there was frost even on the bedcovers at night. Ice broke the boughs of trees. People on the roads died of exposure, the crests of cocks and poultry were frozen and fell off a few days later. Then several further bouts of plague occurred, the first beginning in 1560 and lasting for four years, which left half the village dead, and many more had fled.

Thus life was unimaginably grim when the Trinitarians arrived in Mosset in 1575. 'It was truly a terrible epoch,' says one local history. In 1553 the population of Mosset had reached its lowest point ever. There were only twenty-one hearths counted, that is households, so perhaps about eighty to one hundred people, compared with the end of the fifteenth century when there were sixty hearths, or now when there is a population of about two hundred.

It was hoped that the small band of monks could bring some sort of order and sanctity to the village of Mosset, by all accounts a hotbed of vice. 'A cavern of bandits and thieves', according to the Baron of the neighbouring village of Molitg, who complained that his villagers dared not go there.

The valley of the Castellane was no remote retreat. Instead the road beside the river below the cloister walls saw constant traffic. It was the main route between the Roussillon plain, Prades and Mosset, and thence to the Col de Jau, the high mountain pass into Languedoc, though in those days the route over the pass would have been no more than a stony mule path. Long files of mules in rich leather harness studded with copper nails and festooned with yellow pompons, led by muleteers in espadrilles and red bonnets, made their way up and down the track, bringing wine, minerals and salt and returning to the plain with iron, both raw and worked, wool and wheat, and wood for Collioure, then the main port of Perpignan, to build fishing boats. There were shepherds, monks, priests, soldiers, and desperate army deserters seeking refuge. Many, no doubt, would have sought aid, food or shelter at the monastery.

There was a significant number of foreigners, even in those days. In 1540 there were seven functioning forges and five mills in the valley, and foreign workers came from as far afield as Genoa, Toulouse, Gascony and the Basque country. Iron ore was mined throughout Catalonia at that time and in demand all over Europe, and there were then hundreds of forges in the region. In the winter season when the river was full enough to turn the mill wheels and the hammers of the forges, the valley rang with the pounding of the hammers, the sound of the axes of *charbonniers*, cutting wood for charcoal, and the air was heavy with the smell of burning charcoal and smelting iron.

It was rarely peaceful. There were frequent quarrels and family feuds, which often ended in murder; twelve murders were recorded between 1579 and 1581 alone. Then in 1576, only a year after the Trinitarians arrived, Mosset was ravaged by a rival baron with armed men. In 1580 another threatened attack led the baron Don Garau de Cruylles to arm the population and even the priests of Mosset with clubs of stones.

Fortunately, or, more likely, intentionally, given the flock they had to contend with, the Trinitarians were not recluses. As Augustinian canons, they combined traditional monastic life with an active mission to the world outside, preaching, teaching and caring for the sick; worker-priests, as it were. They did not come to Mosset seeking retreat and solitude, and nor did they find it.

The Trinitarians were an Augustinian order established towards the end of the twelfth century, dedicated to the

79

rescue of Christians held captive by the Moslems in Spain, North Africa and the Near East. Of their income a third was devoted to the ransoming of captives. Like the Benedictines they took the three solemn vows of poverty, chastity and obedience and also a fourth: not to aspire after ecclesiastical dignities. The Augustinians were often sent to restore abandoned or ruinous chapels and monasteries, and Corbiac was clearly a suitable case for treatment. Thus the first restoration began. The small community of monks, with lay brothers or servants to help them, set about restoring the ruins of the first monastery.

Despite their involvement in the community, the primary function of the monks was always prayer, a constant intercession of supplication for the living and the dead, in the liturgy of the mass, the psalms and prescribed prayers recited in the seven offices which took place over a twenty-four-hour day. Theirs was a long-gone medieval world, where everyone believed in God, everyone believed in demons and angels. The function of monks was no idle fancy; people depended on the clergy to keep evil powers at bay and to intercede for them and for their dead. It was pre-Reformation: nobody aspired to a personal relationship with God – that was for the priests – and people paid their dues in order for them to fulfil their role of protection.

The hermits in their chapels burned vigil candles and rang their bells to ward off evil spirits and the priests said regular masses for souls in purgatory. People believed in the magical efficacy of the eucharist, the power of the raised host, in the reality of transubstantiation, the changing of the bread and wine into the body and blood of Christ. The Catholic church comprised both the living and the dead, and the prayers of monks and priests were as much for the dead as for the living. Death was no mystery. It was a close and familiar companion. For many their total acquaintance was as likely to be dead as alive. Most children died in infancy; adults died young and few lived beyond their fortieth year.

Plague and famine were constant companions; pain and suffering were commonplace. It was a world where the flogging of servants, children and wives was taken for granted, considered a necessary discipline; a world without painkillers, a world where the populace regularly turned out to watch a hanging or a burning, an accepted part of the spectacle of life. It was a time when people believed in the efficacy of a double walnut for toothache, the benefit of a thread round a baby's neck to ward off the devil, or the picking of the right combination of herbs on St John's Day to ensure a good year ahead.

The monks had an essential role in a society where people had to believe in building up treasure in heaven since their lot on earth was often so pitiful. At best their example of faith and austerity was inspiring. It was only when they began to build up treasures on earth that they were rumbled by the general populace and tumbled from their perch.

The monks of Corbiac would have followed the same routine as that practised in any Western monastery, a version of the Benedictine rule. This meant observing a strict fast throughout most of the year, chanting the offices and spending time in meditation and silence. They were also expected to do manual work, looking after animals and crops, tending the garden, growing herbs and vegetables.

Others would prepare meals or help make bread in the kitchen. Those who could write might spend time copying out the sacred texts they used in chapel. In winter, with the wind howling, they must have welcomed any opportunity to huddle by the huge stone fireplace in the kitchen, replenishing the logs, warming their frozen hands and their precious inks. During the daily hours of meditation they slowly paced the four sides of the cloister, repeating their psalms.

When they entered the monastery they would take a vow of poverty, and they were expected to relinquish all their personal possessions. According to the Benedictine rule, dress for the average monk could be adjusted to the site and climate but it had to be of cheap local material. The basic Trinitarian habit consisted of a long robe of white wool, girded with a leather belt. Over this the monks wore a white scapular, a kind of tunic that hung to the ground and to which a cowl or hood could be attached. Over the scapular was worn the *frocus*, a shoulder cape. Drawings of the Spanish order show them with flat black hats with wide brims, a useful precaution when working in the sun. The Trinitarian cross, the horizontal bar blue and the vertical red, was fixed to the front of the scapular and the left side of the cape. The same cross can still be seen painted on the walls of the chapel.

In winter a pelisse and hood were permitted, for the long offices in an icy church. They would have had leather boots or shoes for daytime, regularly greased with pig's fat, and a pair of winter night boots lined with lambskins or rabbit fur in winter, and a pair of sheepskin gloves. On Maundy Thursday the chamberlain, who was in charge of the wardrobe of the monks, set out new shoes on four long poles in the chapter house. Old clothes were discarded, consigned to the poor cupboard. Each monk was permitted a writing tablet and a style, a wooden comb, a case of needles and thread, and a knife in a sheath to cut up food. They were shaved once a week, sitting against the wall of the cloister, singing psalms, and every three weeks or so they shaved their tonsures. They bathed twice a year, before Christmas and Easter. Bleeding was often practised; any monk might be bled when he wished, by leave of the Abbot, except in Lent.

One night we sat outside late into the evening. It was

warm and I still needed only a sarong and T-shirt. There was no wind and we could hear the church bells from Campôme, the village lower down the valley, through the still air. It was as if they were reverberating across the centuries. One almost expected to hear the monks' chanting begin in the chapel as they said the vigil prayers before going to bed. We watched the stars appear in a velvet black sky, trying to work out the constellations. Were they still in the same place when the monks were here, I wondered. The light we saw was old, I knew.

Despite their devotions, life in Mosset did not prove easy for the small band of monks, and after only eight months they were near despair. Not only did they have a lawless community to minister to, they were threatened by the Huguenots and almost immediately had to set about building defences. The church priests in Mosset by all accounts were as belligerent as their flock. According to contemporary documents, in 1562 two priests of Mosset had been accused of murder and grievous attack; Pierre Lavila, muleteer of Mosset, accused the priest Jean Brunet of raising his dagger and giving him a blow on the head. In 1583 a priest of Mosset was accused of stealing wheat sheaves from the monastery fields.

The monks by now were living in dire poverty, barely able to support themselves let alone look after their Mosset flock. There were a few meagre legacies to pay for prayers and candles. The Baron's mother tried to help out, and when she died in 1578 she left them a legacy of 200 ducats a year. Unfortunately her generous gesture seemed to be dependent on the successful exploitation of a new mine, which came to nothing. It seems the Baron welshed on them too. There were several bills presented to him by the monks but no sign of payment. In 1593 a meeting was recorded of the little band of monks in the chapel nominating a lawyer in a desperate attempt to apply for a loan.

By 1592 the Baron himself was in debt and all his

lands had been seized. In August of that year eight harvesters had their throats cut in a field by the Huguenots. The soldiers who were garrisoned in Mosset were accused of being in league with the brigands, and the village refused to supply them with wood. In retaliation the captain of the troops chopped up and burnt the furniture and even the roof beams of the château in the middle of Mosset. Then in 1598 treachery opened the gates of Mosset to the Huguenots, and 800 of them poured into the walled precinct of the village. After fierce fighting in the streets the brave citizens, who numbered fewer than a thousand, chased them out.

By then the Trinitarians had had enough. Their efforts to bring peace and order to Mosset were failing miserably. They applied for a transfer and improved accommodation in Perpignan, though there is no evidence that they got it. In 1604 a final assembly took place in the refectory, where the prior, Jerome Strada, and four of the brothers authorized the sale of a house in Mosset. The monastery was abandoned again soon after. In 1605 the Baron, Don Garau de Cruylles, requested to be buried in his mausoleum at Corbiac. Despite his penny-pinching with the monks he still made his will in favour of the chapel and those to be buried there with his ancestors. He was taking no chances with the afterlife.

In 1610 the monastery was taken over by another community of Augustines, who stayed until the Revolution, fulfilling the daily round of the offices and ministering to their flock, baking bread, and caring for the sick with herbs and prayers.

The evidence of the second group of Augustinians is more difficult to elucidate than the Trinitarians', despite assiduous study of the dusty old archives in the *mairie* in Mosset. At some time during the tenure of the Augustinians the west end of the cloister was blocked by an arched doorway which has been moved there from some other part of the building, on each side of which there are two large stones with curious holes through them, which have a groove worn away at the top by some kind of repetitive action, such as a rope. Miles figured that they must have come from the original bell tower and then been reused as spyholes when the chapel was extended and a new bell tower built at the west end. Who knows? Perhaps the Huguenots were still a threat. Above this door is a faded fresco, which appears to be the symbol of the Augustinians: a sacred heart and a book, which is a reference to the original work of St Augustine that inspired his followers.

Come the revolution, there were still four monks left in the monastery. During the intervening period Corbiac is only mentioned in relation to burials. It seems that when the cemetery in Mosset became full, and before a new one was constructed, the poor would sometimes bring the bodies of their loved ones to be buried secretly at Corbiac.

The French Revolution seems to have made little immediate impact on Mosset, though there is a story of one Bonamich who by 1790 had heard rumours of the events in distant Paris, and set off on foot in his clogs to find out what was going on. It took him a long time to return but when he did he was determined to show his fellow citizens and the lord of Mosset, Baron d'Aguilar, that times had changed. After mass on Sunday morning he sat down on one of the stone benches reserved for the seigneur to get his breath back after his walk down from the château. When d'Aguilar arrived his valet was about to chase the upstart from his seat, but d'Aguilar indicated they should go on and ignore the effrontery. He too knew times had changed.

In 1791, after the Revolution, the monastery became a Bien National, a possession of the state, and was sold to Joseph Prats of Mosset, for 26,300 livres. In 1820 it was sold to the Ruffiandis family, who remained proprietors until 1936. They turned it into a farm, and donated the statue of the Virgin Mary to the church in Mosset in 1823. Other fragments suffered a worse fate. The truncated head of a statue was kicked about as a football. In the course of alterations to the chapel in 1870 they found two statues of angels, which were handed over to the government. I wonder where our angels are now. A few other fragments remain. There is a head from a statue over the east doorway of the monastery, and according to the records there remains an altar retable and a stone Virgin over the door of the church in the next village of Campôme, and a mutilated Christ on the cross on the gable of *mas* St Julien on the other side of the river. Perhaps we should try and reclaim them all, like the Elgin marbles.

After the Revolution, the entire place was deconsecrated and used as a farm, lived in by several families. The great vault of the church was divided into two floors, with hay stored above and a huge manger below. The ground floor of both the chapel and monastery was used for animals. Miles noticed the level to which the plaster had been eroded by the constant pissing of animals to about waist height.

Until the late 1970s a family of refugees from the Spanish Civil War were living in the chapel, occupying the upper part of the apse, painting the walls a garish pink but fortunately leaving the fresco. Perhaps they enjoyed it, or perhaps they didn't notice it, so intent were they on their daily grind. The way the farmers simply moved in and inhabited the church and cloisters and adapted them to their own humble needs is a bit like the way the great Roman amphitheatres of Nîmes and Arles were adapted for housing in the Dark Ages: filled with hovels, their original Roman features were barely visible or noticed. But at least the building was not left to fall into ruin, as it might have been had it been more remote.

When we suggested the possibility of an archaeological dig to Jacques he was appalled. 'Leave well alone' was his philosophy. Hating the idea of change, he perhaps only accepted us since we seemed so completely clueless it was highly unlikely we would ever make any significant impact. He took his stewardship of Corbiac very seriously. He told us proudly that any visitors who had the temerity to stop and try to get a closer look at the chapel he would always threaten with a big stick, or even a gun if they seemed particularly persistent. It was a side of Jacques we had yet to see, but his feuds with the neighbours, we discovered, were legendary and the story of his fist fight with the neighbouring horse farmer is still recounted with great relish.

He explained his long-running argument with the mayor of the village over grazing rights for his horses on the mountain pastures. '*Nous sommes comme chien et chat*,' Jacques remarked gleefully. It all sounded very medieval to me – no different in essence from the sixteenth-century feuds over land and animals that racked the village of Mosset during the monks' time at Corbiac.

One day the farmers led us up the mountain to see the wild horses they kept pastured in the valley during the winter and then took to the mountain for the summer. Our little Renault followed their dusty orange Deux Chevaux, another vehicle as singularly battered as the *camion*. We climbed the steep, winding road for about half an hour; a dramatic, sometimes nerve-racking drive with hairpin bends and vertiginous drops, compensated by remarkable views of distant mountain peaks. The lower slopes are typical *garrigue*, a tangle of herbs and low-growing bushes, and the air is redolent with wild thyme, oregano and mint. Then you ascend to a different geographical clime. Fields and flowers give way to pine forest, dark slopes penetrated by shafts of sun slanting through the branches. At the very top is the Col de Jau, 4,500 feet above sea level, one of the high passes of the Pyrenees, often closed by snow during the winter. Here in summer it is like an alpine meadow, scattered with corn-flowers, asphodels, hellebore and wild orchids. Cows amble slowly across the soft, tufty grass, huge brass bells hung round their necks pealing sonorously.

The horses, however, were nowhere to be seen. So Jacques set off to find them, pounding up the hillside at a fast run, until he had disappeared from view. In the meantime Thérèse took us for a walk in the pine forest, where she pointed out the wild treasures to be found there nestling in the undergrowth, tiny pink *framboises*, fragrant *fraises des bois*, and little black *myrtille* berries, which we ate as we walked along and collected in my straw hat. About three quarters of an hour later, Jacques reappeared with the horses, enormous wide-backed beasts with glossy chestnut coats and black manes, accompanied by several foals. They came galloping down the mountain in response to the sound of Thérèse's voice. She patted and stroked their noses affectionately, reserving the best lumps of sugar for the leader, Mandolin. But when we enquired what they were kept for, she explained they were soon to be sent off to Italy to be processed for horsemeat, '*pour manger*'. She seemed resigned to the prospect, even rather puzzled when we asked if this made her sad. Jacques gave Miles his true stamp of approval by inviting him to go wild-boar hunt-ing with him, explaining that this would entail several days of camping out in the mountains. Miles agreed enthusiastically and we imagined larders full of *sanglier* paté for years to come.

We discovered how much we needed to do to the monastery after our first storm. It was August, the heat became humid and oppressive and finally thunder started to roll round the valley; the sky darkened to a muddy glare, and forked lightning slashed the skyline. It was very dramatic, and we opened the French windows to watch and inhale the strong smells rising from the earth and the grass as the rain began. As it drummed fiercely down penetrating the thickly twined trees on the terrace, we could hear a series of steady drips as the rain trickled through the many holes in the roof. There were already a dozen buckets in the attic to catch the worst of the drips, but these soon filled with water and needed emptying and replacing. Without them the water was soon going to run down the walls and through the floors. We had known the roof needed replacing; this, we thought gloomily, was incontrovertible evidence.

5

The meaning is in the waiting

We returned to London after our first few weeks at Corbiac with a carful of rapidly rotting peaches, and a great sense of responsibility. What had we done? During that first summer I had been sitting on the terrace in my sarong one day munching a peach, when several tourists turned up, asking to see the chapel. They looked simply disbelieving when I explained that I was the proprietor. I'm sure they thought we were squatters, and in truth our grasp did seem pretty tenuous.

There was no way we could live at Corbiac in its present state, and we had no money to do it up. Freelance life is always full of promise, but however decent an advance you get for a book it is always spent before the book is written, so we were always in debt. Our Bohemian life in the South of France began to recede like a mirage. I bottled the peaches in brandy and lined them up rustically on my kitchen shelf, arranged another new basket on top of the wardrobe. Miles put up a collage of photos of the building, and optimistically contacted SPAB (the Society for the Protection of Ancient Buildings) to find an architect, and send him off to survey the monastery.

Then life, death and the whole damn thing intervened with a vengeance. By the following year I was pregnant. True, this was all part of my master plan, but I had little idea what working while looking after a baby would involve. I fondly imagined I could put the baby in one of those Moses baskets and keep it under my desk. Writing and rocking the cradle at the same time like Harriet Beecher Stowe. Not so.

We spent a few weeks at Corbiac the following summer, 1990, while I was pregnant. We moved quarters, selecting the best of the two bedrooms in the farmers' wing – the one that didn't seem to leak too much – and painted the walls and ceiling beams white. Even with the little furniture we had, it looked pretty, and I loved to lie in bed and look out of the window to a vista of green trees on the other side of the valley. It was so peaceful, the air so fresh, and I wished desperately I could have my baby in such a place. I looked longingly at the old high chair we had found, and thought again of painting it ready for the baby.

Being pregnant was fine, and Theo was born in October. I even had a good birth, but I didn't cope at all well with the actual baby. The first night home from the hospital he screamed unceasingly and we had every baby book open and scattered all over the flat. He didn't sleep through the night for four years, and neither did I. I would spend hour after hour rocking him on my shoulder while I sang 'In the Bleak Midwinter' (a carol that was the only song of which I could remember both words and tune) and peered at the sliver of moon I could see between the London rooftops. Miles rearranged his books and we squeezed another room out of the flat.

I found myself increasingly frustrated at being in London, and anxious for more space, a cleaner, more tranquil environment. I took Theo to Regent's Park daily, but I hated pushing the pram across Marylebone Road through the noise, traffic and pollution. Trying to work was a struggle. I was fortunate in being freelance in that I could choose how much time for work and baby, but it was hard and the work suffered. Trips to America stopped abruptly, though I did manage to produce several guidebooks to France, travelling with Theo, but it wasn't easy. My abiding memory is breast-feeding Theo, aged six months, sitting in the car on the Promenade des Anglais in Nice.

Meanwhile, life in England was increasingly difficult. My father, a retired Baptist minister, died suddenly of a heart attack, fourteen months after Theo was born. Theo walked for the first time at the funeral, which I have always thought significant though I have no idea why. Eight months later my brother told the family he had Aids, and the world turned dark. He was an Anglican vicar, in a South Yorkshire mining village, and his prospects, inevitably, were grim. We knew he was gay and he seemed to manage to combine his priesthood and his parish work with his gay life. This was different, though, and for the next two years family and close friends struggled to keep it secret, sure there would be a terrible scandal. My own media contacts did not reassure me.

Trips to Corbiac had become more difficult, as it was hardly suitable for a small child. I did put Theo in the high chair at last, but there was no time to paint it as I had fondly thought in my prelapsarian childfree state. As soon as he could talk, he grumbled, 'Mummy, this house keeps falling on my head.' It was worse than camping, since tents don't crumble round you. We had patched up the building where we could, making temporary improvements such as replacing broken windows, but as we knew it all had to be rebuilt there was little point in doing more than the minimum necessary. We tried to tackle the plumbing problems, and Miles succeeded in fixing the worst leak in the kitchen with one of Theo's balloons. It held for a year or two. We blundered on, learning, invariably, from our mistakes.

The peach farmers continued to be supportive and loyal, and would send us Christmas cards with brief news. They emptied the leak buckets regularly, renewed the rat poison and protected the place fiercely from all comers. They always gave us presents: eggs, fruit, walnuts, jars of jam, and home-made *sanglier* (wild boar) paté. I brought them presents of Scotch whisky and Stilton cheese, but they had only the haziest idea of where we reappeared from every year.

When Theo was three we went again for a long stay, for about two months of the summer of 1994, both with book projects to work on. We scrubbed and swept again, tried to eliminate the large black beetles that had invaded the kitchen, and cleaned the mouse droppings out of the cupboards. We managed to create an office for ourselves this time, though if it rained there was always the danger of water in the computer. Theo had the other bedroom next to ours in the farmer's wing, but we had to position the bed away from the drips and rotten floorboards. Every time it rained we went up to the attic floor to empty out the buckets.

Miles tried to rescue the thirteenth-century oak doors we had taken down and replaced, to stop any further damage to them. He removed seven levels of repairs, layer upon layer of wood applied over the years to fix cracks and rotted planks. The accretions of centuries were removed, but as Miles stepped back to admire his work he stood on a rusty nail, and had to be rushed off to hospital for tetanus and antibiotics. For the next week he hobbled about with a broom to lean on, was forbidden alcohol and grew a beard for the only time I have known him in over twenty years. All his suppressed loathing of country life reasserted itself. The weather was terrible, with heavy oppressive clouds and torrential rainstorms. The best solution was to light a fire in the smoky fireplace, play music and dance. At least, Theo and I danced while Miles nursed his foot.

I was obliged to take on his macho tasks, disposing of dead mice, emptying the roof buckets and gutting trout. The farmers had left us a large rabbit – gutted, fortunately – but I had to chop its head off. I gritted my teeth, aware, as Miles reminded me, that this was the rustic life I had always wanted.

Theo coped with it all brilliantly, learning to say 'Bonjour' and almost as quickly 'Allez!' to the dogs that were always sniffing around. He wanted to help with everything, refusing substitute toys and demanding real hammers, trowels and brushes. His most vivid memory now, which he recounts with pride, is of the enormous thunderstorm that flooded the house and how he helped sluice the water out of the door.

The river proved a natural adventure playground for Theo, with huge boulders, shallow pools and little water-falls. Deeper pools were perfect for dipping in on a very hot day. Large trees created a shady green nave, and iridescent dragonflies flitted over the surface of the water. All Theo's experience of years of playground climbing was applied as he scrambled from stone to stone in his purple plastic sandals. He was intrepid yet careful, testing each stone, assessing the climbs and jumps before he attempted them. Pretty soon we abandoned our sandals and wellington boots and together scrambled barefoot.

We needed a direct path to the river, so my first task with my newly acquired garden shears was to hack a way through. I liked the shears: the big scissoring action needed to chop vicious prickly brambles and nettles compensated for months of typing. Afterwards my muscles ached from the unfamiliar activity but my wrists, which had been susceptible to chronic pain and weakness for years, suffered no damage at all. Indeed, the action of using the shears was very similar to the wrist-twisting exercises the physiotherapist had taught me to do every day. It was good to find a productive purpose for the exercise, like cycling to buy bread instead of pedalling an exercise machine.

Theo was determined to help me cut the path and we prepared ourselves carefully, with wellies and long trousers, Factor 25 and straw hats against the sun. I chopped away at the large brambles, clearing the debris with a rake. Theo followed with his little plastic seaside rake zealously scraping away at roots and branches. I found it much easier to involve him in my activities than to create imaginary play for him, much as I admired parents who invented games for their children. Theo appreciated joining in real tasks rather than play-acting with toy tool boxes and miniature kitchens. Not that I made the most competent instructor, since I had ignorantly chosen the worst time of the year to clear the land; we should do it in winter when the vegetation is least abundant.

From time to time Miles leaned out of his study window upstairs, pausing between grappling with the forest of technology he was trying to install, to watch bemusedly as we struggled with the natural world. We hacked and slashed and raked over a period of days, starting from the terrace steps above and then working up from the lane below. The bushes were already covered in huge juicy blackberries. While I chopped, Theo followed, picking blackberries to eat or pointing out particularly tempting ones for me to pick for him. I took the opportunity for some simple arithmetic. 'If you have five blackberries and take two away, how many do you have left?' But usually he spotted another one before completing the sum. 'Six!'

At last a narrow path through the undergrowth was complete. We were both scratched and bleeding but triumphant as we marched to the river through waist-high grass and flowers in the meadow. At the river bank I snipped away at overhanging branches and dense vegetation beneath until we could climb down easily to the water. We crossed to the other side; I kept one foot on a boulder while I swung Theo over to the next one. He helped to haul me up the bank, an achievement he boasted about for months. 'Like Big Ears,' he said. 'Big Ears is always helping.'

On the other side was a lime-blossom tree, *tilleul*, and I picked a big bunch of flowers to make a *tisane*. It is wonderful for sleep and delicious mixed with mint. The blossoms looked splendidly rustic hanging from a wooden beam in the kitchen. I discovered later that I picked them at the wrong time; the flowers need to be newly opened and fragrant, and picked straight away. I could foresee a critical time in the spring when I would have to struggle across the river every morning to test the *tilleul*.

At least Theo didn't eat all the blackberries, and we made a fine blackberry sauce to go with grilled duck breasts. I first consulted some recipe books, then extemporized with what I had in the cupboard. Put the blackberries in a pan, add about half as much water and a sprinkling of sugar. Bring to the boil. Add two or three tablespoons of matured vinegar (Balsamic, or *vinaigre de Banyuls*) and a little red wine, port or fortified wine (*muscat* or *Banyuls*, the local sweet fortified red wine is nice). Add two or three cloves, or maybe cinnamon, and simmer till the blackberries are cooked and there is not too much liquid left. Grind lots of black pepper over. Serve with duck.

It is also good cold, and works well with puddings and ice cream if you omit the vinegar and pepper. I pressed some of the blackberry juice through a sieve and some muslin, into little cocotte dishes; it set into a natural jelly overnight, and was delicious next morning with yoghurt.

That was also the year almost the entire family came to visit. 'Families are tough,' said Tolstoy. Or something like that. I found myself wondering quite how the French manage these month-long August sojourns *en famille*. I dragged them all to see the other sights of the region, including the Romanesque monasteries.

We went to see St Michel de Cuxa (pronounced 'Coosha'), the pre-Romanesque monastery just the other side of Prades, with its great remaining square Romanesque tower, surrounded by silvery olive trees silhouetted against the massif of Canigou. It was built in AD 950 and you can still see the awesomely simple barrel-vaulted nave with tall keyhole arches and a lovely vaulted crypt. Next to the church is the cloister, in ruins until the 1930s, with many of the stones looted and used in local buildings, including the altar stone, which was spotted supporting a balcony. (The rest, as we had discovered, were in the Cloisters museum in New York.) The remaining arches and carved capitals of local pink marble, now restored, surround a tranquil garden with a gently flowing fountain at its centre. The monastery has become famous as the setting for the Pablo Casals music festival, established by the maestro in exile from Franco's Spain and now a highlight of the classical-music calendar in Europe.

We climbed up to St-Martin-du-Canigou, perched on a rock a third of the way up Mount Canigou, founded in the early eleventh century by Guilfred, Count of Cerdagne. We saw the little tomb he carved for himself from the living rock, and the original church, now a dimly lit crypt. We observed the nuns who now occupy the restored monastery, silent and a little grim in their white

97

habits and black wimples, as they presided over a shop selling religious icons and canned drinks. I was glad to spot a homely row of wellington boots beside the gate of the vegetable garden and, once we had climbed above the monastery buildings to get a better view, their washing flapping in the breeze in an inner courtyard.

We took the hairpin bends up to the priory of Serrabone, first pausing at the bottom to buy a picnic from a shop selling local produce where the proprietor had set out great bowls of dough, covered in cloths, to rise in the sun. Serrabone too is on the side of Canigou, with a spectacular view of the surrounding peaks, which rapidly became even more spectacular with a massive electric storm that hit soon after we arrived. We watched the lightning flashes from the shelter of the single-sided cloister. The interior was cool and serene with its splendid tribune of pink marble columns, carved with mythical beasts, flowers and the rose of Roussillon. When the rain stopped we wandered in the lovely botanical garden of vines, shrubs and fragrant herbs.

There was an additional element of strain that summer. The cloud of Simon's illness hung over us all. What was going to happen? Would there be a massive scandal? How ill would he be; how would he die? Where? How would we all cope with it? How were we to tell the children?

I set off to drive back to England at the end of the summer blinded by tears, feeling the dream slip through my fingers. That winter was one of the worst I have ever known. I now had a full-time assignment working for a travel publisher, editing a guide to France, and Theo attended a nursery. My abiding memory is of walking hurriedly through London streets on dark afternoons to pick him up on time, worrying over what would happen to Simon, and how we were ever going to restore Corbiac. We knew the sensible course was to sell it and abandon the whole sorry folly. But still the dream persisted.

I worried all the time – I think that must have been when I got the first white streak in my hair – but one of the things that struck me most forcibly about Simon was his contrasting approach. 'I'm not a worrier,' he once said. Either through faith or the knowledge of impending death he had found a way to live in the present which I could hardly imagine.

It was as if the past had caught up with me. When we bought Corbiac the fact that it was a church was of architectural interest, and I gave little thought to its spiritual significance. Although I came from a religious family, I had left it all without a backward glance and gone in search of sex, drugs and rock 'n' roll. But I was used to having priests in the family: it was oddly reassuring. Somebody was doing the praying even if I didn't believe in it.

In the summer we had stopped at the tiny chapel of La Trinité on the slopes of Canigou. In the dim interior was a figure of Christ on the cross. It was twelfth-century, painted simply in gold and brown, a naïve figure with a patient face, quite incredibly moving, and I felt a profound association between this medieval carving and Simon. It tapped into a deep level of emotion that felt important, something I had left unplumbed too long, and I knew Simon's experience and suffering was something I had to share.

In his journal Simon noted that the Chinese pictogram for crisis also meant opportunity. Through his illness he saw an opportunity to continue his vocation and make some sense of his death. He felt that through his own suffering he could perhaps identify more with the pain of others; in an odd way it made him more of a priest. As he became more ill, he increasingly needed support, he became the carer in need of care himself. Gradually he told his parishioners about his illness. Although few were comfortable with the knowledge that he was gay, let alone had Aids, they loved their shy, bookish priest and supported him in his determination to stay in his parish rather than disappear discreetly as others had done. Until his death he continued to hold services and celebrate mass, offering the bread and wine to his flock.

As his health deteriorated he needed to be fed medicines and food via a permanent Hickman line in his chest, often for several hours a day, and in order to remain at home needed carers to stay with him through the night. The parish organized a nightly rota, and it became an oddly familiar sight: the vicar sitting in a corner of the sofa presiding over a meeting, or writing his sermons, with his IV line hooked up.

His archdeacon, a liberal, sympathetic churchman, was deeply impressed by the parish's ministry to their priest, a response that was so surprising in that hard mining village, and he suggested making the story public through a television documentary. After months of agonizing about the publicity, Simon finally agreed, taping his own video soliloquies about his illness, his homosexuality and his approaching death. Simon's honesty and courage detonated a remarkable response and he was briefly celebrated as 'the Vicar with Aids'.

At the same time, my roles as elder sister and journalist combined inexorably. I wanted to get to know this priggish little brother of mine better. We had always been fondly distant and I had regarded with detached amusement his ecclesiastical robes and liturgical chanting, his calligraphy and bow ties, his fondness for monastic retreats and photos of angels and rainbows. I used to joke about him becoming 'my brother the bishop' one day, and always rather fancied the Bishopric of Wells with its moated palace and swans fed at the sound of a bell. I wrote a newspaper article to accompany the TV programme and we decided I should write a book about what had happened in Dinnington.

It was one of those decisions that you know will affect your whole life. It was a profound responsibility and an extraordinary opportunity as a writer. I had to decide whether to engage or not, to watch from the sidelines or get involved. One day I knelt to take communion from my brother, not believing in the sacrament (he didn't mind) but profoundly moved by the love and faith I could see at work in Dinnington. I began to pay more visits to Yorkshire, to interview Simon, who was often in bed with his drips attached.

The Pyrenees, the leaking roof of the monastery and the mice nibbling away in our kitchen seemed very remote. Then a kind friend offered to lend us money for the roof at Corbiac. We figured optimistically that once the roof was on and the house no longer leaked we could manage to live there. If we could also start improvements, create bedrooms and a new bathroom we would be relatively comfortable. We could cope with the old kitchen, and the other rooms for a while longer, despite their crumbling state. We had already found an architect, a young Englishman passionate about old buildings, with his own property in the Ariège.

We needed a builder, so off I went in the spring of 1995, along with Martha. We stayed in her house, an old mill, Le Moulin, just outside the village. A solid stone house, with wooden shutters and a heavy wooden door of horizontal planks in the Catalan style, it straddles the river and is imbued with the sound of running water.

Martha was Swiss, a little older than I, tall, lean, spare, with short blonde hair. She spoke excellent English with only a slight accent, as well as French, German, Spanish and her own Swiss-German. We had bought our properties within months of each other. 'I walked in the door, saw the old lady sitting by the open fire in the kitchen, and I just knew straight away this was the house I wanted!' Martha recalled. The old lady, who had been a

101

pianist, used the house for a summer retreat from the heat of Perpignan. She had been friends with Pablo Casals and other musicians, who had often visited the house and played the grand piano in the mill. She had left her vintage cream-coloured *mobylette* behind, with a little plaque inscribed: 'Jacqueline Dussol, pianiste'.

In the kitchen Martha had kept the red-tiled floor, the old wooden *armoires* she had bought with the house, the typical shallow Catalan sink of red marble, the open fireplace and all the smoke-blackened fire irons. I think she rather regretted not being able to keep the old lady by the fire too.

Although it was only February, during the day it was warm enough to sit in the garden, where we ate the baby artichokes and new asparagus we had found in the market in Prades. We had bought a box of oysters and Martha taught me how to open them, how to protect my hands with a dishcloth and use a special oyster knife to tease into the muscle and break open the shells. In the evening we grilled duck breast over the open fire in the kitchen.

For five days we discussed love, death, children, food, wine, art, psychology – all the essentials. We had become good friends in the intervening years since we first met in Mosset in 1990, and she had often visited me in London after Theo was born, simply holding the baby and sharing the burden. She never doubted that I would realize my dream of Corbiac.

Martha was one of the few people I confided in about Simon's illness. She knew about death: her husband had died suddenly of cancer when her daughter was only three. Her experience of Jungian analysis gave her an understanding of Simon's metaphors for coping with death – for instance, the image of himself as a little boat cast adrift, heading one day for an endless sea.

Martha had settled with her husband in England, where she ran an art gallery and vineyard. Even after her husband's death she had no desire to return to Switzerland. 'Swiss culture is very narrow-minded, not very open to the rest of the world. They pride themselves on their neutrality but they isolate themselves in the process, they cut themselves off.' I began then to realize that the different nationalities I was now meeting were far from typical of their countries. It was not, we agreed, always escapism that made people want to leave their country, but, rather, a desire to remake themselves, find a space where they could develop more freely.

I envied Martha's ability to speak several languages. I felt very strongly that I wanted for my child this ability not just to speak French in addition to English, but to be able to learn other languages easily too. The primary reason was of course communication, but it was also to enable him to appreciate better the rich diversity of other cultures and languages.

I had rarely been to Mosset in spring. I walked down the hill from the village to Corbiac, revelling in the cold, clear air. I could hear cowbells and smell the faint whiff of woodsmoke. There were carpets of violets under the trees, tight balls of mimosa in blossom, and clumps of purple irises just coming into flower. Birds twittered, hooted and trilled all around me. Below was the monastery, the faded red brick of the arched bell tower etched against the backdrop of Canigou, still covered in snow. Around the building were the peach trees in full pink rig. It was ravishing and I fell in love all over again.

On arriving, I opened all the shutters to air the house, leaning out of the windows to admire the mountains. Then I emptied the buckets in the attic for what I hoped was the last time, and contemplated the prospect of a new roof.

We had asked for quotes from several builders, believing we should use local labour if we could. One firm came and measured it all up very carefully, and then they

went bust. Another firm didn't turn up at all. Then I met
Paul, a brusque Yorkshireman with a long ponytail who
had been living in France for seven years. When I saw the
magnificent supporting wall he had already built for
Martha, and heard he had learned his trade building dry-
stone walls on Ilkley Moor, I somehow knew this was our
man, and so he was. Whenever later I was asked why we
had an English *maçon*, I had only to explain that he was
de ma région, and all was perfectly understood.

6

From Soho to the Pyrenees

I grasped my chance; finally with a roof it all seemed possible. I had the book about Simon to write and a modest advance so I planned a long trip to Mosset, arranging to rent Martha's house and put Theo, now four, in the school for a month. Miles, who needed to be in London, would visit, and it would be a good opportunity to see how I coped on my own. I knew if we ever were to move he would need plenty of urban respite and I had to be used to managing things myself. It was a challenge, and one of the things I wanted most was to become stronger, more independent, to chop wood for myself, sleep alone in a house in the country, not shriek when I saw a snake or a mouse.

We overlapped briefly with Martha and her daughter, Sarah, and had a short holiday together, barbecuing in the garden and picking cherries. The children scrambled up the branches, stuffing themselves with the fruit, while I held the ladder and filled baskets below. Children from the village came to help, and immediately adopted Theo when I said he would be going to school with them for a while. They were intrigued by this little blond English boy, with his big blue-green eyes and spectacles and no French.

We got to know the village better, now we could walk up the steep path through the old streets every morning to buy bread and croissants. We shopped at the *épicerie*, often buying their celebrated Roquefort, which was perfectly matured in their cool cave next to the Mosset church. People came from as far as Perpignan to buy it, Yvette informed me. There was a post office open for two hours each morning with an old-fashioned telephone *cabane* where you paid for the call afterwards. The post-mistress, Dominique, was friendly, and helpful with my letters and parcels to England, assiduously looking up the correct postage in an ancient well-thumbed book of instructions.

Early in the morning Mosset almost bustled as people came for their bread and newspapers. Everybody said '*Bonjour*' as a matter of course, whether they knew you or not, and I loved this common courtesy. Intrigued by this small community, I sat one day with the *annuaire* (telephone directory) and looked at the list of names in Mosset, so many of them Catalan, and wondered if I would ever get to know them.

Then Martha left, finishing off the champagne to help with the car packing, and I was on my own. She told me to be sure to listen out for the nightingale. I felt nervous alone, checking the lock on the door several times before bed and starting up at unusual sounds. But I heard the rats before the nightingale. They had been a problem while Martha was there, and someone from the village had been round to lay down poison. We called him the ratcatcher but it turned out that in fact François did everything, from collecting the rubbish to checking the water meters.

I had been deeply impressed when Martha went up into the attic and removed the corpses of the rats herself. This

106

was the sort of thing you had to do if you lived on your own, I thought with dread, thankful they had been eliminated. But then one night as I lay in bed I heard a plop and a scuffle over my head: the rats had found a way back into the roof. I knew they couldn't get into the house and anyway weren't really rats, but some sort of water-rat (as if it made any difference to my fevered imagination), and of course they were harmless to humans. All the same, the sound of them scrabbling about overhead was nightmarish and I could sleep only with cotton wool stuffed in my ears.

Once we were on our own, Theo immediately went on hunger strike, his chosen power gesture for several years. Any doubt that it was a deliberate protest vanished when he said, 'I am not going to eat anything. And I'm not going to drink anything either.' It was a protest against the total control I had over him, was obliged to have over him, especially when there was no-one else around. It was always a problem, one not easy to resolve. I knew I had to accept my role and try not to exploit my power, but I was very aware that here more than ever I was his only conduit to the world. Since I had no intention of giving up eating, we compromised on French fun food – for example, when I cooked *moules* we used a shell to extract the mussel from within another, or in the case of artichokes we stripped off the leaves with our fingers and dipped the tender heart in melted butter and lemon.

He struggled to talk to Martha's gardener one day, following him about saying, '*Je m'appelle Theo*,' the only French he knew, and finally managed to ingratiate himself. I was so moved at the effort he was making, his struggle to be accepted, how desperate it seemed he was to communicate. I wondered if I was making the right choices for him, whether it was all going to be too tough. Was I expecting too much of him? Did I have the right to uproot him and start such a precarious new life?

107

The path from Le Moulin joined the old road into the village, now just a cobble-stoned street, and entered through one of the old stone gateways near the church. We passed old ladies outside their houses, watering plants, all in the same uniform of faded black dresses and flowery pinafores. '*Vous allez à l'école?*' they asked curiously, and seemed pleased when I said yes. The church bell in the village was loudly chiming nine o'clock; children all over France were arriving at school for a morning of lessons.

A couple of small boys were running with their satchels bouncing on their backs, a little pigtailed girl was walking with her father, and the white school bus drew up to deposit several more children at the school door.

I took a photo of Theo that first day at *l'école de Mosset*, standing in front of the great double doors. He looked so small and English, his new little blue rucksack on his back, his eyes huge behind his glasses. The small school of Mosset is a standard turn-of-the-century French school building, with two doors, one sombrely marked GARÇONS, the other, FILLES, above the peeling brown paint. These days neither the classes nor the entrances are divided by gender, since all schools in France are co-educational. The school serves the three villages in the valley and outlying hamlets and homesteads, and at that time had thirty pupils altogether. About ten years ago the numbers had dropped to less than twenty, and there was a threat it might close, much to the distress of the villagers, most of whom had attended the school themselves. Now it seems to be thriving again, helped by the foreigners and outsiders coming to the area. The mayor of the village and the teacher had been happy to enrol Theo, although I was rather vague about when he would arrive permanently. But an extra name on the enrolment helped their chances of keeping the place open. Almost all the local children attended the school; it is the only one in the valley and an essential link in the community.

We were welcomed by 'Maîtresse', as the teacher was always known by pupils and parents alike. A short, jolly woman, with a face as round and cheerful as her Smiley watch, she had run the village school for the past seventeen years, educating both her own children there in the process, and lived just outside the ramparts of the medieval château that dominates the village. For the first few days I stayed with Theo at school, sitting in a corner on a low child's chair, and trying to learn more French myself. I was very pleased to identify the story 'The Ugly Duckling'. Then the class did some drawing, and while the country children drew cherry trees, ladders, horses and goats, Theo drew a large red bus, reluctant to relinquish his urban roots so easily as all that. There was an emphasis on Catalan history and culture, and this day one of the first lessons was Catalan, an even more daunting prospect than French for Theo. Still, by the end of the day he could say 'moo' in three languages, and so could I. He was fortunate that Abigail was also at the school; the daughter of the English artists Bob and Gwen Royston, who lived in the village, she helped him with translation and held his hand on the way to lunch.

The church bell chimed at midday, the hallowed hour when everyone in France stops for lunch. The door of the village shop was firmly locked, and soon the sound of clinking knives and forks could be heard from behind shuttered windows. The schoolchildren formed a crocodile, older children holding hands with little ones, and they trooped through the village square to lunch.

School lunch is served, logically enough, and much to my delight, in the village café, which has been reopened to encourage tourism, but which has few guests during term time. Here the children eat a proper three-course meal, complete with bread served in baskets and water in wineglasses. The chef sends out the menu every week so parents don't duplicate their child's meal in the evening. (The menu for secondary schools is also published every week in the local paper.) A typical meal at the village café might include *salade de tomates*, *rôti de veau*, *frites*, and yoghurt. They all have their own napkins, and at the end of the meal one of the older children goes round with a flannel and wipes the sticky faces of the younger ones.

Lunchtime at Theo's London school was a grim affair by comparison. The children were given an oval plastic plate with three compartments, one for veg, one for meat and one for pudding, and a slot for a drink. They queued up with their plates, indicated what they wanted, and found themselves a place at a bench. As soon as anyone finished eating they cleared their plate and left for the playground.

Serving schoolchildren a proper lunch has always been part of the French system. According to Laurence Wylie's classic account, *A Village in the Vaucluse*, the schoolchildren he observed in the 1950s were served a three-course lunch, consisting of two substantial dishes such as stew, thick soup or spaghetti, and a dessert of stewed fruit. Each child in those days was expected to bring their own piece of bread with them. Children were strictly disciplined and expected to finish everything on their plates. This taught them not to waste food, and it also saved on dish washing, since when the main course was finished and the dish wiped clean with bread the dish was turned over so that dessert could be served on the other side. The spoon could also be inverted so that jam could be eaten from the handle.

One day a pottery teacher came to Mosset and made a kiln in the school playground. A bunch of excited small children assembled wearing a motley array of plastic aprons and hand-me-down old shirts. They pummelled great lumps of red clay into pots, which varied from

110

the smoothest, roundest bowl to the most twisted little thumb-printed offering. The process took several days and involved every single child. The older ones helped to build the kiln, constructing a base of papier mâché that was then covered in clay. When the kiln was finished, the youngest children picked bunches of wildflowers and excitedly pressed coloured petals all over its outer surface of wet clay. Then a fire was lit below and the pots inside were slowly baked. At that moment in the school yard cradled by mountains the scene was idyllic.

I was completely hooked by the time Miles came out for a week, flying into Perpignan. The sun came out and we sat in the garden, eating bountiful meals, revelling in the fresh, fully-flavoured melons, plums and cherries in season and gorging on figs from the two twisted old fig trees at Le Moulin. We explored the village and the remains of the château, now converted into apartments around a central *place*. From outside, the high walls remained forbidding and there were only fragments of former glory. Theo delighted in the arrow slits and the possibility of dungeons. He was already becoming familiar with the village and loved to play hide-and-seek in the narrow streets, where he was safe from cars and already known as 'le petit anglais'. He had begun trying out French words and was constantly asking for translations; once, he even asked what 'phew' was in French.

In the middle of June the lime-blossom trees that shaded Le Moulin blossomed. Jacques said the *tilleul* would soon be ready to pick, but I must wait until they had just opened, and pick the smallest ones for the best *tisane*. He chuckled and shook his head when I asked if he drank it himself. On the appointed day I assembled my baskets and spent hours stripping the pale-yellow flowers and tender green leaves from the branches. It was a warm day and the scent was so beguiling I was in heaven. It was

111

delicate yet almost intoxicating, the essence of early summer. I filled every basket I possessed and put them all over the house to dry, turning the leaves frequently to encourage the drying process, releasing the fragrance, till the whole house was perfumed. Each night I brewed a soothing tea. I even packed up a box of the blossoms and sent them to Simon – who, against all the odds, was celebrating his fortieth birthday – hoping the scent would travel to him.

Paul was working on the roof at Corbiac, and we went to observe his progress. The mulberry trees had been cut down; it was sad to see them go after they had provided us with shade on the terrace all those years, but I also remembered the way the mulberries were constantly tramped into the house, staining everything a livid purple. They had not been a very good choice of trees for shade, and were more likely planted to feed silkworms, the cultivation of which was at one time a substantial industry in these parts. I wonder if somewhere there are bolts of Corbiac silk.

Now the monastery looked strangely naked and vulnerable, with its peeling shutters, patches of cement and tumbledown walls. Several workmen in frayed cut-off jeans, boots and little else were clambering over the roof, already deeply tanned from working outside. There was Tom, an Englishman who had moved to France a year before with his family, and Tim, who although English had grown up in a tepee in the Ariège and spoke perfect French. Even Paul's wife, Polly, had been recruited to operate the crane. Tall, long-legged Polly was the kind of woman who cheerfully chopped logs, rode motorbikes and drove lorries without any ideological fuss and bother. She and Paul had lived in an army truck for a year after leaving England, while they rebuilt their house themselves in a village nestled up to Canigou.

The roof was over a hundred feet long and required

lorryloads of tiles and vast quantities of cement to be swung up in buckets by the crane. Apart from tiles, the wooden beams were the most critical items and the greatest expense. Paul followed local practice whenever possible, so he used pine, as well as some of the existing beams.

Miles wanted the main beams back in their original position spanning the width of the building, not the length of it, where they had been put when the farmers added an extra attic floor. This had weakened the building since the beams no longer held it together. Both Paul and the architect had wisely advised us to think of the building as a whole and so the roof was made to cover not just the cloister wing that was still in use but also the ruined section to the west, in the hope that one day it too could be restored. Until then we had mentally discounted the ruined west end, so it was a challenge to think about its future use. Below the roofline the top stone lintels of the five original dormitory windows were restored and strengthened. They had been blocked up by the farmers, and new ones knocked out to suit their needs. Now they were waiting to be fully reconstructed when the time came, and they looked like eyes half closed in sleep: Rip Van Winkle windows waiting a hundred years to come to life again.

The garden became a building site, with cement mixers, sacks of cement, stacks of beams and tiles, and a growing pile of old tiles and rotten wood tossed off the roof. I imagined the monastic building site, with the monks themselves perhaps clambering up ramps with hods of tiles, securing the scaffolding, operating the primitive hoists of wood and leather belts needed to lift the wooden beams, and hammering in nails. I collected the cast-off nails, centuries-old handmade nails – blunt, stubby ones, thin elegant ones, many bent and twisted – cherishing their uniqueness.

113

Paul's own equipment was almost as antique as the monks'; he introduced us proudly to the Captain, the second-hand crane he had bought and trundled behind his truck all the way from Perpignan, its panels red with rust and every tyre different. He had a passion for old machinery (Polly said he had so many old motorbikes there was even one under the bed) and was keen to start up the engine, which chugged like an old steam train. Somehow the Captain fitted right in with the dilapidated building. It was to become a familiar companion, loosely tethered so it did not resist the wind, like a weathervane turning and squeaking through the night.

Theo was intensely interested in all the building activities. Declaring that he too wanted to be a worker, he dug a stick into the ground to make a hole, then stood back, hands on hips, lips pursed, assessing his work. Paul soon became his hero. He treated the child like an equal, a buddy, letting him help. It was good for Theo to understand how a building was constructed, see people at work, and meet different male role models. The peach farmer, also willing to let him help, took him off to ride the tractor, collect eggs, feed the rabbits or give hay to the horses.

We wanted to learn more about the building, and were invited by the mayor of Mosset to see his collection of old photos of Corbiac and the village. Madame Mestres served *muscat*, the sweet wine that is often drunk chilled as an aperitif here, while Monsieur Mestres bent his shiny brown head, fringed with straight grey hair, over the old black-and-white photos spread out before us on the table. There were several views of Corbiac in the early twentieth century, including photos showing a farmer and his wife with a cow and a plough in front of the church; workers in a field planted with potatoes; a woman standing on the unsurfaced road, beside a field full of rows of corn. We examined them closely, trying to discern where walls and windows had fallen down or been replaced, trying to learn what was behind each photo.

The mayor and his wife had only recently retired; both had been teachers and he was a professor of mathematics in Perpignan before they came to live full-time in Mosset. M. Mestres' own connection goes back a long way. '*Je suis un pur Mossetan*,' he stressed, with all the emphasis on the pure. He rummaged in the old dresser to produce a fat folder, which was a genealogical table of his family. He thumbed through it and ran his finger down the page, to 1614, back before the Treaty of the Pyrenees in 1659 when the region became part of France, a date which he made sound like only yesterday. Then it was still Catalonia, of course. René Mestres was born in Mosset because his mother, like so many of her generation, followed the tradition for women to return to their parents' home to have a baby, with the help of the midwife in the village, the *sage-femme* as she is still called today.

Nevertheless he spent most of his school days in another village, returning to Mosset for long summer holidays. 'Although I haven't passed all my life here, it is still the village I feel most attached to,' he said. They in turn have brought up their own children in Perpignan but returned regularly to Mosset for holidays. For their children, too, Mosset is their village.

The French, I was discovering, have a profound attachment to the country. It is not so much the sentimental love of landscape that I grew up with, but a deep, almost mystical, nostalgia for the *pays* and the life of the *paysan*, still in touch with the earth. Even many city dwellers remain attached to a particular place, their own *pays*, or a village, and return there for holidays, proud of their idealized peasant ancestry.

Mme Mestres found a photo of the *capelletta*, a tiny chapel opposite their village house. Before it was restored, the roof was as thickly overgrown with plants as Corbiac.

115

Restoring the *capelletta* had been one of their first priorities when M. Mestres became mayor. The roof had fallen in, letting in the rain, and the villagers had been using it as somewhere to dump their rubbish for twenty years or more. M. Mestres raised his hand as a measure. 'There was a metre of rubbish,' he said, shaking his head in disbelief. It was easier to dump it there than struggle down the winding streets of the village. More pictures of Mosset appeared: wheat-threshing in the village square; old women bent double with baskets of kindling; pigs in the streets; the coffee-grinder roasting coffee beans at his doorstep; washing spread out to dry on the rocks above the village.

Until the middle of the twentieth century Mosset had hardly changed since the Middle Ages. It was a typical mountain village with a rural agricultural society of people who lived by the rhythm of the seasons, working in the fields in the daylight hours and returning to the protection of the village at night. M. Mestres pointed out on the wall an oil painting of a shepherd following a great flock of sheep through the village. There are still a few traditional shepherds left, taking the sheep out to pasture in the morning and bringing them back at night.

Mme Mestres picked out a photo of a procession in the 1950s, carrying the statue of Notre Dame de Corbiac. There was a priest in white vestments. 'He was the last curé here,' said Mme Mestres. 'That was when the presbytery, next to the church, burned down,' said her husband with a chuckle. Mme Mestres smiled. 'He liked to *faire la fête*,' she said, nodding. 'He liked a drink.' After the presbytery burned down, he had been defrocked and got married. Now the priest came only once a month to say mass for the few old ladies who still went to church. It seemed as if the clerics here had always had a somewhat disreputable quality. There was the one caught stealing from the monks at Corbiac. Then there was Abbé

Perarneau, who was very fond of hunting and fishing. He was notorious for poaching (in which he was accompanied by the fire chief of Perpignan, also a child of Mosset) but said that, in his position, God would surely forgive him. He reckoned it was as easy to say mass outdoors, when he was out hunting, as in church.

I asked M. Mestres about the story of the priest in Mosset who was executed by the Resistance for betrayal. The curé, a Spanish Francoist, had apparently given a list of members of the Col de Jau Maquis to the Gestapo. He had also denounced Pitt Kruger, the German pacifist exile who had established a school at La Coume, a remote farmhouse in the mountains above Mosset, and given sanctuary to children fleeing the Spanish Civil War and Jewish refugees from the Nazis. Towards the end of the war, in August 1944, the priest was taken by the Maquis to the Col de Jau, where he was tried and executed, then left hanging naked from a tree. There is still controversy about the story, explained M. Mestres, and some still deny that the priest was really a traitor, insisting that the list he was carrying was never intended to be seen. As in so many places in France, the wartime history was still a sensitive issue in Mosset.

Wartime life in Mosset had been relatively easy compared with that in the cities, since they could grow their own crops and peasants were used to subsistence living and foraging and hunting for wild food. They could always plant a secret patch of potatoes and M. Mestres remembered his father trying to hide a pig from the Gestapo one day. Mestres gestured down the valley to the river. 'I remember how close the Germans came,' he said. He was a young teenager, playing down by the river, when, hearing a rifle shot, he hid himself. A column of German vehicles had been spotted coming up the road, and immediately all the young people scattered into the hills they knew so well.

Later, when I passed the parapet in Mosset again, I looked at the old men. They looked at me, though I don't think they really saw me. I think to them we foreigners all look the same, with our jeans, our sunglasses, our haircuts. They knew who hanged the priest. Lots of people knew. It was a village secret, just as they knew who had been in the Resistance and who had been collaborators.

Throughout the twentieth century the village had declined, and like many other hill villages that have crumbled back to the earth, it risked total abandon. Now there is change, as more and more people buy rural properties and increasingly try to live in them all year round. Tourism helps, with the popular system of *fermes auberges* and *chambres d'hôtes* providing local employment and supplementary income for farmers. Mosset even has a small ski resort constructed further up the mountain. The new settlers need an infrastructure of schools, shops and restaurants, and a successful outcome to the campaign to keep the school open is probably the most important factor in Mosset's survival. It was one of M. Mestres' most important tasks as mayor, since the life of the village depended on it.

I was determined to keep Theo on the school roll however long it took to get here, encouraged that my own desires coincided so well with the needs of this newly discovered community. When we took our leave of the Mestres, I was busily planning the future when Theo could go full-time to l'École des Trois Villages, as it is now called.

We were further inspired by a visit to Albert and Robert, two gay Dutchmen who were in the process of restoring a barn on the edge of the village. We always pronounced their names in the French way, and soon reduced them to simply 'the Bears' for short. When we arrived at their rustic wooden door tucked away under a little stone street bridge, Theo asked wonderingly, 'Are they really bears?'

They were hard at work. Robert was painting shutters with yellow paint. 'We brought it specially from Holland,' he said, with a flourish of his brush. Albert, clinging to a ladder, was dressed in bright red overalls and a red helmet. They were doing all the work themselves, from installing sewer pipes to laying tiles and painting windows.

Albert and Robert have been together for twenty-two years, living in Amsterdam, where Albert, a trained singer, ran his own theatre and opera company and Robert taught English and Dutch. Then tragedy struck, when Albert very suddenly lost his hearing. 'I thought the singers were miming until I realized something terrible had happened.'

They sought refuge in the little house they had in a nearby village, but they needed somewhere bigger. 'We told everyone, we want electricity and water, and a bigger house,' said Robert. 'And near a village. I'm not someone who wants to sit alone on a mountain top.' Then Gerard van Westerloo, a Dutch friend and long-time resident of Mosset, said he knew of something there. 'But everyone said, oh, it's cold in Mosset. It was true: every time we came it was the Tramontane or rain.'

When they took a first look at the building through binoculars, Robert exclaimed, 'But it's a ruin. There's no roof on it.' There was certainly no water or electricity.

'I don't want to go there,' said Albert. But they did, and fell in love with the place. And like everyone who has fallen in love with a house they like to recount all the details, a bit like one might describe at length a birth or a love affair. It took a year to buy the barn, Gerard negotiating with the owner on their behalf. 'Then Gerard called to say the man wants to sell. Now,' said Robert. 'I said, "I come. Now."' They went to see it with the vendor, who had inherited it, and had probably only been there

119

himself once or twice. It was raining and looked terrible; the roof had fallen in and thick brambles and small trees were growing inside the walls. 'It was just a barn,' said Robert. 'Someone did say he was born here but he couldn't say where exactly!'

Next door was a narrow house, which they lived in while they did the renovation. It bore a remarkable resemblance to a tall Dutch house: three rooms, one on top of each other, connected by steep ladders, and low windows with lace curtains and bright-yellow shutters.

They spent five years renovating, working half the year six days a week. 'We were very disciplined. It was all we did here,' said Robert. 'And it was good therapy for me. Slowly I went up and up,' added Albert. Albert, beginning to recover, turned from music to painting and sculpture, inspired by the landscape around him. 'I took the colours from here, from the mountains, the blues, the stones, the forms.' Looking at the work they were doing and the way Albert had transformed himself, I reflected that gay Dutchmen must be some of the more evolved people on the planet.

We made further visits over the next year or so to see how the work on Corbiac was progressing. Once the new roof was finished, Paul began to reinstate the floor at its original level, but only in one half of the cloister wing; we couldn't afford to do it all at once. He reopened two of the original windows, then constructed two bedrooms and a new bathroom for us.

We stayed at Le Moulin one last time in February. I suppose I was trying to experience the weather at its worst, and I certainly succeeded. It snowed and was so cold that the pipes froze solid. The very first night there was an earthquake. I sat bolt upright in bed. It was as though I was in *The Wizard of Oz*, as if the house was about to take off, but my first characteristic thought was, 'Oh, now what have I done?' thinking perhaps it was the gas tank that had blown up. Miles, also characteristically, simply said, 'Oh, it's probably an earthquake,' rolled over and promptly went back to sleep. It turned out that it had been quite a dramatic tremor, wrecking houses in nearby St Paul de Fenouilledes, the epicentre of the earthquake.

The *tilleul* blossoms were in a bowl on the kitchen table when I went back to Dinnington again. They still harboured a faint scent of the South but I don't think Simon ever made any tea. Many more trips to Yorkshire followed as Simon's health declined. As I grew closer to him, visiting him in his peaceful house, sitting sometimes in his quiet room full of candles and icons, and entered into the rhythm of his services – the mass, the Easter vigil, the chants and hymns – it all started to resonate. I began to understand the meaning of what the monks were doing at Corbiac; its spiritual function, the role of retreat and meditation, the daily round of chants, psalms and prayer that was its wellspring.

Though he had no desire to be a monk himself, Simon made regular retreats to the holy island of Iona, and his beloved Bardsey, a remote island off the coast of Wales, once an important point of pilgrimage and still only accessible by boat once a week. It is described by the poet R. S. Thomas, who had his parish in Aberdaron, the embarkation point for Bardsey, as 'that green island, ringed with the rain's bow, that we had found and would spend the rest of our lives looking for'.

Simon's own description of Bardsey helped me to understand better than anything else the religious philosophy that sustained him, a spirituality that made him feel deeply rooted in the world. 'On one corner of the island is a hide for bird watchers, low, stone with a slit to look out of across the sea as it breaks on the rocks ahead of you. If you sit in there your vision is filled hour after hour with the waves of the sea, with the clouds of the sky and the sun . . . If you sit there for any length of time you join the rhythm of the place, the tides and the days, the times and the changing light: your hiding for observation becomes an invitation to participate in the rhythm that underlies the world . . . It is about deeper engagement with the world, about more pain, not less, about exposure and vulnerability not seclusion and privacy.' A deeper appreciation of monastic life grew in me, one that resonated oddly with the Be Here Now hippie philosophy that I had youthfully embraced.

Simon was writing the biography of a monk, an Anglican Benedictine whose own book about the liturgy had become a classic. So I met my first monk, Father Basil, the abbot of the monastery Simon was writing about, when we both stayed with Simon for the weekend. Father Basil observed with intrigued bemusement the demands of secular parenthood as I rushed about serving breakfast, mopping up spilt milk, strapping Theo into his stroller. The abbot, on the other hand, dressed in his long black monastic habit, leather belt and silver cross, disappeared at regular intervals to say his offices in peace. I found myself envying this monk the rhythm of his quiet, contemplative life, and suggested we did a life swop.

The fact that I was already involved, had tried to understand how Simon was finding such reserves of strength to cope with his illness and accept his dying with such grace, was a great aid when he finally took his leave in November 1995. We lit candles and listened to repetitive chanting and music as he lay in his hospital bed. It didn't seem to matter whether you consciously prayed, whether you believed; the words did not need to mean anything, they touched another part of you, beyond language. It was like a long, shared meditation. His curate said a final mass for the friends and family around his bed. I sat with him the night before he died, alone beside him, my own vigil, and felt strangely content; as Simon had tried to explain, the meaning was in the waiting. Never have I felt that I was so much in the right place. Slowly I understood how close this moment had been to the monastic experience; how the chanting, the intense focus, the universe narrowed to a single point, had driven everything else away, and even though it was all so deeply sad we were left feeling strangely uplifted. There was something profound about it that I merely glimpsed.

It was strange to realize after my father and my brother died that after all we still had a church in the family. For several years after Simon died, I found myself wearing his coat and jacket, literally taking on his mantle.

I started writing *Scarlet Ribbons* about six months before Simon died and it took another year and a half to finish. Slowly we turned our faces towards Corbiac again and I took leave of the family, to whom I had become so close through his death. Mother understood, and was in any case beguiled by the holidays she could spend sitting on our terrace, contemplating the mountains.

Theo, nearly six, had started school in London, an Anglican school near to the flat. He was happy enough, but we were increasingly disturbed by the clearly evangelical approach of the staff, who were preaching Jesus to a school which was at least half Hindu. It had been almost impossible to find a non-religious state school in the centre of London, as we would have wished. We liked the idea that in France Church and state were clearly separated and schools did not teach religion. Theo's schooling was one of the reasons we moved when we did, before the house was ready or we could really afford it. I was anxious Theo should start school and French as soon as possible, before it became too difficult.

I had work commissioned in France, both guidebooks and articles, for the first few months, and felt reasonably confident that it would continue. The Internet was developing and we hoped technology would make communication easier. Miles had a book to write, but he remained extremely dubious about living in the country full-time. We continued to rent the flat in London, in order to spend as much time there as he needed.

I felt ready to spend some time on my own. In many ways I craved it, and sometimes thought of the hermit of Corbiac with envy. Since Theo was born, my bedroom had also been my office. With a baby it was always difficult to find space, either actual or psychological. Miles and I had lived together for almost twenty years and we felt that we could survive, perhaps even benefit from, more time apart. We hoped that friends would visit. In the end I think I psychologically moved to France, whereas Miles was only ever visiting. It became apparent that I had more stamina for solitude. Miles needed the stimulation of the city in a way I didn't seem to, then.

So we left lunches in the Groucho club, the second-hand bookshops of Charing Cross Road, the temptations of Liberty's, the museums, the art exhibitions, the dinners with friends, the murmur of the Tube train beneath the flat, the lilacs in bloom in Regent's Park, steak and kidney pie, bacon sandwiches, Cox's Orange pippins, English clouds.

We also left behind the gloomy, damp November days when it gets dark in the afternoon, sash windows, pollution, crowds, the guy coughing upstairs, the English tabloids, the Royal Family, a Tory government, the health service, catered children's parties, trying to find a parking space, litter, dirty streets, and pallid tomatoes.

Most friends were supportive; a few were mystified. Some said I was wanting too much: 'You can't have everything, Rosemary.' And I would seriously think, why not try? I read a story once of St Thérèse of Lisieux. At age four, when offered a handful of ribbons to choose from,

'I choose all,' she said. A few friends felt offended and asked what was wrong with England. Some called me brave when really they thought me mad. Best were those who understood the dream.

I think Simon understood. We had shared the stories as children, the magic kingdom of Narnia, the wonderful tree house on a desert island in *Swiss Family Robinson*. There was always a desire for a magic special place, what Simon called 'the Kingdom'. Perhaps it is what we all are looking for but rarely articulate. For years I wanted to visit Bardsey, Simon's island, and it took a long time to realize I had to find my own.

7

Moving to France, lock, stock and barrel vault

When we finally moved from London in 1997 it really seemed as if there were malign forces trying to hold us back. We had hoped to leave the previous autumn, but one thing after another delayed our departure and now it was February, the coldest time of the year. In some perverse way I thought if we started then, things could only get better. We finished our packing by the skin of our teeth, poking odd shoes and toothbrushes into every corner of the car. Inevitably, despite the enormous amount of stuff we sent by removal truck, the car was loaded to the gills, with the cat perched precariously in her basket next to six-year-old Theo with a bottle of Rescue Remedy near at hand, recommended by the vet in case she needed to be calmed down.

We set off in good time the next day but only got as far as the Strand, about ten minutes away, before I crashed the car. Bang into the back of someone at a red light.

Maybe the driver stopped suddenly, I don't know, but it was clearly my fault, if only technically. There was a dreadful slow sense of everything falling apart: this great loaded car, all our commitments, the vast truckload of stuff arriving at Corbiac the next day. But apart from the cat, who had shot to the front of her basket and had her nose pressed up against the mesh, no-one was hurt. One indicator-light cover was broken but the light itself still worked, and the front and side were bashed in, but the car still seemed to work fine, and we just thought, go for it. Let's just get there. I had no idea if the Shuttle or the Motorail would let us on with a car in such a state, and the prospect of the Motorail inspectors examining the car for existing scratches was a bit daunting. I knocked back the Rescue Remedy myself and on we went.

When we arrived at the Shuttle there was a big notice saying no guns and no animals. Now what? Instinct prevailed again and we flung a blanket over the poor cat, who fortunately is not much given to miaowing. Given the beaten-up state of the car, naturally we were waved over to be inspected. Some sort of electronic search was done, but I think the amount of stuff and Miles's ingenious packing defeated the security inspectors. Anyway they didn't even find the cat.

Then we had to drive to Paris, since the Motorail from Calais did not function at this unseasonal time. In normal circumstances it was a journey of about three hours and we calculated we had allowed plenty of time. The weather, however, had other ideas; there were gale-force winds, driving rain and even hailstorms, so the entire journey took about five hours, with the car blown all over the road. It was monstrous – I think truly one of the worst drives I have ever had to do in my life.

But then karma kicked in. After a night on the train we arrived in Narbonne to warm sunshine and palm trees. We bowled along the Autoroute de Catalane, one of those wonderful French motorways that are so well designed they seem positively to enhance the landscape, perhaps because it follows the old Roman road, the Via Domitia, right along the coast. We drove past vineyards and sea lagoons, past the giant ochre sandcastle of the Château de Salses, the Mediterranean glittering seductively in the distance. Then we headed west up into the mountains, the air freshening every minute. As we turned up the winding mountain road from Prades to Mosset – our street, as it were – I opened the car window and inhaled the air. It was mimosa time: great clouds of tiny golden blossoms glowed as we passed. The air was fragrant with that distinct honeyed scent, which seems so exotic in the winter months. As I sniffed I felt like Mole in *Wind in the Willows* when he smells his little underground burrow after months of adventure. 'Home!'

As we rounded the bend the monastery came into sight, starkly visible – we had rarely seen it in a winter landscape – looking like a great ship, with the round apse like a prow, about to sail off down the valley. The peach trees surrounding it were leafless and skeletal. The air was sharp and crystal clear, the mountains in the distance covered in snow, the peak of Canigou reigning supreme with its cold white crown. It was undoubtedly beautiful. It was also very cold.

We released the cat indoors and set about exploring our new quarters, anxious to assess it before the great Cotswold Carriers truck full of most of our possessions (that is to say, ninety boxes of books and a few dilapidated items of furniture) arrived from London. Theo, meanwhile, was thrilled to find a horse called Faustine grazing our field and fed her the last of our Marks & Spencer's apples.

The next few days were a blur of scrubbing and cleaning, fixing beds, looking in vain for all sorts of things we knew we had packed. We determined to get at least one room as cosy as possible, damning the expense with a battery of electric heaters and gas stoves to supplement the woefully inadequate wood fire. Paul and Tim cheerfully helped us unload the truck and fix innumerable things we had only just thought of. They had organized cleaning and painting and prepared the building as much as possible, patching up the great acres of crumbling ruin that surrounded the few rooms they had actually reconstructed thus far. It was only later I heard Paul had said in his typical gloomy fashion, 'They are going to hate it.' Paul's wife, Polly, helped in innumerable ways, with painting and cleaning, advising on shops and services, looking after Theo sometimes, and bringing us fresh vegetables and raspberries from her freezer.

We had suggested various improvements to make habitation possible. So now we had two bedrooms, with heaters installed, the walls painted white, the big wooden beams stained brown. I was determined to make the bedrooms a priority, to provide a retreat – I had seen too many renovation projects where the bedroom got left till last. It didn't take long, since we had so little furniture; in our case, books had to furnish the room. We hung a wooden rail for clothes, added a little yellow table and chair, painted with a border of flowers, I had bought years ago in a local *brocante* shop, Miles's mother's oval mirror, and on the bed the faded blue-and-white American quilt, one of several Miles brought back from Kansas while visiting William Burroughs. There were no curtains: I was still revelling in the prospect of a sky full of stars and bathing in moonlight. Theo had a tiny room next door, but there was space for a bed, a table, a chair. He had no curtains either and even when I succumbed later, when cosiness beat out romance, he refused them, saying how much he liked the sound of the wind in the big pine tree in the garden.

The bathroom was lovely, with the bath by the window, and a view of forested hillside to contemplate from the shower. We even had hot water, as long as we remembered to change the butane gas tank which also supplied hot water downstairs.

As far as civilized, renovated accommodation was concerned, that was it. The rest of the building was rudimentary though just about usable. Half of the cloister building was still at the old level, about two metres lower than the restored floor, with a rudimentary wooden staircase between the two. Our old bedrooms would make a spare room and office for me. The room next to it, which had been Theo's leaky bedroom before the roof was renewed, was now a mezzanine of sorts, where the new floor level met the old, with a temporary staircase from the old floor level to the new so we could use the room. This became Miles's office temporarily. We had plans to expand as soon as possible into the section of the west end which already had a new roof. We figured it would not be too expensive to create another room there, at least on the upper floor, for Miles to have a big separate office. (This turned out to be over-optimistic, to put it mildly.) For now there was a rudimentary door of wooden planks installed at the west end of the corridor so we no longer had a view straight through to the west-end ruin. Finally, at the east end was the big room we had previously used as an office, once the farm kitchen with fireplace and bread oven. It was not in good shape, despite valiant efforts by Paul's team to decorate it. The floor was rough boards, ventilated by several holes through to the cave below. The ceiling beams were painted with grim dark-brown paint and also had several large holes through which the rain had leaked before the roof was fixed. The holes had been covered over with hardboard and we simply decided to leave it as it was. The walls had had one coat of white paint, but various yellow stains were seeping damp, and the big fireplace was coated with years of grease and soot. The window frames were still painted agricultural-itinerant-labourer yellow.

The views were superb, however. From the east window there were exquisite pink-streaked dawns, a perfectly framed view of Canigou and a cherry tree. From the south window we could see the opposite side of the valley, with its covering of pine and beech trees. The hill was called Mt Poux, which amused Theo greatly. We were determined to turn this room into our library and sitting room and Miles finally began to whistle, sounding content for the first time, surrounded by dozens of boxes of books. He categorized them in his usual methodical manner, into travel, biography, art, fiction, all neatly aligned on the plain wooden shelves Paul had constructed. Hearing people whistle as they worked became for me a measure of wellbeing; as long as somebody is whistling as they work somewhere in the building I feel reassured.

Downstairs proved even more difficult. There was a big room at the west end of the cloister, which had been 'restored' already. This had French windows that could not be opened from the outside so was no use as an entrance. We had ripped out the ugly new fireplace, which didn't work, but this had left a huge black chimney-shaped triangle on the wall and a gaping rubble-filled hole beneath. There was no ceiling, just the underside of the bedroom floorboards. We could not complete the work, because although the ceiling had been raised to its original level we still needed to do all the floors, windows and wiring as part of opening the cloister arches, some-time in the future. So we had to make it liveable as it was, half done. The huge wooden table was still there but had been severely warped by a torrential rainstorm while the roof was off. There were several places on its top where dishes and plates tilted dangerously. Still, a table that could seat as many as ten at a pinch was too good for firewood and we had a new plywood top made for it.

There was the small adjacent kitchen, which had three doors and a bathroom off it, and not much else other than the ancient stoneware sink, a two-burner stove, a by now decrepit fridge and the elderly *armoire* with wobbly doors and drawers, of which the mice were still particularly fond. Hot water for the upstairs shower and kitchen was provided by one gas heater, fed by butane gas from a cylinder that had an infuriating habit of running out in the middle of cooking or, worse, mid shower – which was bad enough if there was someone downstairs to change it, hopeless if not.

Yet again I cleaned the mouse droppings from the big wooden *armoire* in the kitchen and lined the drawers and shelves, then arranged my pots and bowls; we already had basic kitchen equipment, which I had supplemented with Spanish terracotta pots. I had found a shop in the old town of Ceret that still sold good-quality terracotta, which lasts well and does not crack, as much of the new stuff does now. I stacked round bowls, shallow platters and big rectangular oven dishes; each was slightly different – some had darker glazes, some were deeper than others – and I enjoyed their lack of uniformity, the earthy connection with their origin as simple clay.

The monks' kitchen equipment would have been carefully specified. The best records of monastic kitchen arrangements in France come from the customaries (sets of instructions for monastic life) of Cluny Abbey in Burgundy, the greatest of the medieval monasteries, whose customs were followed by many others throughout France and Spain. Three great cooking pots called *caldaria* were required, one for boiling water, one for cooking beans and one for other vegetables. Another on three legs was required for lye. Four large bowls were also needed: one kept for half-cooked beans, one to stand under the water faucet to wash vegetables, one for

132

washing-up, one to hold the hot water for the weekly feet washing, and one for the brothers to shave with. They also had three great cooking spoons: one for stirring beans, one for other vegetables and one for fat. A shovel was needed for putting coals on the fire; also a pair of tongs, four pairs of cooking sleeves, two hand screens to protect the cooks from the heat of the flames, three cloths, to be cleaned every Thursday, a knife for lard, and a stone to sharpen it with, another saucepan for heating water and melting fat, a skimmer for fat, a salt cellar and spice box, a pail for water, two brooms, two netted dishcloths, two saucepan boards, two stools, a stand for the vegetable bowl, a stone base on which to set the hot cooking pots, a pair of bellows, a wicker fan, two pot hooks, a washing trough, and two pulleys to move the vessels for hot water from the faucet to the fire.

I looked with new eyes at the jumble of bric-à-brac and unnecessary items that crept into my kitchen – the oyster knives, the olive pitter, for example – and wondered if I too would achieve a higher spiritual level if my kitchen was so carefully prescribed. I congratulated myself on at least leaving behind the pasta maker, on the principle that life was always going to be too short to make my own pasta.

New wiring had been installed in the renovated section and we had a temporary system installed in addition, since the old wiring looked really dodgy – bare wires strung from the rafters, frequently deluged by rain. The electrician was a small, squat Catalan with black hair and beard. Although he had a very strong Catalan accent, he said everything with such emphasis, and repeated himself so many times for my benefit, that we managed to communicate. Shaking his head in disbelief at the numbers of sockets we required for each room (hi-fi, computers, vacuum cleaner, lights, TVs . . .), the electrician did as we asked, and even installed the security light we had brought from London. (They do have them in France, it turns out, but we weren't taking any chances at that point. And it would have taken us for ever to work out what they were called and find them anyway.) This was a major new technological development, flashing on whenever anything passed (including dogs and bats) and astonishing the farmers.

I set to work cleaning and scrubbing, vacuuming up the dust of centuries, and began coating everything possible with white paint. Most of it was due to be ripped out at an unspecified later date, when we raised the rest of the floor level and opened the remaining cloister arches, so my only concern was to make it look as fresh and clean as possible and disguise the most infelicitous excrescences. I have never worked so hard in all my life as I did those first few months. I quite literally worked my fingers to the bone, as finally my finger ends started to split and crack.

But every morning there was consolation as I arose to spring. Dawn came late enough for me, about 8 a.m. in the winter, and the east window gave a perfect view of the most splendid artistry. Often I would go straight outside in my dressing gown, revelling in the opportunity after years of watching the sky from my basement window in London, where I craved the chance to go outside without going to the park, without crossing busy polluted roads, before I could breathe. The faintest blush of pink on the peach trees in many of the fields around promised peach blossom. Already there were fairy clouds of white blossom, the almond, which was always the first to appear in February or early March. There were still large fields of snow on the far peaks, luminescent in the sunlight behind the darkly shadowed hills in the foreground. Beyond to the west is the mountain called Madres; I liked the idea of a mountain called 'Mother'.

There was a symphony of birdsong. The only one I could identify at first was that of the blackbird, since we had one that sang outside the bedroom window in London; every year it seemed the same blackbird returned, or perhaps his son or granddaughter, to sing for us. In the cherry tree one day I saw three blackbirds, with glossy ebony coats and bright egg-yellow beaks, arranged so elegantly they looked like a Japanese painting or some kind of heavenly visitation. Then there were the buzzards soaring way above us, cawing, wheeling magnificently. At first there was always a pair and then one day we saw there were three.

Like us the birds were all nesting madly, plucking up all manner of loose twigs, hay, even hair, to make their nests. They popped busily in and out of holes in the building – we could supply an entire housing estate of commodious holes, *tout confort*. Any time anyone passed by they chattered furiously in defence of their territory. I saw one little finch, with blue and yellow feathers, poking its beak-full of grass into a crack in the wall, and I wondered how many generations of little blue and yellow birds had built their nests here. How many monks had watched them too, contemplating their industry. No doubt they had a psalm to sing about it. Miles found a nest in the wall, visible if he quietly slid out a stone; within were perhaps seven cheeping little beaks. But later there was carnage, with three of the tiny fledgelings, all beak and bone, dead on the ground.

The cat, prosaically named Kitty, who had adapted better than anyone, was clearly discovering a whole new world. In several doors there were already rudimentary cat-flaps, obviously made for the farm cats, and she could get outside through a narrow aperture in the wall of the blocked-up cloister. The wind whistling through the hole was less convenient for us, but since the slit was just her width it kept her slim. We fully expected to find her stuck in the gap like Winnie the Pooh, and Theo waited hopefully for the day we could hang tea-towels from her legs. She had spent all her time until then in one block of central London, and at first was horrified by the great outdoors, sniffing the grass and then scuttling back inside to hide in the attic rafters. We thought she might live up there for ever, but then we heard her squeaking one evening and saw a little black face appear at the kitchen window. She had clearly been outside for hours and we began to see her prowling across the field, and stalking the birds and the red squirrel that lives in the pine tree opposite our bedroom window.

Finally Kitty went completely native, shitting outside and seeing off the other cats stalking her territory. She became a killing machine, slaughtering rabbits, squirrels, birds, mice, even a fully grown rat. She watched patiently, poised in intense concentration; and we found her victims strewn about the garden. Sometimes her prey was dragged inside, with a special triumphant mew we had never heard before, and proudly displayed in the middle of the floor for our approval. The farmer warned us that there were lots of foxes, though, and they ate cats. 'C'est la nature,' he said with a shrug.

There were more red squirrels living in a hole in the wall above the apse. Sometimes we caught them dashing vertically up the wall, or saw their tiny dark-brown faces peering inquisitively over the stone ledge. But Kitty had her eye on them too, and lay in wait for hours, and they became more cautious, eventually disappearing altogether once we had cut down the big cypress tree next to the chapel wall.

Soon the peach trees were in full pink flower, dramatic against an impossibly blue sky and the snow still glazing the top of Canigou. I swear I literally saw the cherry tree come into blossom, its little starry white flowers popping out as the sun struck them. And when I scrambled one day along our overgrown river bank I found clusters of violets, tiny shy flowers nestling within large fleshy leaves.

If I knelt right down with my face close to the ground, and snuffled gently, I fancied I could detect the faintest delicate scent. All my friends and relations had been keeping their fingers crossed or praying for us, and their good vibrations seemed to have resulted in the best March the South of France had seen for years.

Our daily life continued fraught with novelty and decisions about every imaginable thing. Even going to the bank was an adventure as I tried to work out how to use my pin number with my new French debit card. Cash was offered in francs or pesetas, reinforcing just how close we were to the border. Spain was only an hour's drive away. It is said that many people in this region had no idea if they were French or Spanish until they were called up for the First World War. The bank was remarkably casual, with open counters and no security grilles. I was there one day when a woman handed her baby over to the cashier to be looked after while she worked out her transaction. Another time the entire façade of the counter fell off. A man in the queue promptly stepped forward, produced a hammer from one of his pockets and hammered it back again. The down side inevitably was long queues while elderly peasants in overalls and berets slowly counted out their takings from the market, or while the bank teller talked on the phone, repeating everything, especially *oui, oui, oui*, over and over again. When I finally figured out how to connect to the bank phone line for recorded information, and could even understand the figures recited to me, I discovered they played John Lennon's 'Imagine' while you waited. Miles was highly amused by this. 'I wonder if they understand the lyrics,' he said. 'Do they realize he's singing about a world with no possessions?'

Our shopping lists were always a bizarre mixture: clothes horse; mattresses (for the second time, since our original purchases were soaked when the new roof was being built); candles; cup hooks; door hooks; rubber gloves; washing line; phone line; gas fire appliance; bucket; loo seat. Even buying run-of-the-mill groceries and domestic products was a challenge, since I still didn't know the brand names of anything and would spend ages bemusedly trying to decide between washing powders, with only the name Zip or Skip to help. Only later did I find out that I had been doing the washing for the first few weeks with fabric conditioner instead of detergent.

It took a long time to get used to the business hours, with midday closing between 12 and 2 p.m. observed even by the supermarkets in Prades most of the time. I also had to adapt to a much slower pace, as assistants wrapped parcels with assiduous care and discussed each purchase in detail with their customers: the quality of the meat, the freshness of the eggs, the taste of the wine. Nobody is in a hurry. Nobody is in it primarily for the money – the best *boulangerie* in Prades closes for *les vacances* during high season, when they could be at their busiest. At first I thought the supermarket assistants were ignoring me when I said '*Bonjour*', but soon I understood that each transaction had to be fully completed, and she would not greet me until she had said, '*Au revoir, merci*,' to the previous customer.

Best of all was the drive to the supermarket, in contrast to the struggle through London traffic I had been used to. I listened to Elvis, Puccini or Verdi as I swept down the magnificent gorge of the valley, past craggy towering rocks with the magnificent sight of Canigou visible ahead. It always gave perspective to even the most harassing day.

Even going to the garage was not the negative experience it had always been in London. I had to contend with cars and garages rather sooner than I had really hoped, since the front side of the poor Renault had been bashed in before we left London behind. It clearly had to be

138

repaired. I considered the local *garagiste* in Mosset, but the steep track down to his garage looked daunting; I figured if your car hadn't needed fixing before, it certainly would by the time you reached the garage. So instead I went to the local Renault dealer in Prades, where I was greeted by Madame Taurinya, a large, handsome woman with a huge bosom, who smoked cigarettes constantly, not least when she was leaning over the engine. Her husband, a slender man, smoked small cigars. He was impressed to hear we were writers and told me he was the grandson of one of Roussillon's best known poets, Alain Taurinya. He immediately presented us with a copy of the poetry, and told us about his own work with Didier Payré, one of the teachers at Mosset school, researching local legends and traditions, recording the memories of old people. For the first time ever, going to the garage became a pleasure, as we exchanged books. Only in France, I thought, could one talk poetry with the *garagiste*.

Discussions about the insurance of the car, however, revealed that since it was nearly ten years old it was not going to qualify for European cover under an English policy any longer. I was also aware that keeping your car longer than six months in the country meant you were supposed to register it in France. This I knew to be a long, arcane Catch 22 kind of project which I was loathe to embark on. It was the kind of gruesome future problem with which other English ex-pats delighted in regaling you. I was once stopped outside the Prades post office by an Englishman who, having spotted my English plates, enquired how long I had been in France with the car. He was anxious to warn me that I would soon be in trouble if I didn't register it with French plates.

We were by now completely broke, so somebody had to start remunerative work immediately. In preparation for an article I read several books about downshifting to a

139

simpler life, all of which said before you make any dramatic changes in your life you must assess your finances very carefully. We disagreed. If you start assessing finances you would never do it. In fact I suspect that the kind of people who assess their finances carefully are not the kind of people who do anything as mad as this anyway. Typically the magazine that commissioned the downshifting article folded before I delivered, and didn't pay any of the contributors.

I had very little time to work those first months, but one project I had to complete was the book about my brother. It had been hard to finish, hard psychologically to let go. It was easier to write it at Corbiac, to relinquish it in a new place, especially a place Simon would have loved. I was always sad that he never visited. So, failing an office as yet, I installed myself in the calm, white-walled bedroom with the Powerbook, and wrote my final chapter. My younger brother had criticized me for 'dwelling on' the subject of Simon's death, and he was right, I *had* dwelled on it, but now it was time to move on. Here and there about the house I put his lovely earthenware bowls, his little Celtic boxes, his photographs of rainbows.

We hoped that modern technology was going to make it relatively easy to work here, and since divesting fortunately had not applied to Miles or to work we did have a fax, two phone lines, hi-fi equipment, French TV and a video recorder. Miles struggled to set up his office with two Macintosh computers, including what was then a state-of-the-art black Performa. We had no desks or filing cabinets yet (I was still trying to find out where to buy them), or even book shelves for our offices, so the precious Macs had to sit on white plastic garden tables. When the wind was in the wrong direction a stream of dust and fine rubble, remnants from the new roof, would trickle through the wooden beams of the ceiling and down the back of his neck.

We also had Internet access, just about, though the trials of connecting to and operating through the French telephone system were long and bitter. I think sometimes I must have sounded like Inspector Clouseau in my efforts to communicate with telephone engineers and marry our ambitious technological requirements with the reality of the crumbling walls where the wires had to go. At this stage in 1997 few of the publishing companies or newspapers we worked for were on line, so e-mail was rare and we were still dependent on traditional methods of communication. We installed a shiny new mailbox at the end of the drive and going to get the post became a major daily event (the only major daily event, as far as Miles was concerned). I rather enjoyed choosing when to collect the post, rather than having it plop uninvited through the letterbox. It reminded me of an architect friend I used to live with in Bristol, who never opened anything in brown envelopes, and if he hadn't opened his mail considered it had not actually arrived.

We must have doubled the Mosset postbag immediately. Sadly, the mailbox didn't last long in its pristine state. Attached to a pole cemented too close to the narrow road, it was horribly mangled when the next large truck arrived, delivering the office furniture we had finally ordered by catalogue. As the lorry tried to turn into the driveway between the two overhanging cherry trees the mailbox was crushed. Miraculously, it still opened, and stayed there for another year, looking like something steamrollered in a cartoon. I imagine it matched the generally ruinous aspect of the entire edifice to anyone driving by.

Nor did the post appear very promising as a means of communication with the outside world. The village did have a post office but it was open only between 9 and 11 a.m. When I tried to insure a parcel of books, the postmistress insisted that over a certain value the parcel must be secured with string and sealing wax. Someone did kindly produce a stick of red sealing wax, but that we thought was hardly the point.

The first time a courier parcel came for us, the local Federal Express agent phoned to ask if it would be all right if he left it in one of the cafés in Prades for us to collect. No, we said. Another day, when I went to buy my bread in the village *boulangerie*, I happened to spy a Chronopost package left for me on the counter. They had been wondering who it was for. Once Federal Express lost an entire shipment of photos. 'Don't worry,' they said. 'We've lost the entire plane load. All the packages from the South of France have gone missing.'

There were compensations, however, like the time a Federal Express courier begged to take one of the Ardoise slate roof tiles we had stacked up outside the chapel. He explained it was a favourite cooking method in Andorra, and perfect for barbecuing. As he stood at the door with his receipts to sign in one hand and the slate he had selected tucked under his arm, he enthusiastically outlined his recipes for fish, duck breasts and steak. We tried the method out, putting a slate onto the barbecue grill instead of cooking directly over the open fire in the traditional way. It worked brilliantly, the slate absorbing and spreading the heat; the skin of fish, duck or chicken crisped well without sticking to the bars of the grill when you tried to lift it off. I recalled eating sardines stuffed with ricotta and herbs in Corsica years ago and tried it with a large *daurade* (bream), stuffing it with a mixture of fresh *chèvre* (goat's cheese) and chopped fresh thyme and marjoram, which had melted nicely by the time the fish was cooked. Perfect served with wild rice, and a salad of mixed green leaves and toasted almonds.

Food became more significant in our primitive new life. We bought fresh free-range chickens and guinea fowl from the neighbouring *ferme auberge*, and unpasteurized milk and yoghurt from the newly established dairy in the village. We could see the cows that gave us our milk grazing the field opposite. The local beef, *rosée des Pyrénées*, was excellent, fed only grass and hay in open pastures. The butcher in Prades always displayed a picture of the beast the meat came from to reassure his customers. The steaks were particularly delicious with Roquefort sauce, a local speciality, made with butter, *crème fraîche*, melted Roquefort and sometimes meat stock. For some reason the Catalans eat more Roquefort than anyone else does, despite the fact it originates in the Massif Central, matured in caves with a particular humidity that creates the correct conditions for the famous blue mould. In the supermarket there are seven different sorts of Roquefort on offer.

Accustomed to a wide range of exotic vegetables in Marks & Spencer's and Sainsburys, I was disappointed at first by the meagre supply of vegetables in winter – mainly cabbages, cauliflower, turnips and carrots. Gradually, though, I began to understand that people ate local seasonal fruit and vegetables, not dwarf French beans flown in from Peru, or out-of-season Dutch tomatoes. If they couldn't grow it or preserve it they did without it until it came into season again. We learned to eat according to the seasons and take pleasure in anticipating the new walnuts, the *cèpes* and chanterelles, winter spinach and sorrel, oysters and tuna.

After our first asparagus season that year I was content to wait another year, to savour fully the prospect of eating it again. I realized why someone like Jacques might eat a single perfect peach of his crop or seek out the best *cèpes* on one superb autumn day. Eating one peach picked at just the right moment of ripeness is perhaps better than gorging on crateloads. Miles says this is nonsense, a hangover from my puritanical background. 'What would be wrong with crateloads of perfect peaches?' he queried.

'And it would be nice to drink good wine every day, not just on special occasions.'

Anyway, it was asparagus season a few weeks after we arrived and the market stalls were loaded down with stoutly tied bunches; both the fat white variety, which is never exposed to light, and usually favoured by the French, and the thin, dark-green stalks, the wild asparagus preferred in the Midi. Advised by a market trader anxious I should enjoy his product at its best, I learned that if droplets appear when the stalks are cut it is a sign it is fresh, and that I should keep it in water like cut flowers. Early one morning the farmers had left us on the doorstep a parcel of eggs – all sizes, brown and white, one or two downy feathers still clinging to the shells – wrapped precariously in newspaper. We found the best way to eat asparagus: dipped into the raw yolks of newly laid eggs, and drizzled with hot butter and shavings of parmesan. They are also delicious roasted in olive oil, then strewn with black olives and parmesan cheese.

Whatever the season, there seems to be something in the countryside to forage, and it took us a while to realize that the folk busily combing the roadsides and edges of fields with sticks, hopefully carrying plastic supermarket bags, were looking for the wild asparagus. I was reminded of the first meal I ate in Provence, prepared by a Swiss woman who was a wonderfully inventive cook. It was almost entirely wild food, an omelette of wild asparagus followed by a tart of wild sorrel and spinach. To our surprise we found a single rogue asparagus stalk growing in the wilderness of our garden, so we cooked it and ate it with relish.

But then after several weeks of sunshine the clouds descended. Never had we known anything like it. For several days we were shrouded by a dank pearly mist, sometimes unable to see beyond the garden wall. It felt as if we were marooned or bewitched. Miles compared it to

144

being in a *Rupert Bear* story, 'Nutwood and the Grey Cloud', perhaps, and told Theo we needed the Professor to make a machine to blow it away. The damp rose from the old stones, and with it the animal smells of centuries past. Prints and pictures began to curl up and, worst of all, the books began to buckle. We surveyed the rippling pages with deep dismay, noticing also that strange insects had nibbled little tunnels through some of them.

Medieval monasteries, it transpires, do not have damp courses. At least we didn't suffer the problems of the original monastic libraries. The library of the great abbey of Cluny in Burgundy sometimes lent books to sister monasteries. A plaintive letter still exists from the Abbot of Chartreuse seeking the loan of a volume of the letters of St Augustine, 'for the greater part of our copy, that was in one of our granges, has been accidentally eaten by a bear'. The Book of Durrow, a famous Celtic illustrated manuscript, suffered an even worse fate. After the dissolution of the monasteries in the sixteenth century, the precious book was acquired by an Irish farmer, who used it as a magical treatment for his sick cattle by regularly plunging the holy book into water for them to drink.

Deep in the cloud, we all snuggled up by the fire with our books and the kind of mountain of buttered toast the Hobbit used to dream of on his long, hungry adventure. It was the idyllic snug scene I used to crave in an efficient, but unromantic, centrally heated London basement on dark winter days. We were reading to Theo *The Lion, the Witch and the Wardrobe*, one of the Narnia books by C. S. Lewis. It was my brother's copy, which he had underlined in places, which made it even more nostalgic. We had so often wished ourselves in Narnia when we were children, hiding hopefully in wardrobes, in case Mr Tumnus turned up.

Miles began sorting out more boxes of books. For Theo he produced several *Famous Five* books we had not yet

145

read. I took great pleasure in reading Theo my old favourites, what I considered to be an essential part of his cultural education. We even tried them in French translation, *Le Club des Cinq*, to discover them eating croissants instead of buns, and *paté en croûte*, *tarte aux fraises* and Camembert instead of egg-and-lettuce sandwiches, pork pies and ginger beer. George had become Jacques/Jacqueline and poor old Timmy the dog was called Dagobert. Miles countered this with an equally essential diet of rock music, jazz and Charlie Chaplin films. While I worried that Theo hadn't read *Swiss Family Robinson*, Miles thought it a serious gap that he had not heard of *Wayne's World* or James Bond.

Theo himself seemed to be able to source a perfectly conventional contemporary diet of dinosaurs, Batman, Spiderman, Dragon Ball Z and Pokémon, and liked nothing better than to go to bed with the *Beano*. He seemed not to have lost touch in that respect at all, or perhaps such children's entertainment is now so universal it transcends language barriers – a positive form of globalization linking kids across the world with a common language of McDonald's, Disney and plastic superheroes. Like most of his contemporaries, Theo watched too much television and best of all liked to have the TV and his GameBoy both at the same time. 'I like noise, Mum!' he would say. He had little interest in books, although he liked the *Bande dessinée*, the comic books that are so popular in France, among adults as well as children. But when I started muttering about Shakespeare I knew I was fighting a rearguard action.

For the monks the idea of communal reading was essential to their worship, both as part of the daily offices and during mealtimes, when they would take it in turns to read to their brethren as they ate in silence. It was the duty of the cantor to look after the precious books of the monastery, which used to be kept in special chests in the cloister. Not until the fifteenth century were there libraries, special rooms devoted entirely to books. Miles fulfils the role of cantor for us to perfection.

Finally, after several days in the depths of the cloud, we heard a nightingale singing its complicated little song, always the same theme over and over as if its heart would break. It was exquisite, magical, as if what we had really needed was the nightingale to come and sing the cloud away. There is a lovely Catalan song summoning the *rossignol* – the nightingale – to soothe the children in winter.

But in truth it was the great wind from the Pyrenees, the Tramontane, which really blew the clouds away. It blew for several days, rattling the windows and piercing every crack in the walls, of which there were many. Outside it tore at your clothing and made your eyes water. It left us begging for mercy, but it swept all before it, and the valley was left washed and fresh as dawn. All the impurities were blown from the air, and the grey clouds vanished. We hated the wind howling round us, but wise friends told us we must learn to love it. Canigou reappeared angelically crowned by a little halo of white fluffy clouds. It was like the beginning of the world.

8

French without tears

By March it was time for Theo to go to school. For the first few weeks I took him by car and picked him up at the end of the day. At first he hung back when I left him and sometimes he cried, but, I was assured, cheered up pretty soon after I'd gone. Although it was nearly two years since he had spent a month there, it was all at least vaguely familiar and most of the staff were the same. We decided that this time – he was now six – it was better he began straight away without me and stayed for lunch every day in the café. The new teacher – still called Maîtresse – made valiant efforts to understand him with the aid of a large, dog-eared French–English dictionary.

The other children remembered him and were very nice to him, eager to hold his hand when they went for walks in strict crocodile formation. Abigail, his English friend, was indispensable. She was in the older class, and in the first few weeks when he could hardly communicate at all she sometimes had to be summoned from the classroom next door to translate for him. He came home one day and said he had been sick at school and had had to ask Abigail the word for 'vomit' in French before he could be excused. Soon after that he announced brightly over supper one evening, 'I learned the French word for fart today.'

He was naturally cautious and at first refused to play with the other children in the playground, preferring to observe everything from a safe distance. Before long he demanded to travel by the school bus like the other children; in the end it was more important for him to feel he belonged with his peers. Then we simply had to walk with him to the end of the drive and wait under the cherry trees for the little white bus to wind its way up the valley road. At the end of the day the bus, which does a circuit of the valley every morning, lunchtime and evening to pick up and deliver the children, dropped him off again and he made his own way to the house. One day I happened to watch him unobserved, and I was happy to see him skipping down the drive, singing and throwing his coat in the air.

He spoke very little French when he first went to the school, although we had tried to teach him some vocabulary. But the easiest time to learn a foreign language is as a child, and it is a great pity this has yet to be recognized and seriously included in the education system in Britain or France. Most children in either country only start learning foreign languages at the age of eleven or twelve, when it is already too late. The capacity to learn foreign languages diminishes rapidly after that. When they are very young, children learn by ear, unhampered by spelling or reading. Until the age of six or seven they learn a foreign language as they do their own; after that it becomes a more formal affair. Even the facial muscles remain flexible until the age of seven, so it is much easier to adapt the muscles to the various jaw movements required for the pronunciation of other languages.

149

The contrast with Theo's central London school could hardly have been greater. That school, which was only a quarter of a mile from Oxford Circus, was surrounded by tall, redbrick Victorian buildings and heavy traffic. There was a needle exchange around the corner which always had a line of dejected junkies outside. In Mosset they are surrounded by mountains, with only an occasional vehicle passing on its way up to the mountain pass. In London they went on school trips to the London Transport Museum in Covent Garden; from Mosset they could go for walks in the forest and learn about birds and mushrooms, or go and sail paper boats in the village *lavoir*, the old wash house, which still had a huge basin of water.

The level of provision for the children in French schools is generally excellent, with primary-school-children particularly well provided for. They can start at age three, attending the *maternelle*, or nursery, full-time, as preparation for school. There is also a *garderie* after school, where the children can stay and play until 6 p.m. There is no charge for any of these services. (In London, by contrast, parents themselves had to organize after-school childcare and employ someone as a carer. The school made a room available but took no other responsibility.)

The strangest thing to get used to was that there was no school on Wednesdays, which is supposed to be devoted to sports or arts activities, but there was school on Saturday mornings. This is difficult if both parents work or you like to go away for the weekend, but many women in France work a three- or four-day week so they can have Wednesdays free for the children. *Le weekend* is, anyway, a pretty recent development – they don't have a word for it after all; for most people Sunday is the only day off, and the idea of *dimanche* and long family lunches is still treasured.

The pupils in Mosset, and in most *écoles primaires*, are aged between two and a half and eleven. In Mosset they are divided between two classrooms, with two teachers. This is the old system of *classe unique*, where the teacher teaches children in one class at several different levels, and the children are encouraged to help one another. In the younger class where Theo began, *les petits* played and drew at low tables, supervised by a nursery assistant, while *les grands* sat at desks and were taught from the blackboard by the new *maîtresse*, a brisk, extrovert woman, with a penchant for playing the accordion, who had spent many years teaching in a large Paris school. She had moved to the next village with her husband, a distinguished entomologist who preferred insects to people. The children loved hearing Maîtresse's stories of car trips with her husband, who liked to drive with the sun-roof open and a large butterfly net sticking out of the top to catch insects.

Theo was lucky to join the school when he did. I had been so anxious for him to start, knowing how critical it was he should learn French early. Even then it seemed very late. He was able to spend a few months in the younger class learning French, before moving up to the older class, where he would be expected to know how to read.

He was learning to read in English, but was hardly fluent. The French class he joined was engaged in simple reading and writing exercises, matching text and pictures. With 'Le chat mange le poisson', for example, he had to match drawings of a cat and a fish to the words; or they had to draw the subject corresponding to the word – for instance, to distinguish between *un clou* (a nail) and *une clé* (a key.) At this level Theo could simply learn the French along with the reading and writing. The French approach is to teach reading through writing with great stress placed on draftsmanship; letters had to be correctly drawn, within upper and lower lines of special school paper. They learned cursive script, proper joined-up writing, from the beginning, with elaborate curly French 'R's and 'T's. Several exercises were designed simply to teach the correct shape for a letter – for example, that of the letter 'U' was reinforced by drawing the repetitive scales of a fish.

Apart from tentative encounters with other parents our acquaintance at this point was pretty limited. Few of the people we had met during summer visits lived there all year round. Nobody in their right mind, it seemed, was there in February or March. The village, which is relatively lively in summer, with people sitting outside the café, old folks perched on the wall watching the traffic, was cold, windswept and empty in the winter.

When I went to buy bread one day, the wind was howling cruelly through the Place next to the church, which has been sliced through the middle by the main road. Until 1908 the main thoroughfare wound through the village streets from gate to gate, but then the track over the Col was improved and surfaced, making it the main route over the Pyrenees into the Aude *département*. Now it bisects the village, and although traffic is infrequent except in the brief summer season, it is divisive and dangerous. Nevertheless, there are usually enough stray dogs in the Place to slow up any diehard French motorists.

Though the café windows were steamed up it was easy to see there was only one hunched figure at the bar. An old lady shuffled past in her black dress and slippers, with a basket of carrots and onions from her garden below the ramparts. (Most of the villagers who live in small village houses without gardens still maintain a vegetable *potager*, or allotment, outside the walls.) '*Bonjour, Madame*,' I hazarded and she responded with a quizzical look.

I went to the *épicerie*, an old-fashioned shop that supplied all the needs of the older folk of the village, especially the women who had never learned to drive. Here Yvette presided, always dressed in a standard-issue pinafore, with her dark hair in a tight old-fashioned bun. I commented that the village seemed very quiet, and she intoned gloomily in agreement, '*Il tombe, il tombe*.' As far as she was concerned the village was finished, irremediably changed by foreigners like me, but as a steady influx of foreigners has been the norm for this valley since the time of the Phoenicians one suspected she is playing a role that has been part of the fabric of village life for centuries.

The *boulangère* is also called Yvette. Even in March she still had Christmas decorations in the window and won't take them down till she substitutes fluffy Easter bunnies, which will stay at least until summer, or until she gets out the dried corn and gourds in the autumn. This Yvette is very taciturn, and several winters passed before she acknowledged me and smiled. Her shop is basic, stocking *baguettes*, *croissants*, a few packets of pasta and an array of *bonbons* in glass jars, which the children select painstakingly one by one. In the corner is an old wooden bread table, a *pétrin*, looking rather like a small coffin on legs, once part of the basic furniture of every village kitchen, for holding the dough while it was rising, along with a lockable wall cupboard to store the bread for the week.

There was still snow in the air, and on the col, and I asked Yvette if she liked to ski. '*Ah oui, j'aime beaucoup le ski*.' So did she go often? 'Every year,' she said firmly. She would wait for the right conditions – clear weather, good snow – and then ski, just once each year. The idea of this small, feisty woman waiting for the perfect moment to ski, being satisfied to ski just once a year, fascinated me. It was like waiting for the wild asparagus to make its brief appearance, for the one dish of *cèpes* gathered on a warm autumn day, or savouring the taste of that perfect peach. It seemed to me a kind of contentment that was impossible to imagine in contemporary life. There was something about the restraint, the ability to be satisfied with so little, which somehow reverberated with the austere lives of the monks.

At Easter I went back to England with Theo, and it rained for the next three weeks at Corbiac, where Miles was alone, trying to write and keep warm. He described opening the door and being hit with a great wave of water that soaked him to the skin. He was not a happy man by the time we returned. He greeted me with the news that the septic tank was overflowing and that he had fallen off a wall at the edge of the field, where he had been investigating what the neighbouring farmer was up to. The farmer had set fire to the undergrowth to clear it and then gone to lunch, allowing the flames to spread to our land. Miles had hurt his leg quite badly, and his eye. I told him he was not allowed out of the garden any more without carrying flares in his pocket. He had also had several tourists demanding to see the church, after which he resorted to putting a notice on the door. He had looked up how to write 'piss off' in French and written '*Fous le camp*', which is very rude. I was horrified, thinking of the embryonic relationships I was attempting to develop with other parents and what they would think if they saw it.

His fall was the beginning of a nightmare for Miles, who left almost immediately for London himself. His eye was very cloudy and it transpired he had a torn retina. He had to have two emergency eye operations and in the end was away for three weeks. It was the downside of living in two places, since he had no-one to look after him there. Later that summer the other eye began to show similar

154

symptoms and he had to have another laser treatment. This was done in Prades, our small local town, by a very efficient ophthalmologist and I was impressed that treatment of such quality was readily available here. It was the beginning of an unprecedented accident-prone year for us all, with broken bones and car crashes the like of which we had never experienced before.

While Miles was away, I was left for the first time in sole charge of the great, creaking, wind-blown abbey. I had Theo for company of course, and sometimes he slipped into my bed at night, a warm, cosy little body of great comfort. But during the day when he was at school, I was alone. It was a sort of survival test, I suppose. The first night or two I lay awake for hours, twitching at every creak and groan, waiting for the roof to fall in or the local axe man to arrive and chop us into small pieces. Having a house like this is a bit like having a new baby: unpredictable things happen, you never know what to expect; in the same way that you fear a tiny cough is the beginning of terrible illness, you worry that a creaking beam is a herald of forthcoming disaster. If you were ever to do it again, ever to have another baby or buy another monastery, experience would tell you it was just a cold or the wind in the rafters.

But mostly I felt happy alone, unafraid. I sat by the fire one night with no music on, and it was so quiet I could hear my own body rhythms. Miles had pointed that out. I think I thought it was the dishwasher before that. It felt as if I was finally taking possession of the house. It was imbued with several centuries of prayer and chanting, and for me the atmosphere was utterly benign.

One of the lowest moments of this first time alone was caused by the fire. Technology notwithstanding, I had been determined to get a decent wood fire going – my great romantic dream. ('More dust,' groaned Miles.) I hauled logs, collected kindling and even bought myself an axe. Standing in the queue to pay at the hardware store, two men in line behind eyed me quite nervously. 'What are you going to do with that?' one asked with a chuckle, but I think they saw me in red lipstick, grasping my axe, and remembered the film *Basic Instinct*. I got a sudden depressing insight into their view of women.

I felt an extraordinary sense of power as I hefted the axe and brought it home in the back of the car. A bit like riding shotgun. Unfortunately I failed miserably to make the slightest impact on the most modest log, despite advice on the *t'ai chi* of the axe swing proffered by a local Dutch hippie with bright-red hennaed hair, who arrived at the door on horseback not long after we moved in.

The fire in the library did indeed look wonderful, with its big, curved, white plaster mantel flanked by a bread oven, and the scent of woodsmoke on the air outside was nostalgic. Cosy as it looked, though, the fire was woefully inadequate and the room was beset by gale-force draughts, despite Miles's efforts to plug the worst holes with newspaper. Most of the heat went straight up the chimney, and unless you sat within about a foot of the fire it hardly warmed you at all. Miles and I had argued for years in a hypothetical way about the pluses and minuses of a log fire; now Miles seemed to be proved right.

We did have plenty of dry wood. One of the big pine trees in the garden had blown over in a mighty storm several years before and we had cut it down, with the help of the peach farmers and visiting friends. We had a huge stack of dry logs ready cut with Jacques' chainsaw and piled in the chapel. Pine, it turned out, though, was notorious for spitting. The fire could not safely be left once it was lit. Moreover, the fire was upstairs and the temporary kitchen was downstairs. Worst of all, we had no fireguard because I hadn't come across one in a style I could tolerate. Now with Miles away, I found myself with the fire lit, red sparks spitting all over the floor, and supper to cook. Unable to leave my dream fire un-attended, I wept with frustration. The solution finally was to put Theo in charge of the fire, under strict instructions to shout for me if anything sparked too dramatically. I reasoned that small boys (or, I suppose, grandmothers, but ours was wisely absent at this point) had been employed keeping watch over fires for millenniums, so I might as well uphold the tradition. It was the first of many times when my choice whether to allow Theo to take a risk and learn something was in fact mediated by necessity. Even at the early age of six he had a role to play.

By late spring, although the weather had improved, it was still cold in the house. It had been boarded up so long it had had no chance to absorb winter sun. I decided it was warmer to work outside and sat on the terrace to write, struggling to see the screen in the blazing sun wearing sunglasses, sunscreen, a hat and a quilted waistcoat. Sitting outside the cloister I thought about the monks here. This was where they would have done their writing. Not surprisingly, it was this south-facing north walk of the cloister that was most favoured traditionally as a scriptorium; here the monks could sit and laboriously copy out the manuscripts of psalms and gospels they needed for worship, their tired fingers warmed by the sun.

The cloister would not make a very suitable scriptorium for writers today since the sun would reflect off the computer screens. We of course do not have to make the basic materials to work with; in those days, however, pages had to be created from vellum of calf or lambskin, or more modestly of waxed wooden tablets tied together with leather thongs. Lamp black or soot was used to make ink, and the colours that embellished the manuscripts were made from shells, lead, malachite, various rocks, and even insects; the *kermes illicis*, for example, is an insect that creates warts on a species of Mediterranean oak, which when crushed produces a brilliant red. Flowers of the yellow flag iris yield a yellow dye, and the black dye from the roots was used as an ink. Fish oil or egg white was employed to fix the colours on the page. Bluebell roots were sometimes used to make paper glue for book binding. The magnificent blue of lapis lazuli was keenly sought. It was pleasing to discover that the Abbot of Fleury, a grammarian, mathematician and historian, who died in 1004, noted that, 'After prayer and fasting, the practice of literary composition did most to bridle the lusts of the flesh.'

The nights those first months were often as clear and splendid as the days, deep darkness studded with thousands of stars. I was so greedy for them I sat out on the terrace after dark and simply stared. I wanted to know all the constellations, to be one of those people who can glance up to the heavens and say, 'Oh, there's the plough, and look, Orion.' As it was, I had just about managed to identify Mars as the red planet, after reading an entire trilogy of science fiction and with patient guidance from Miles.

The moon too was becoming a new acquaintance. After years of occasional glimpses through London roof tops, it was miraculous to be able to watch its slow progress across the heavens as it waxed and waned. Sometimes it shone into our uncurtained bedroom window so brightly it was hard to sleep. I remained baffled as to its cycle, however, and glazed over when Miles tried to explain the complexities of the moon and its orbits.

The peach farmers say they work by the moon's cycle: a waxing moon is best for planting, and a waning moon for chopping wood when the sap is not rising. But how does anyone ever work out how to plant by it, I wonder. A prosaic English neighbour told me he had done a control planting, putting in some potatoes according to the moon rule, others at random. He reckoned he could perceive no difference.

The farmers had been acting very mysteriously since we arrived. They were distant, reluctant to stop and chat as they used to, as if the relationship was different once we were installed as real inhabitants, not just amusing patrons who turned up for a month or two in the summer, got everything wrong and went away again. They emptied out of the chapel all the tractors and equipment; in fact there was a distinct scorched-earth feel to their departure: everything of any possible use was garnered up, nothing was wasted – newspapers, old yoghurt pots, jam jars, bits of rope and string, all carefully husbanded and reused. If they left eggs or peaches in an old plastic carton, they always wanted it back. Woe betide me if I threw it away. As he headed off, waving, down the drive, Jacques picked up a piece of old wire mesh and asked if we wanted it, then squirrelled it away purposefully in the back of the ancient 2CV as soon as I gave him permission. I invited them for a drink as I used to do on our summer visits, but they demurred, and ever after found an excuse to refuse. We were never invited to their house in the village again. They still gave Theo packets of sweets when they saw him, but invitations to view the rabbits or feed the chickens were no longer issued, and my fantasies of them as substitute grandparents, eager to teach him country lore, faded fast.

We discovered the worst thing about peach trees is that they have to be sprayed with unspeakable chemicals several times a year but especially in spring. The peaches were hybrids producing identical-sized perfect science-fiction fruit. One day (despite my tentative requests to him not to) Jacques started spraying at 8.30 a.m. just as we were about to set out to wait for the school bus at the end of the drive, and the air was thick with toxic fumes.

I waved ineffectually at Jacques, gesticulating my disapproval, and wanting to explain that pollution was one of the urban ills I was trying to escape. In the end I decided it would be safer to get in the car, leave the windows fully wound up, and drive Theo to school. Jacques was oblivious, head down, driving the battered old tractor, carefully swathed in mask and gloves, to protect him from the chemical onslaught. Thérèse, however, was walking a few paces behind the tractor in her usual flowery pinafore and wellington boots, completely unprotected. No doubt they were following the letter of the law.

The neighbours, meanwhile, watched warily from a distance. No welcome wagon here. Only slowly did I learn the ways of these mountain people: there if you need them, but unlikely to press themselves upon you. Later I met Madame Gomez, who lives in the farm adjoining the Corbiac property, overlooking the monastery from the east, and she complained that it disturbed her that our chimney is on the other side of the building so she can never see the smoke from our fire. For her this would be a traditional signal that all was well with the neighbours: the fire lit meant that the daily round was under way. Perhaps it is just as well she can't see our smoke, since it appears much more erratically than peasant tradition demands; sometimes we don't light the fire till the afternoon, and in any case we don't use it for cooking. Still, I like the idea of my neighbour, while maintaining the discreet distance appropriate in this small hamlet, taking it for granted that she should look out for our welfare.

Only Sylvie made any real gesture of welcome. She came from the stables two fields away; the white-painted fence of the paddock is visible from our property. It is no doubt significant that she too was an incomer, even if she had lived there for fifteen years or so by that time. She is sturdily built, not tall, but with the upright carriage of a horsewoman, full-bosomed, with streaked blonde hair piled in artistic dishevelment on top of her head *à la* Brigitte Bardot circa 1956.

She arrived, one afternoon while I was writing on the terrace, with a spray of purple irises from her garden. I invited her for tea, English-style, with milk, which she accepted with amused interest. Most French people drink it without milk, though they do often add sugar, and English tea bags are still one of the things I bring back. Tea bags are made deliberately weak for the French. Sylvie and I had met before, when I took Theo riding one day, and now she suggested that Maxime, her son, who is a year older than Theo, would be a suitable friend and it would be good for them both to learn each other's language. And perhaps Garance (the name means 'rose madder' in French), her fourteen-year-old daughter, might come and get help with her English homework?

She invited Theo to go riding again, so a few days later we walked up the Mosset road and through the hacienda-style gateway with Sylvie's hand-painted sign, Domaine St Georges. The path, which wound steeply down the valley side, was deeply rutted and rocky. On the banks either side horses were grazing and chickens, bantams and guinea fowl were scrabbling around under the trees. The enormous black dog of childhood night-mares came running up and grabbed my arm in its teeth. 'She is only playing,' explained Sylvie indulgently, as she approached.

When I paused to smell the lilacs along the path leading to the house, she snapped off a few sprays and deftly transformed them into a handsome bouquet, explaining that she once worked as a flower stylist in Paris. Inside the house a log fire was blazing with the wood-stove door open; beside it, a big wicker chair. Pretty flounced curtains of Provençal fabric, sewn by Sylvie, draped the windows. Beyond, under a mezzanine floor, Garance was watching television. She rose to greet me politely with kisses on both cheeks, as well-brought-up children still do, even when they are first introduced to an adult. In the corner was an easel with one of Sylvie's paintings of pumpkins on it. George, her husband, greeted me with an English ''allo' from the stove. He is tall and dark, with a moustache, and a sprinkling of English, learnt as a waiter in London. He reminds me of José Bove, the swash-buckling anti-globalization campaigner and peasants' hero. George did most of the cooking for the family and guests, though Sylvie did a good line in rich chocolate gâteaux and home-made fruit liqueurs.

Sylvie coaxed me to sit down in the chair by the fire and gave me a glass of rose-hip tea. They showed me a dog-eared photo of the house, no more than a small shack when they arrived. Horses are their mutual passion and they have established a stables and simple lodgings where they accommodate guests, give riding lessons and take people trekking in the mountains. They seemed content, and live very frugally, growing vegetables in a village *potager*, fishing for trout from the river, keeping their own chickens and guinea fowl, rarely travelling or taking holidays. Even the newspaper is passed on from someone else. They have a car, which gets them to market once a week, but Sylvie said she hated driving. 'If I ever have to drive I find it so stressful, George always knows I will need to eat an entrecôte afterwards,' she said quite seriously. Sometimes George gave us several of the small trout he caught, which Miles liked to cook in the Catalan style, dusted in flour, fried in butter and oil, then covered with a sautéd mixture of minced garlic, parsley and chopped *prosciutto*.

One day in the spring we drove up to the plateau between the Castellane valley and the Fenouilledes range of hills. It is savage open country, strewn with great boulders that look as if they have been flung down by a giant hand, some rearranged into mysterious dolmen and menhirs by neolithic forebears, who must have had gargantuan resources of strength.

It was only April but the sun was so hot, the sky so blue, it was like a summer's day. We stopped to climb up the hillside, a stark, barren expanse of goat tracks, scented herbs, rough gorse and, everywhere, silvery-leaved olives with ancient twisted trunks, now abandoned, but once a vitally important crop. There was a scent of yellow broom in the air, and pink cistus flowering, returning swallows diving in the clear sky, and a busy world of ants and lizards darting over the stony ground.

The view was awesome: the peaks of the mountains stretching away, their flanks still striped with snow, small fields of cows tucked into any available level space of land below us, a lonely little chapel on the hill opposite. It was a tenth-century hermitage, which made me think again of the monks and hermits seeking solitude in the deep peace of these mountains. Gently we dug up two small thyme plants to put in the garden.

We decided we would make our own maquis garden, on a promontory of rocky ground that faced due south. We would try to recreate the natural *garrigue* of the mountains with cystus, broom, thyme, rosemary and lavender, and maybe aloes and cacti too. The little thyme plants were dug in and watered and we waited hopefully.

The garden was in truth a terrible mess. We had never done very much during our summer visits, apart from chop down dead trees and attempt to curb the brambles and weeds. Now building work had added to the chaos: half the terrace had been ripped up to tackle the dodgy plumbing beneath; a teaspoon, it transpired, was the main cause of the blockage, but by then half the terrace had gone. A huge pile of stones and rubble from the walls that had been removed from inside the building was heaped in one corner of the garden. Fortunately the weather held, the sun continued to shine, and we could contemplate the mess with equanimity.

As usual our interests were difficult to reconcile. Miles was interested only in preserving the building, while I wanted to decorate it and make it pretty. Whereas I was inclined to train wisteria to drip romantically over a ruined wall, he wanted to tear back all the vegetation to reveal the stonework and protect it from further incursions by evil, invasive roots. I looked longingly at stone walls imagining them as a backdrop for roses and clematis, but Miles resisted any planting that might damage the fabric.

He was determined to dig out a thriving bay tree whose roots had caused an ever-widening crack in the cloister wall. He had poured in gallons of caustic soda, but finally brute force proved necessary to get the roots out. Meanwhile, I was busily trying to grow another bay tree in a little pot. I resigned myself to planting my herbs in beds in the middle of the garden, a plan that would in any case fit in better with the original cloister garden of the monks, which would have had herbs or trees and maybe a fountain in the middle of the enclosed arched galleries. We still had the original holy-water stoup for the church; it was crude – not like the sculpted marble basins often seen in churches here, but simply a big hollowed-out round stone like an Anish Kapoor sculpture. It would have stood by the main entrance so that the monks could sprinkle themselves with holy water as they came into the church. The stoup had been cemented on the end of the terrace by the previous owner but had now been moved by the builders. I imagined it in the centre of the cloister, perhaps as a fountain, or maybe simply brimming with a meniscus of water. Reconstructing the cloister would have obvious advantages, we decided, not least of protecting us from the fierce wind. There were enough fragments of arches to show the position of the rectangular cloister garth around which the monks would have walked, meditating or chanting their daily offices.

In the end Miles's approach proved more sound than mine. He decided to reconstruct the devastated corner of the terrace in stones, and we then gradually filled the space with wheelbarrow-loads of earth, and planted small bushes of rosemary and lavender, which grew gratifyingly quickly.

All the chaos and mess was of course paradise for a six-year-old, and we rather hopelessly kept warning Theo off the piles of rocks and rubble, but then he pointed out that he had never fallen and that it was good practice for mountain climbing. 'Mountains often have slippy rocks, Mum, so you have to learn to test them before you stand on them.' It was true: it was a lot better training for the terrain than a super safeguarded children's playground. We climbed up the hill on the other side of the valley, to Rabbit Rock, so called by us because of its silhouette at certain times of the day. Theo was intrepid scaling up dizzy rocky outcrops, obliging me to follow and attempt climbing feats I would never otherwise have considered. He was going to set the pace.

Theo requisitioned a pile of builder's sand as a sandpit and it rapidly became dinosaur land. Then he created different countries with rocks and slates to represent them. One had a kangaroo on it: that was Australia, Theo explained. England had lots of cars and France had lots of dogs, which just about summed up his perspective, I suppose. He found large animal bones all over the place and began to arrange them into shapes and sculptures, including an entire 10-foot long dinosaur of cow bones. Encouraged by this level of creativity, Miles returned from his travels one day with a $2 remaindered book on how to construct a dinosaur out of two chicken carcasses. First, boil the chickens . . .

Having also purchased a strimmer, he attempted to

mow the grass or at least the cloister area that was latterly covered in brambles. There seemed little point in seeding it until all the building work was done, but even cutting it had made a huge difference from the wilderness that was there before and Miles's satisfaction in his lawn was positively suburban. What is it about men and lawns? Ideally, though, he said, he would prefer to see it all paved over like a courtyard. No grass at all.

We congratulated ourselves on our manual labours, taking pride in the fact that we were already fitter, and our hands and faces were surprisingly tanned. My arm muscles were even beginning to impress Theo, who was keen on Popeye at the time. Manual labour, at least in the early days of the monasteries, was considered an important part of the monastic life, following the original rule of St Benedict. There were variations, but in many monasteries – certainly small ones like Corbiac – it would have been essential. Planting crops, raising animals, building walls and tending the garden were all part of the daily life of the monastery.

Later on the rule was relaxed, and in a feudal society it is likely that the monks would have had servants for many of their tasks. Perhaps they became more like the decadent monks of Cluny, sniffily criticized for going through a mere ritual of manual labour, counting the work of the monastery, the psalm singing and liturgical chanting as their proper labour. Indeed it is hard to see how it would have been possible to fit in a proper agricultural day with the three or four hours of offices required.

The monks at Cluny, according to one account, would proceed solemnly to the garden after matins, bow to the east and begin weeding the beans, only to be recalled to the abbey soon after to sing the next offices. They would return to the fields again later but would be more likely to sit in the shade of a tree to receive a lecture on the benefits of manual labour.

My new rusticism was equally ambivalent. I spent as many hours reading books about herbs as I did planting them. It was clearly more efficient to buy vegetables than spend the time required to grow them, however good they might taste. As I pottered about the garden in my sun hat with my latest basket on my arm I sometimes felt like Marie Antoinette playing at being a milkmaid.

9

Village d'Europe et du monde

We went that year to the village *foire*, an event that had recently been revived. It was the beginning of May and turned out to be bitterly cold. I still thought we had moved to the South of France and I dressed up in silk trousers, sandals and jewellery. I froze. Nor was my attire suitable for inspecting sheep, cows and chickens. The fair was traditionally an event held for the farmers to display and sell their livestock. There were still pens of animals to be seen, and one elderly shepherd was presented with a prize for his sheep by the mayor. Few of the old shepherds are left now, but this one is distinguished enough to feature on one of the village postcards. I have once or twice seen him crossing the village street with his flock and disappearing up the narrow street to the pastures above, where he sits under a tree with his traditional blue shepherd's umbrella and the black-and-white dog that is grandfather to many of the other dogs in the village.

Until the mid-twentieth century everyone had goats

that would be sheltered in the village at night. The ground floor of all the village houses was where the animals were always kept and wood and hay was stored. People lived above them, benefiting from the warmth that rose from the animals.The goats were taken out to pasture by the goatherd every day, responding to his whistle as he passed their houses. When they returned at dusk the goats all headed happily, without prompting, for their own stables. Today most people in the village still use the ground floor *cave* for storage and live on the second floor, as did the farmers at Corbiac.

These days the village *foire* is an opportunity for all the local food producers to display their wares. The *ferme auberge* sold its *foie gras* and chickens; Isabelle, the dairy maid, set out her stall with Mosset unpasteurized milk, yoghurt and home-made tarts; Jacqueline presided over trays of cheese – rounds of fresh white *chèvre* and matured cheeses rolled in dried herbs. André Perpigna, one of an extended family of Perpignas in Mosset, sold his honey produced from hives dotted over the mountainside, *miel de la montagne*. Other stalls lined up local wines, oils and vinegars flavoured with herbs and garlic.

There were plenty of hippies from the hills too, selling leather purses and belts, embroidered waistcoats, strings of beads, macramé potholders, dried herbs, hand-made pots and rabbit-skin jerkins. It was clear that the mountains around were riddled with ramshackle small-holdings, as the *soixante-huitards* (as the 1968 generation are termed) and their children carved out a primitive eco-existence with their dogs and donkeys, dancing at the full moon, playing guitars, bathing in the rivers and growing giant pot plants.

This year for the first time the *foire* had been extended to include the artists of the village, who had opened their studios to show their work. The standard was high for such a small village. Bob and Gwen entertained a steady stream of visitors, who were as curious to see their house as their paintings. Bob had applied his artistry to the walls too, painting them white and leaving stones revealed that he particularly liked, to handsome effect.

The couple had been planning to move to Wales from Suffolk but Martha had suggested they looked at a house in Mosset. Within a few days they had bought it, sold their English place and begun a totally new life. Bob, who had been a professional footballer and hairdresser before he trained as an artist, had never even been to France before and spoke not a word of French. They had converted a large house in the village, doing almost all of the work themselves. I particularly admired Gwen's skills as an electrician. In the meantime, they had lived in a tent and washed their clothes in the traditional village *lavoir*. Gwen recalled a group of visitors being given a tour of the village. 'We could hear them saying, "Of course no-one uses the *lavoirs* any more," as they came round the corner, "except for *les anglais*!"'

Robert and Albert's *atelier* was also full of people, seriously studying the abstract paintings on zinc and the lead and zinc sculptures, which Albert was now selling very successfully, as well as examining the doorknobs, shower screens, woodstove, tiles and windows. Robert said that the villagers had always watched the progress of 'the crazy Dutchmen' with fascination, astonished at what they proposed to do with a collapsing barn. 'One old man came straight away with a bottle of wine and three plastic glasses, and asked about everything we were doing. He came back every week after that.' I wondered if they had encountered any animosity because they were gay, but they said they had been warmly welcomed. 'The old man did say one day that it was a shame Albert was not a woman. He said, "He is a very good man for a woman!" And then he saw the washing hanging out and said, "At last. There must be a woman." But we said, "No, it is our washing."'

We too were stunned by the transformation they had made, and beadily made mental notes as we admired the Spanish tiles with their rough texture and varied shades of terracotta, the chalk-stained wooden floors, the step made from a boulder in the shower, the huge new glass windows in Albert's *atelier*, the rocky outcrops at the base of the wall that had been cunningly turned into counters and seating. They had even made a garden, a pocket-sized corner with a magnificent view of Canigou. There was a little table for two, decorative vegetables and shady trees. How did they manage to grow vegetables when they still lived in Holland half the year? 'Oh, we just plant them when we arrive,' said Robert with a wave of his hand. 'They grow very quickly.'

That year the new mayor invited all the foreigners for aperitifs on Europe Day in May. Alain Siré was young, dynamic and determined to drag Mosset into the twenty-first century, pushing ahead plans for a modern new *mairie* and the Tour de Parfum – the key element of his attempts to create tourism in the village – a place for exhibitions on perfume and related local products. However, there were no lavender fields, no scent industry of any kind and never had been in Mosset. There was some muttering about this and someone remarked bitterly, '*Mais alors*, what are the true smells of Mosset? Cow shit, horse shit and dog shit.' (It sounded better in French.)

Aperitifs were served in the village square, with soft drinks and *muscat*, plates of *saucisson*, and slices of pizza from the *boulangerie*. There was an extraordinary babel of languages as English, Dutch, Spanish, Belgian, Finnish, German and Chilean all attempted to talk to one another.

But it was a wonderful confirmation that the folk welcomed us and understood that new blood was necessary if the village was not to die.

Some indeed of the new blood is French, like Marie-Jo, a retired teacher who has set up a library just behind the village square, a rare thing in such a small place. Most of the incoming French are northerners fleeing the cold for a sunnier alfresco life in the south, numbering among them a carpenter, a social worker, a teacher, an electrician and several shepherds. The family who set up the *ferme auberge* originally came from La Rochelle in the Sixties and Sylvie came from Paris.

I was particularly struck by the number of young French people in Mosset. There seemed to be a kind of reverse exodus, of young people escaping to the land rather than away from it. The twentieth century has seen a complete reversal in the image of the country, *la campagne*. In the first half of the century the peasants left the land in droves to go to the cities, looking for work and an easier life. When the Popular Front government established the forty-hour week in 1936, the railways were obliged to recruit 85,000 new employees. They were deluged with applications from peasants, attracted by an unimaginably short working week as well as the prospect of urban life. Over the following three years 300,000 French peasants, many of them under thirty, deserted the farm.

By the 1970s the *soixante-huitards* had begun colonizing remote mountainous regions like this, bringing with them new ideas about eco-friendly land management and conservation. They are called *néo-ruraux* and are attempting to cherish and preserve some aspects of the *paysan* life that is rapidly disappearing, struggling to survive as basket weavers, goat's-cheese producers or leather workers. Increasingly to many young people the rural world looks more attractive, especially since so

172

much of the farming is subsidized. A recent survey estimated that 44 per cent of the French now dream of a life in the country, away from the city grind of *métro-boulot-dodo* (Tube-work-sleep). In the last decade of the twentieth century over 500,000 people left Paris for the provinces.

Most live very simply, grow vegetables in the traditional *potagers*, chop their own wood, go mushroom hunting in the autumn, swimming in the river in summer, drive incredibly beaten-up old cars or rattlebang *vélos*. They roll their own cigarettes and grow their own grass, wear second-hand clothes, and pride themselves on living frugally. Some work for the commune, gardening, fixing walls, collecting rubbish. Many of them paint or sing, are carpenters, potters or gardeners. A hardcore live up in the hills in the old *cortals*, the summer refuges now abandoned by the villagers, working as *bergers*, looking after sheep, or simply subsisting on the land, reviving a way of life which had been sustained until the mid-twentieth century.

The *cortals* were simple stone shacks, two or three hours' walk up the mountains, with pasture and sometimes woodland, where many of the villagers lived from spring to the end of October, taking with them their chickens and rabbits, turkeys, pigs, dogs and cats, to pasture their cows and grow wheat and barley. They returned to Mosset only on Sundays and fête days, though the women had to do the round trip at least once a week to make bread or to irrigate the gardens.

These *nouveaux paysans* don't travel much or take holidays, but they are not simple peasants either; critically they have chosen this life, they have TV, radios, increasingly the Internet, and they know what they are rejecting. I reflect that this is the case for most of the people here. The few who are still genuine peasants, like the peach farmers, cannot conceive of another way of life, are utterly content with what they have, while the young French and the foreigners have made a deliberate decision to live a simpler life.

It occurred to me that there were two Mossets. There is the Mosset of the incomers, some French, some foreigners, most of whom live here all the time and struggle to make a living, establish small business enterprises, tend gardens and revive the daily life of the village. And there is the Mosset of the 'vrai Mossetans' who feel passionately attached to their village and family roots but many of whom have only ever been here for holidays, and then retired here. They are often the ones who grumble most about the village changing, not realizing that if it stayed the way they remembered it would die.

One day all the village was invited to herrings and schnapps in the square to celebrate the wedding of Lettie and Ludovic. They had been married in the church, Lettie, warm, rosy-cheeked, with streaked blonde hair in a loose bun like a Vermeer milkmaid, Ludo, tall, loose-limbed, his face deeply smile-lined with a day's stubble, kitted out in a faded white suit. Lettie had retreated to the Pyrenees, exhausted and burned out from her job as a social worker, and had found solace in the big skies and mountains. Both potters, they lived in a house they built themselves from a ruin in the village, still with bare stone walls and a single wood stove.

We met the Dutch ghetto *en masse* that day and were thankful that it was the Dutch foreigners who dominated the village rather than the English. Among them there were musicians, an opera singer, artists, gardeners, a brain surgeon and several donkey owners, including Marianne, tall, red-haired, brusque and gravelly-voiced, with a sardonic sense of humour which I discovered was typically Dutch. She had given up a career leading holiday groups in Greece to run donkey treks in Mosset.

When we asked Marianne where she lived, she

174

explained that she moved between two houses, one of them belonging to her mother and both of which were rented out in summer. One was a converted olive mill by the river, a simple basic dwelling with a wood stove. 'But then I looked at the house of my mother one day, and thought I was crazy to be carrying wood all the time. It has central heating. You just have to turn a switch.' Sometimes she slept on her terrace if there were too many guests, and had hung her clothes outside. 'But the bats nested in my dresses,' she said resignedly. I asked her once if she had had a good season with the donkeys. 'I have no idea,' she said; she still hadn't done the sums. I got the feeling she probably never would. So long as they produced enough money to live on, it didn't matter, it was what she wanted to be doing anyway.

The lynchpin of the Dutch community was Gerard van Westerloo, who had first arrived in Mosset over twenty years ago. He used to ride down to the village on horseback from his *cortal* in the hills, looking like a Wild West cowboy, but now had moved into the village. He is gay and many of his gay friends have moved to the region on his advice.

'You must ask Gerard,' people would say, about everything from fresco restoration to gardening, horses to ceramic glazes, the best path over the mountains to the relics in the church. Gerard was small, with a natural elegance, his body honed and skin deeply tanned by years of outdoor activity. He was always accompanied by one or two dogs he had rescued.

He had also rescued several buildings in Mosset, and was painstakingly restoring the interior of the fifteenth-century church. Anyone else who had been in Mosset that long, and owned so many properties, would have been well-off by now, or at least have a decent house of their own. But then those were not the kind of people who came to Mosset, it seemed. Gerard was a most unworldly character. Money simply slipped through his fingers – he just wasn't bothered – and he was always losing his possessions or simply moving to another house and leaving them behind. Once he won 4,000 francs in an art competition and left the money on top of the car when he drove away.

He was one of those people who perch lightly on the earth. Years in South Africa had given him a passion for open spaces, for a life close to nature and animals. Eventually he left because of apartheid, and spent a year walking back to Holland. He trained as an artist and became an accomplished ceramicist, but eventually abandoned it to come to the Pyrenees, breed horses and paint. 'Ceramics were too limited. I was always trying to do things that were impossible,' he explained. He ran riding holidays for a while, which were very successful, but never made any money. 'We always spent all the money. We ate too many good meals,' he said, chuckling ruefully. But in the end 'There was a lot too much people' for him and he retreated to live with his horses and dogs in a primitive stone house up in the mountains above Mosset.

Lettie had first come to Mosset on one of Gerard's riding holidays. She described it to me later. 'We were always getting lost,' she said with a laugh. 'We never ever reached the mountain refuge until it was dark. And once we had got to the top of Madres, the mountain west of Mosset, and we could not find the refuge. So we had to tie up the horses and sleep out in the open.' The top of Madres is bleak and almost treeless, however, and by morning the horses had all escaped. 'Gerard says, "Oh, it's no problem: they will have stopped at the next bit of grass and they will all be together." Well, he was right but they were nearly at the bottom of the mountain and we had to go all the way down and all the way up again.'

Access to land was always an issue, and riding through

a field Gerard warned them that the owner did not like them coming through. 'But it is an ancient right of way,' Gerard insisted. 'Sure enough,' says Lettie, 'halfway across she appeared, with a raised shotgun, and Gerard just told us to gallop!' Crossing another field of horses that included a stallion, Gerard warned Lettie that the horse she was riding was *en chaleur*, on heat. She had to gallop fast with the stallion close behind. 'They don't wait for you to get off or anything . . .'

For us the Dutch were to prove critical. They were the cement of the community, a bridge between all the different nationalities. They have usually grown up speaking English and other languages as well as Dutch and, although we could not understand Dutch, sometimes when we overheard it the tone and the rhythm were so close to English that we felt on the verge of comprehension. It seemed to us that the Dutch were key to European integration. Miles commented that they were much closer both culturally and geographically to the English than any other European nation. 'Instead of squabbling with the French, who are so different, the English should treat the Dutch as their door to Europe.'

One of the Dutch women I talked to at Lettie's wedding party said that all the foreigners had one thing in common: that they were brave. All had made a choice, whether they were escaping or pursuing their dreams; all had thought harder than most about what they wanted from their lives. As a result, perhaps, they were also more committed to the life they had chosen, having stepped sideways from traditional paths, and they often had more awareness of the community of which they were part and of their environment. Of course there was also a higher proportion of eccentrics, the folk mad enough, dreamy enough or unhappy enough to make the break from a conventional life. There are more people without children, more women alone, more gay people, more of those

177

English expats that had the vision to move rather than retire to Eastbourne.

Not that all the villagers welcomed foreigners of any sort, French or otherwise, and there were still plenty of diehard peasants who resented any change at all. Occasionally they were obstructive, like the neighbour of Lettie who tormented her for years with his *droit de passage* along the little lane beside her house. First of all he insisted he needed to push a wheelbarrow through it to get to his garden, then he wanted to pass with a trailer; finally she baulked when he began to tease her by saying he had to get a car through the narrow alley.

But most of the villagers can see these mad foreigners spending money on crumbling old ruins that none of them would want to live in themselves. They are busy ripping out their rustic Catalan kitchens and installing Formica and microwaves as fast as they can. Nor is beautifying their village high on the agenda, and the dog shit remains, like everywhere else in France a major source of contention.

When a *nettoyage de printemps* was announced to clean up a section of the river outside the village, the *nettoyage* team consisted almost entirely of civic-minded foreigners, who laboured all morning filling black plastic bags with years of accumulated rubbish that had obviously been chucked into the river by the locals. I later discovered that the French members of the team who had turned up actually lived adjacent and were cleaning up their own bit of river. My hopes that the *nettoyage* would be an annual event were never realized, and the rusting old car and abandoned refrigerator deep in the river gully that runs beside Corbiac are all still there.

The more we hear the more medieval the village still sounds, with people squabbling over fences and boundaries, fighting in the bar and stealing chickens. They complain about someone else's chimney smoke coming in

178

their windows, or a neighbour who has stolen their lettuces. Recently a thief tried to make off with somebody's chickens and sheep in the back of his car. Unfortunately for him he was not familiar with the village and ended up stuck down a little alley that went nowhere. He was still there when the *gendarmes* came, hauled him out and arrested him. The *gendarmes* who have to come up from Prades groan every time they get a call from Mosset.

A fair number of the men still go out hunting, and village freezers are full of sides of venison and haunches of wild boar. Some of the menfolk still get their hair cut in the village square by a travelling barber. One day they are all looking scruffy and shaggy, the next day they all have neat short haircuts.

The twenty-third of June is the eve of the Fête de St-Jean, celebrated in France with bonfires and feasting, especially in the South. Four special herbs, leaves and flowers – St John's Wort (*millepertuis*), the everlasting flower (*immortelle*), the mayflower (*orpin*), all wrapped with a walnut leaf (*feuille de noyer*) – are picked the next morning just before sunrise and made into posies to bring good fortune the following year. One year I did get up before sunrise to collect the right flowers, and I made them into posies and posted them to my mother and friends.

St John's Day is 24 June but the fête is celebrated the evening before, something I discovered too late the first time, turning up in the village on the 24th when it was all over. It is nominally the feast of St John the Baptist but undoubtedly has earlier, pagan origins, being two days after the summer solstice on 21 June, the shortest night of the year. If the night is clear it is possible to see the flames of the fire that is lit on the peak of Canigou and then carried down by torch to light the bonfires in the

179

villages, a tiny light winding its way down the mountain.

The event has been taking place in Mosset for centuries, and although there have been years when the population was severely diminished – years of plague and of war when there were no young men to leap the fire – it is still maintained. The children of the village, dressed in white, including Theo in one of Miles's big white T-shirts, formed a procession which wound its way up the street to the village square, carrying lighted torches aloft. It was led by Sylvie's husband, George, and his daughter, Garance, straight-backed, tall and proud on their gaily caparisoned horses. The bonfire was lit with the torch in the village square and sausages were set to sizzle on a giant grill, so that all the village could eat together. Everyone was offered a drink of *muscat* wine from the traditional Catalan *pourron*, a long-spouted jug. The idea was to try to pour it from a height straight down the throat and not all over your face and clothes. As the square is now the main route through the village, several bemused motorists struggled to pass, one of whom was only allowed to proceed once he had drunk from the *pourron* through the car window.

These were not all traditional villagers running the show. These days such fêtes are as likely to be kept alive by incomers, whether French or foreign. The man who grilled the sausages was José, the school-bus driver, an exile from Pinochet's Chile. When the new mayor wanted to put up a sign outside the village reading 'Mosset, Village d'Europe', it was José who insisted he added 'et du Monde'.

The curly-haired, bespectacled fellow in shorts who organized the children was Belgian. He has achieved a consummate balance in his work schedule, working at the spa hotel down the road in the summer and serving the dead as an undertaker in Prades in the winter. Another Belgian, Véronique, served drinks, along with Michel, who is half French, half Algerian. Dutch Marianne offered bread to go with the sausages and Bob passed the *pourron*, challenging one of the old men of the village to drink from it (which he did with consummate skill). However, the young guy who cranked up the sound system with a spliff of grass wedged in his mouth and a distinct fondness for *l'Hard*, what the French call heavy metal, was a local. Several of the guys normally seen propping up the bar helped to tend the fire. Alain, the suave new mayor, patted backs and shook hands with Tony Blair-style aplomb. René Mestres, the previous mayor, was there too, smiling, happy, I think, to see Alain – rather than a political rival – as his successor following in his footsteps.

Behind the fire a row of young boys, not much older than Theo, waited excitedly. When the fire died down a little they all started to run and leap over the flames. I was appalled and tried to stop them, standing with my arms akimbo. '*C'est dangereux. Arrêtez!*' I shouted. Another mother whose son was in the thick of it remonstrated with me – '*C'est la tradition, madame*' – and I retired abashed. Theo naturally was intrigued and I thought with dread of the moment he too would want to jump the fire.

Bob's use of found objects in his artworks got him into trouble the next morning after the fête. He took a fancy to a piece of charred wood left over from the bonfire and was just carting it off in his wheelbarrow when he was challenged by one of the villagers, who ticked him off because it was not his wood. It was an insight into the passions that wood rights still evoked even today.

The villagers turned out again for the summer school fête, which resembled a 1950s English church fair, with games, tombola, home-made cakes and sales of pottery made by the children. Prizes for the tombola included horse-riding lessons, donkey rides, home-made preserves, local cheese, supplies of milk, watercolours and, most coveted of all, a large jar of *foie gras* from the *ferme auberge*. Here, too, there was a surprising mix of people. Although agriculture and rural tourism remain the main sources of income, there are also nurses, forestry workers, singers, artists and writers among the parents, and there is a truly international mix of pupils, reflecting the population of the village. Theo's best friend was Belgian and when a Dutch girl arrived with no French at all he was sympathetic. She didn't speak English either, but they seemed to communicate all right.

Theo had begun to make friends, to invite them for *goûter* – to tea – and visit their houses too. One day he proudly announced he had watched *Aladdin* in French at Maxime's house. My attempts to communicate with his friends remained rather pathetic and they were often astonished at my laboured efforts, especially when I tried to tell them off and needed to look up words such as 'mess', 'tidy up', and 'stop fighting'. Theo tried to correct my accent, saying '*Arrête!*' with such a roll of the 'rrrr's it was almost frightening. I thought it must be like having a mother who is handicapped in some way, and I tried hard not to embarrass him.

Theo had coped well with his first few months at the school, and was even doing well in *mathématiques*, but of course he was not yet reading. For the next year the school decided he should divide his time between the two classes, until he could read, so that he could move to the older class with his friends. I was very concerned they would feel it necessary for him to *redoubler* and stay down for another year, which would have been very demoralizing for him, but this seemed a very sympathetic and intelligent solution.

He knew his way around the village, and lots of people, already. Most of all he seemed to know the animals. Out for a walk he could identify all the dogs we met by name. 'Look, Mamma, that's Popeye, he has a

182

broken leg.' 'There's Bamboo. He was stuck to another dog the other day and they had to throw a bucket of water over them to separate them.' Thus he was also learning about sex and knew already more about the sexual habits of dogs than I did. He always welcomed the pilgrim dogs who came and begged food, and went on their way. They should wear little scallop shells round their necks, I reflected, like the pilgrims on the route to Santiago de Compostela. Miles took a more robust approach to stray dogs, threatening to follow the example of William Burroughs, who, though very fond of cats, abhorred dogs. He always found a can of Mace very effective.

Rose, an English neighbour and great animal lover, would have been horrified by such a suggestion. We met through the inefficiency of the French postal system. I kept finding letters in the *boîte* for 'Rose Murray': Rose Mary. I suppose the confusion was understandable – in French they sound almost the same. I had heard of her, an elderly Englishwoman of seventy or so, living alone outside Mosset. Bob and Gwen had been to see her in hospital recently. I imagined a rather strict, retired teacher. I looked her up in the *annuaire* and phoned her and she came round to get her letters. She was not at all as I expected: a small spry woman in stretch pants and Lacoste T-shirt, with bare tanned feet slipped into dusty old espadrilles. She had delicate features, in a face lined as much from sun exposure as age, though she was clearly not someone who would ever have much time for sunbathing. Wiry white hair sprang back from a high forehead. She stayed for a drink on our ramshackle terrace, sitting in the chair hugging her knees like a girl, then followed me on the inevitable tour of the monastery – which she always referred to as 'the abbey', making it sound like something out of a 1950s boarding-school story.

Rose had been in Mosset about three years by that time, having decided after her husband died that she did not want to retire to the safe haven of Hampshire like the rest of her sisters. France offered the space, landscape and reasonably priced property she needed and once she saw the little house outside Mosset she knew it was the right place. One balmy summer's day I walked up the lane to see it, tucked away in a sheltered ravine with the most magnificent view of Canigou. The house was simple, fairly new, with French windows opening out of all the downstairs rooms and one large room on the upper floor, accessible by an outside staircase. Rose had transformed it by adding a wooden veranda round three sides so it looked like a bungalow in Simla. Now, covered in climbing roses and clematis, it provided a shady private space for reading on a *chaise longue*.

On the banks around the house Rose had created an exquisite garden of trees and shrubs, with paths that wandered through the surrounding woodland and down to a waterfall. There were holly bushes, roses, lots of lavender, crab-apple trees, lilacs and mimosa. Rose, dressed in a practical pinafore and wellington boots over her jeans and T-shirt, fondled the leaves lovingly, pointing out the silver bark of the birch tree, or a wild columbine that had sprung up. 'Look, here is my little pond,' she said. 'Last year there were salamanders.'

Rose took particular delight in the wildlife she had encouraged with her eco-system, the butterflies attracted by the nettlebed, or the birds that fed on the crab-apple. She cleared the trees from the back of the house so she could see the fox that ran along the bank above. She even enjoyed watching the mice that had taken up residence in her shed, and exclaimed with affection at the spider's webs that had appeared again on her gate. I was impressed by how strong and active she was, and that she seemed so happy to be alone, with just a cat for company.

She didn't seem old though she made no pretence to be young. Old age could be a state of grace.

One day Rose mentioned quite casually, 'I'm an Eden, you know,' by way of explanation. Perhaps it was after mention of the butler tumbling downstairs with a tea-tray and his teeth falling out. She was an eccentric scion of one of Britain's old aristocratic families, the niece of Sir Anthony Eden, the British prime minister. I was intrigued, not least because I had never really met a Conservative I liked before. The wicked Tories were an unquestioned mantra of my uncompromising Socialist upbringing, and most of my actual experience was restricted to reporting on the bring-back-hanging bigots of the Conservative Women's Conference as a young journalist. Rose lent me a book about her grandfather, written by her father (Sir Anthony's older brother, Sir Timothy, who inherited the title after his elder brother Jack was killed in the First World War), entitled *The Tribulations of a Baronet*, about the great family estate of Windlestone in County Durham that Rose could recall as a child, before it had to be sold. She represented a lost period of English life, when great estates were run by paternalistic lords who took care of their tenants and felt completely sure that this was the right order of things. I understood the regret for the loss of an estate that had been in the family for four centuries, and could believe that someone who owned and loved it might take best care of the land.

Our friendship gave me some insight into the mindset of a Tory. My own family were from Durham too, though they came from the other end of the class scale. Miles's parents had been servants in West Country houses similar to Windlestone and his father had an abiding hatred of toffs. It was perhaps only outside England that we could all be friends.

Rose married a diplomat and he and she spent sixteen years abroad. They lived in Portugal (in Byron's house, as

185

it happened) and Romania, and had two children. Rose was not at all a suitable diplomat's wife, and clearly loathed all the dressing-up and cocktail parties. Nowadays she never dresses up; the only concession she makes is the occasional piece of ethnic silver jewellery. Her husband became High Commissioner in Jamaica, and when he moved on to Haiti Rose remained in Jamaica where her children were at school. Rather than stay in Kingston she took a house on her own in the country, to be nearer to the children, where she lived alone without water or electricity. She had an innate confidence in herself, in her value, a kind of self-assurance from her background that I found myself envying.

She told us about her exploits with the Animal Liberation Front after the family returned to England and I loved her story of her driving the getaway car after liberating several beagles from a vivisection laboratory. She was very fond of donkeys and was planning a trip to Morocco to visit a donkey sanctuary. But since she liked camels too she also planned to visit a nomad village and go camel riding for the first time. She had travelled a great deal, visiting Peru and China after her husband died. Several trips to Morocco followed, and she took intimate black-and-white photos of the nomads she travelled with, sharing their tents in the desert and the women's quarters in the village. She agreed that she could do this because she was old. 'It is easy to be inconspicuous. You just buy bread, a few oranges, and you look like a local.'

Rose had an inexhaustible interest in marginal folk, from the slums of Jamaica to the prisons of Britain, and all the most eccentric characters in Mosset seemed to flock to her. She clearly preferred the company of the Dutch hippies, gay artists and local hermits to the retired expat English community who were always asking her to lunch and musical soirées. She never thought twice about

186

giving someone a lift in her car, whereas I would only do so if they were female or I knew who they were.

Soon I was hearing further exploits of several of the more eccentric inhabitants of Mosset. I had met Franz and Joan on an earlier visit, and visited their tiny village house, which was hung with mysterious dried plants and herbs and furnished in part with rabbitskins they had cured themselves. Joan unnerved me particularly by telling me the dreams she had about me. They planned to organize what they called 'mystical mountain walks', and started a yoga class. Rose, typically, let them give a yoga class in her garden, and had awoken one day to find a group of devotees stark naked doing asanas on her lawn.

Rose always liked to know what was going on. 'What's the gossip?' she would say eagerly as soon as she sat down in my kitchen (or '*Qu'est-ce qui se passe?*' if it was the kitchen of Marie-Jo, the village librarian). You didn't need the English tabloids with Rose around. She arrived one day to tell me about a terrible tragedy in the next village. A woman had committed suicide. Before her husband left the house one day she had asked him to sharpen the kitchen knife and once he had gone she had slit her throat. Actually Rose gives credence to the idea that gossip has been a word which has become unjustly pejorative. It derives from the old Saxon word for 'godmother' (*godsibb*, or *godakin*) and originally meant 'spiritual affinity', and 'sharing information about friends and relatives' – a perfectly reasonable activity rather than the spiteful malicious activity that is suggested by the word today. That, anyway, is my justification for being as keen as Rose to hear the latest local news.

Not long after we met her, Rose took up photography again. She had many pictures of Jamaica she had taken twenty years previously – remarkable pictures, born of long intimacy: children dancing in the street; mothers breast-feeding; old women crouched in the squalor of

187

their backyards; dreadlocked rastas smoking huge chillums. Gradually the idea of an exhibition in the village library emerged, and then the photos were accepted as part of the fringe show of the Visa pour Image festival in Perpignan, the main world event for photojournalism. Suddenly Rose became totally focused on her photography, turning her spare room into a dark room, and declaring a distinct distaste for visitors. It was as if she felt she had only limited time and still so much to do.

10

Pecat de gola Deu el perdona: (God pardons the sin of gluttony)

As the days grew warmer I began to do yoga outside under the pine tree, looking up through its filigree branches to a blue sky and circling swallows. My salutations to the sun felt like a faint echo of the prayerful genuflections of the monks. I liked to think of the monks contemplating Canigou as I do. Around me were so many birds trilling, chirping and whistling. I could identify a few: the little robins, lots of big colourful jays, lovely yellow-breasted orioles, a nightingale, the hoopoes with their extraordinary black-and-white-striped plumage which fleetingly land on the lawn.

The herbs I had planted were growing fast. There was lavender and rosemary and several kinds of thyme, vervain, camomile, chives, dill and sorrel. I loved going out to the garden and plucking the freshest leaves of thyme or rosemary for a sauce, grabbing large bunches of sage to add to roast potatoes, or making tea from

189

camomile, vervain or mint. I made a hair rinse from sage and rosemary by steeping the leaves in boiling water. It is good for the scalp and smelt so refreshing when I poured it cold from the jug over my head after I washed my hair.

In the field beside the monastery were great rolls of golden hay, which lacked only a peasant with a pitchfork to look truly picturesque. The cherry trees were heavy with fruit and we were overwhelmed with cherries, dark red and sweet, hanging in perfect clusters. We filled basket after basket with fruit, Miles and Theo climbing a wooden stepladder to pick from the highest branches. There were still plenty for the birds. Garance, Sylvie's teenage daughter, helped to pit them, sitting on the terrace with me, several large bowls between us. Our hands were stained purple and our clothes splashed with juice, and we tried to speak English and French together. I have attempted to help her with her homework, but sometimes I was as foxed as she was by the grammar questions, which seemed very complicated when she could barely speak the language at all. They would ask what was wrong with an English sentence, which looked perfectly all right to me, accustomed to the flexibility of the English language.

I filled every empty jar and bottle with cherries. I made jam, stirring the bubbling fruit, skimming off the scum of impurities, and lifting the spoon until the liquid began to cling and drip sufficiently slowly to be done. I pickled them in sugar and vinegar, drowned them in port and brandy. We made cherry tarts, *clafouti* (a dessert of cherries cooked in batter, which is a bit like Yorkshire pudding with cherries) and sauce for duck breasts. Theo's favourite was chocolate cherries made by dipping the stemmed fruit in melted chocolate.

Once we had picked from the tree nearest the house, we went to gather a basketful from the two old trees that flank each side of the entrance from the road. Suddenly there was a great bellow from the barn where the peach farmers worked a few hundred yards up the road over-looking us. Thérèse jumped into the battered 2CV and drove up in a cloud of dust. I was roundly abused for taking their cherries, because those trees were in the peach fields, part of their land. It made me realize how seriously the rights over the terrain are taken, and from then on I was always anxious about trespassing in ways I knew nothing about.

We were invited to a *cargolade*, a Catalan snail feast, to celebrate Pascal's birthday. Directions were typical: 'Take the ancien chemin de Mosset, past Yves' land, over the arrosage canal, to my uncle's old peach field.' Traditionally a Catalan *cargolade* (Catalan: *cargols*) is celebrated with old friends, but new ones, it seemed, would do just as well.

On a long trestle table under the shade of trees at the side of the field were big mesh sacks of *escargots*. Pascal, who was labouring over a fire of vine cuttings, looked tanned and muscular from his outdoor work, already a different person from the pale, hunched boy who had turned up at Corbiac to cut the grass for us, part of a village initiative to create work for local young people. I was immensely touched to be asked to his party. José was helping lower a huge iron grill over the flames, ready to grill the snails. Theo and I joined in the preparation, intrigued. Carole, the *assistante maternelle* from Theo's school, tall, with a mass of red hair, showed us what to do. Carole was always easy to talk to because she was so used to speaking to children she always said everything at least twice, which was very helpful for me trying to follow her French.

Each snail had to have its little hibernation lid, the veil, removed, and then be dipped in a salt-and-pepper mix until it started to dribble, then hundreds of them (just waking up) were laid on the grill to cook. The usual reckoning is about a hundred snails per person. They were small, these snails, what are called *petit gris*, not the big fat *escargots de bourgogne*, most often served in restaurants. At Corbiac we have lots of the big fat snails, most evident when you go out on a damp night and crunch them underfoot accidentally. After every rain there are hundreds. One even nibbled my toe one night as I sat on the terrace looking at the stars. I was puzzled for a long time why they were there, until someone told me there used to be a snail farm the other side of the river. An enterprising colony must have set up house *chez nous*.

I had once been for a walk late at night outside the village, and been baffled by the people I saw poking about with sticks and torches in the bushes. Finally I worked out they were foraging for snails. So when I saw our own abundant colony, I had to try and harvest my own. First, I learned they must be purged – a wonderfully biblical word – kept in a box or crate for a week or two, and fed only on a few sprigs of thyme, which theoretically adds to the flavour. I collected a dozen or so and put them in a cardboard box with air holes in it, and bedded them in nice fragrant bunches of thyme. Somehow, though, my enthusiasm dwindled and when I found one morning that all but one had escaped, I tipped him out as well, bid him '*Bon voyage*', and left Theo to try to organize snail races instead.

There were already about thirty people scattered about the field, sitting on rugs and blankets under the trees, plus the usual contingent of dogs, about one for every four or five people, who turned up at every party. By now I knew many of the people a little and Theo knew all the dogs. With a whoop, 'Hey, Guillaume!' he discovered his school friends and they vanished into the trees with several dogs barking behind them. I hardly saw him again.

I suppose he might have fallen out of a tree, but otherwise there was no danger, and most of the kids in Mosset run around together unsupervised all the time.

It was all wonderfully casual, with people drifting by throughout the afternoon. We sat around under the trees, drinking beer and passing bottles of wine. Isabelle Mestres, the dairy maid, daughter of M. Mestres the old mayor, arrived with a tray of cheese and yoghurt to put on the table. With her skin as white as her own milk, her dark eyes and plaits, she looked as though she had walked out of a Fragonard painting and straight into cut-off shorts and cowboy boots.

I enquired about the milk which she had recently started to deliver, and ordered milk and yoghurt. I have heard that local yoghurt and local honey, full of most local anti-bodies, is the best antidote to hayfever, a new affliction. Now I could find out for myself. Isabelle unloaded the baby into the arms of her husband, Nenes, who looked after their herd of cows. He had the broadest smile of anyone I had ever seen, and looked like a cross between Keith Richard and Jungle Boy, with wildly tangled blonde locks and incredibly furrowed skin, from his years of exposure to the elements as shepherd up in the mountains. He fell in love with Isabelle when she was running the café in Mosset, and had come down from the mountains to a life of domesticity and cows. In a way they had united old and new Mosset – the outsider, a Frenchman from the Vosges – marrying a scion of one of the oldest families, and were emblematic of the changes taking place in the village.

Le look for all was distinctly downbeat – jeans, combat pants, Doc Martens, even – especially throughout the summer. Rarely sandals and never shorts. They were for tourists or schoolboys. Most of the women wore their hair long and flowing if dark, or scrunched up in a clip if blonde. No-one seemed to wear makeup or even much jewellery, though some of the men sported earrings or occasionally neck chains.

The table was loaded down with contributions, dishes of tiny black olives, medallions of marbled *saucisson*, sliced tomatoes and raw onions, roasted red peppers, bowls of rice salad, and slices of pizza. The snails were ready, and we ate them with cocktail sticks, digging out the reluctant molluscs from their shells, and dipping them in *aïoli*, rich creamy yellow garlic mayonnaise, which contrasted pungently with the encrusted salt. The snails had a wonderfully smoky, earthy flavour from the fire, and I ate dozens, though not a hundred. Theo reappeared, looking unimaginably filthy, waving a large prize stick, and was now eating his snails with studied deliberation while two little French girls from his class, Clemence and Claire, watched and squealed in disgust. He took great delight in this, being more French than the French; he once tried to send his *menu enfant* steak *haché* back because it wasn't *saignant* (bloody) enough for him. He couldn't get over the fact that these French girls didn't like snails. He still declares *escargots* to be one of his favourite foods (along with McDonald's, and Chinese crispy fried duck and samphire).

But there was more. Fat brown sausages, *boudin noir*, and lamb chops were put on the barbecue, and the feast continued. Sweet Rivesaltes Muscat was quaffed with slices of salty Roquefort cheese. Carole picked up her guitar and started to play. Someone else had a set of bongoes. As I, full of Catalan snails and *aïoli*, dozed comfortably under the spreading branches of an acacia tree, with the setting sun streaking through the leaves, I mused that I was as close to a tourist as anyone at the *cargolade* was likely to get.

After a bit more frantic scrubbing and the purchase of a sofa bed to put in my office, Corbiac was sort of ready for

194

summer guests. They came anyway. It was easy since we spend most of the time outdoors, eating our meals at the table under the pine tree or on the ramshackle terrace.

I liked to serve simple meals of one cooked element at most. A fish stew, perhaps, with salad, and bread and fruit; grilled trout with almonds and couscous, and a tomato salad scattered with chives; or a *rôti* of pork with bay leaves and wine vinegar, cold potato salad with *aïoli*, red peppers roasted with anchovies and garlic, slices of fragrant orange melon. We served cold *muscat*, local red and rosé wine, nibbled peppery radishes, cucumbers, melon and apricots.

Actually, simple meals was my angle. Miles took a different approach. He decided to investigate Catalan food (though he forebore to make our own *cargolade*) with the help of Colman Andrews' *Catalan Cuisine*. Andrews is very informative, but rather pedantic, and his recipes are sometimes hard to follow. This is difficult for Miles, who likes to follow recipes exactly, and always groans when I immediately start to adapt them. ('Oh dear, there's no ricotta – I'll use *chèvre* instead'). Miles, on the other hand, has been known to miss a page and continue blindly following instructions with another recipe entirely.

We had not even heard of Catalan cuisine when we first came but we became intrigued by unusual items on the menus of restaurants: *ragoût* of rabbit, snails, monkfish and cuttlefish; rabbit with apple and honey *aïoli*; squid with chocolate sauce; peppers stuffed with *morue* (dried cod) or artichokes with snails.

It is a very distinct style of cooking – the last great undiscovered cuisine, so they say. There are many influences, Arab and Italian in particular, as a result of the seafaring traditions of the Catalans. 'It came from the cooking of the Romans who occupied this area for almost five hundred years,' said Miles, our new authority on Catalan cooking. It was they who introduced olives and grapes, leavened bread, favas, lentils and chickpeas, and may have introduced the curing of ham. Catalan ham was very popular in Rome apparently. 'Then it was modified by the Moors who also conquered the region, and by French and Italian merchants. The earliest recipes were recorded back in the fourteenth century,' Miles explained. Some of the earliest cookbooks are Catalan, like the Cookbook of the Canon of Tarragona from 1331, which laid down dietary rules for monks and priests, and the fifteenth-century *Libre del Coch* (Book of the Cook).

Catalan cuisine is noted for its intriguing combinations of sweet and sour, meat and fish, and meat and fruit, as well as a variety of original sauces. It has been undergoing a revival as new Catalan cuisine, with celebrated chefs in Figuères, Cadaqués and Barcelona adding a sophisticated modern twist to the old recipes.

Miles studied the recipes closely and set out to master the four basic Catalan sauces. This involved the purchase of a serious pestle and mortar: a huge yellow- and green-glazed ceramic bowl and stone pestle for grinding the ingredients. The key sauces are the *picada*, *aïoli* (*ailloli* in Catalan), *romesco* and *sofregit*. The first sauce he tried was typically the most difficult, *aïoli*, an emulsion of garlic and olive oil, with a little salt added. Provençal *aïoli* often contains eggs and is not at all the real thing, according to the Catalans. Mind you, a lot of places claim to be the originators of *aïoli*, not least ancient Rome. Pliny the Elder is credited with one of the first written recipes. 'When garlic is beaten with oil and vinegar,' he observed, 'it is wondrous how the foam increases.' It is like the argument over the correct ingredients for *bouillabaisse* or whether Toulouse, Castelnaudary or Carcassonne is the source of true *cassoulet*.

For the Catalan *aïoli*, you crush the garlic in a mortar and add the olive oil very slowly, drop by drop. It is a tricky business and the sauce is liable to break down at any moment. Personally I was very pleased to find Colman Andrews had included a recipe for 'drowned' aïoli – that is, aïoli that does curdle, since that is what usually happens to mine – and he recommends adding it generously to fish soups and stews. I was encouraged when a French Catalan friend, who lives in a nearby village and is a superb cook, confessed that she usually asked one of her elderly Catalan neighbours to make her aïoli for her, since it always curdled when she made it. The most unusual Catalan version of aïoli is worked into a paste with fruit such as apples and pears or quince, to serve with roast meat – like rabbit, chicken and pork, for example.

Many Catalan recipes call for a base of sofregit, which is simply chopped onions cooked as slowly as possible in plenty of olive oil until they turn a dark brown. Some recipes also add tomatoes and garlic – for a chicken and prawn ragoût, for instance – or other vegetables. It is also a good base for soups.

The picada was the sauce that Miles most favoured – probably because it is time-consuming and fussy, and very different from conventional French or British cooking. It is a thickening agent, used as the base for a wide range of recipes, made from crushed nuts, garlic and bread. He likes to count out all the ingredients beforehand in little piles surrounding his mortar: fifteen blanched almonds, fifteen blanched hazelnuts, three cloves of garlic, a bunch of Italian parsley, sea salt and a thick slice of country bread. The nuts are roasted in a pan, closely watched because they burn very quickly. The bread is fried in very hot olive oil, then the bread, nuts, garlic and salt are all crushed in the mortar. This takes for ever, but it can't be done properly in a food processor. Then the parsley is mashed in and the whole just covered in the olive oil. Miles usually gives up before the ingredients are properly pulverized but the result doesn't affect the taste, just adds an unexpected crunchy texture to some of the dishes.

Picada is called for in Monkfish with Burnt Garlic. After making the *picada* – the garlic is in the *picada*, not really burnt but sautéd in olive oil until dark brown – you use the same oil to cook bite-size pieces of monkfish that have been dipped in flour, until they too are golden brown. Remove the fish, add a little fish stock to the *picada*, season and reduce by about a third. Return the fish to the pan and cook through.

What is it about men in the kitchen? Men and women definitely have different attitudes to cooking. It's not just the old cliché that when they cook they use all the pots and pans in the kitchen and then leave you to do the washing-up, although that is still true enough. (One friend of mine complains about scorch marks on the lino, which is where her husband puts hot saucepans when every other kitchen surface is overflowing with dirty dishes.)

To Miles cooking is an art, an exciting new experience, a challenge with ever more pinnacles of achievement to conquer; he likes best of all anything that will take three days to cook instead of one, preferably as it sits in an exquisitely orchestrated marinade. Miles took absolutely no interest in beans until he came across a recipe for them cooked in a chianti bottle. Now that sounds really interesting . . . We were driving back from a weekend in Sussex once and saw a sign saying, 'Hay for sale'. Miles demanded that I stop the car immediately. 'I must get some hay!' 'Hay?' I enquired. 'What will we do with a bale of hay in London?' 'Oh, I've got this wonderful recipe for chicken cooked in hay that I want to try.'

While the men wield the bulb baster and the larding needle, the women get stuck with the day-to-day cooking, walking around with the contents of the fridge engraved somewhere in their mind, always knowing what is missing from the larder. ('I know there is some pasta in the cupboard, and I'm pretty sure there's still a tin of tomatoes left, so if I just buy some bacon on the way home . . .')

It's always men who are enthusiastic about computer-programming recipes; women immediately think about floury fingers on the keyboard. Ideally men would have some esoteric piece of hardware for every kitchen procedure: tomato slicers, olive pitters, pineapple cutters, larding needles, asparagus steamers, and, naturally, a cast-iron frying-pan.

We have now at least achieved a frying-pan ceasefire. Miles insists on a cast-iron French frying-pan, the sort that must be laboriously reseasoned with oil and salt every time it is inadvertently washed up, or for that matter every time I used to cook in it when everything always stuck to the bottom. Eventually I gave up and bought my own, a very nice, non-U, non-stick frying pan.

Male chefs would probably like the orderly precision of the monks. The Rule of St Benedict said everyone must help in the kitchen; only the very old and the sick were excused. The customaries gave strict instructions: how the cooks were to take off their capes and hang them outside the kitchen, to wash and soak the beans and put them in the cooking pots with water, how they were to skim and wash the pots, to take them off the fire as soon as the skin of the beans cracked and add salt and fat, how they were to clean the pots and use them to heat water for washing-up and finally to set them to drain on a sloping board. How they were to cover the fire at night to keep it in, and sweep and clean the kitchen on Saturdays. Through all these operations prayers were recited, and when the cooks went to mass they were to leave the vegetables on a slow fire with more water in the pot than usual, and a lay brother to watch them. And when all was finally scoured and clean they sat down in the kitchen and said the Divine Office together.

Our English friend Robin was a typical male cook. Visiting us in mid-August he decided to make paella for twelve. I produced the big paella pan I had bought years ago and which, I admit, does need oiling and salting every time it is used. Robin returned triumphantly from his shopping expedition with all the ingredients. Chicken, fish, shrimps and two large *langoustines*. These last were still alive, glistening grey crustaceans. Our downstairs bathroom, which doubled as a larder then, was the coolest place in the house as it backed onto the stone wall of the church, so Robin filled a bucket with water and put the *langoustines* in there to wait for their moment of death. I was slightly embarrassed by this larder but recalled that Peter Graham, the legendary foodie of the Auvergne, kept his cheese in the downstairs loo, which had just the right temperature, humidity and air flow.

The paella fire was lit, and several hours were spent in preparation, with Miles and Robin getting steadily drunker as they cooked. Suddenly there was a blood-curdling scream from the bathroom. Jacqui, Robin's wife, emerged with a look of terror on her face. She had been sitting quietly, when there had been a fearful scrabbling behind her and, turning round, she saw the claws of the *langoustines* clambering over the side of the bucket, like something out of a horror movie. They were stuffed back rapidly into the water and covered with a lid, but it was clearly time to eat them before they ate us. The paella rice had to be properly crispy on the bottom, but at last in went the final ingredients, the *langoustines* rapidly despatched by the heat of the paella.

The table was laid under the tree with the big Provençal yellow cloth, and blue-and-white plates, dishes of small black olives and green olives with lemon and garlic from the market, in pottery bowls, slices of dark red *saucisson* on a wooden board, rosy pink radishes to dip in *aïoli*. We gorged on paella and drank quantities of chilled rosé wine. Dessert was easy: all we had to do was pick the peaches and pile them in a big rough terracotta bowl lined with vine leaves. It was the kind of lunch that went on until five or six, with everyone eventually sprawled on picnic rugs on what we optimistically called the lawn, snoozing under large hats. But not all our culinary experiences were so pleasant.

Martha was at Le Moulin, and I proposed a trip to Bages to our favourite restaurant. It was an hour-and-a-half drive but worth it, I insisted. Whenever we arrived by Motorail in Narbonne we had always headed straight for it, a small restaurant in a tiny fishing village overlooking the salt lagoons, with herons and flamingos and the kind of luminescent light that made you understand why the artists so loved this coast. Inside the place was funky, with jazz playing gently, black-and-white photos on the wall, the kitchen in the corner, and a big fat grey cat curled under the table. The proprietor looked like Georgia O'Keeffe with white hair pulled tightly back into a bun, and a long dark dress, and you could watch as she deftly opened the shellfish right there and then.

I booked a table, but we arrived late, distracted by the lagoons, the flamingos and picking samphire, the edible seaweed that was growing in the salt flats. We were greeted by a sour-faced woman I had never seen before. She said we had no reservation, though I insisted I had called. She grudgingly indicated a table, but we had to pull two together ourselves to make room for five people. No bread or water was brought, and when I asked what had happened to the usual proprietor I was told she was on her way. Reluctantly the woman took our order for food, but I had to get up again, to ask for drinks, and was beginning to feel rather embarrassed. Eventually she returned to say she didn't have the wine we ordered, and we must make do with a *picher*. And wait. She brought two of the dishes we ordered and I asked again for an extra table setting and a wineglass for me. Finally the other dishes arrived and were banged down in the middle of the table, so we had to sort out for ourselves what they were. Martha declared the mussels overcooked and I still had no food at all. I was by now absolutely mortified. We got angry and started to complain about the service. I began to wonder. It all looked the same – the décor, the photos on the wall – but where was the *patronne*, and where was the cat? At that moment the waitress came behind me with the *bouillabaisse*. From the corner of my eye I saw a stream of yellow liquid pouring onto the table and into my lap. Perhaps she wanted to pour it over my head. I cracked and ran upstairs to the loo and burst into tears. Madame then asked if I was ill – or perhaps expecting a baby? Martha followed me, gave me a hug, and said we must leave immediately. Without paying. A huge row ensued, the other guests in the restaurant shouted at us for causing trouble, and called us tourists. Martha retorted with equal abuse in perfect French and we marched off downstairs to a torrent of curses. When we reached the street Theo said confidentially, 'Don't worry, Mum, I've got some chips in my pocket,' and he revealed a stash he obviously pocketed when he saw which way the wind was blowing. Later it transpired that the *patronne* I remembered had moved to another location across the square, after a disagreement about the lease. I had made a reservation with her on the old phone number, and when she said did I know where the restaurant was I had replied yes, of course, not realizing she had moved. It became one of those stories. And one day perhaps we will go back again and find the right restaurant.

The Mediterranean coast is only an hour away so sometimes we abandoned work and went to the beach for the day. Winter, we figured, was for working. In high summer we avoided the most popular resorts – Collioure, which is a charming, overgrown fishing village much loved by Matisse and his artist friends, but impossibly over-crowded in the summer – and, at the other extreme, Canet, the town beach of Perpignan, which is noisy and raffish with carousels. I preferred to compromise on small family beaches, with little *pension* hotels and rocky coves.

Sometimes we went with friends, and ate cheap, de-licious lunches of *moules marinières* and chips for only 50 francs a head. Theo became adept at extracting the mussels from their shells, declaring them to be his favourite food. We rented deck chairs and sat and gossiped about work and relationships. I talked about Theo and the risk we had taken by coming here – cutting him adrift from an English education and identity. My friends complained about the relentless pressure to main-tain the lives they had chosen – the mortgage, the private schools, the nannies, the career path. I talked about my relationship with Miles, my anxiety about how much I had threatened it by pursuing my own desire to live here, and great tears began to slide down my cheeks. Another friend confided her own marital difficulties, creating a special trust between us by sharing her feelings so openly. It is curious the intimacy that a beach induces.

I thought perhaps it was simply the nakedness, warmth and relaxation that made it so, but then we went to Collioure at Christmas and sat in a café well wrapped in coats and scarves, and looked out to sea. Miles's friend, another man of his generation who was incredibly reserved and never talked about his emotional life or his family, began to speak about his father for the first time in the thirty years or so he and Miles had known each other. Perhaps it is more than the relaxation of the beach; perhaps it is more to do with the sea. It is after all a favourite image of the subconscious, a Jungian image for all that is washing around under the surface, the powerful forces of which we are barely aware. It is as if the sea's movement and limitless aspect unleashes the emotions and allows deep feelings to surface. My brother used the sea as a metaphor for his death, the idea of floating out to sea, like King Arthur on his funeral byre, of being carried endlessly by the waves. Now whenever I walk by the sea I can remember him with that bittersweet sadness that is the key to keeping memory alive, finding places or moments that are pleasurable and yet summon up the connection with the best of the loved one; for Simon, candles and rainbows, but, most of all, the waves of the sea.

We spent one night in a small hotel on the beach at Leucate (on the coast between Narbonne and Perpignan), sleeping with the window open. I was lying facing the sun, which woke me with the first light at about 7 a.m. Theo was still asleep looking utterly beautiful, wrapped in a flimsy yellow sarong, his skin smooth and brown and hair bleached blond by the sun. I lay and watched the sunrise, my eyes filled with the pink, blue and primrose of the dawn, until the sun rose, a fiery red globe over the horizon, casting a long bright path across the glittering empty sea. I went to do yoga exercises on the beach and swam in the calm clear water. It was not too cold, though a shock to go in, but I had no hesitation, there was no-one else. The water was so still and silky, so smooth, in that moment of equilibrium between onshore and offshore winds.

11

The smell of trees

It was a warm evening at the end of that first summer. This time I was not going home. So often I had left sadly at the end of summer to return to London. On one occasion, I remember, I could hardly drive for tears running down my cheeks. An autumnal mist had drifted up the valley, veiling all the colours. The moon was softly focused but above the mist the stars appeared. The cicadas were chirping and the light from the living room shone out onto the ruined cloister wall. The air was so still you could hear the church bells in the distance. There was a smell of damp earth, moisture rising as the warm air drew it out, mingling with the fragrance of the lavender, mint and stocks on the terrace.

That morning there had been a rainbow that arched right over the church. We see so many rainbows: as soon as there is sun and rain I know they will come. We have a house alert. Even Miles, who is usually sniffy about the beauties of natural phenomena, preferring a nicely turned roof line any day, will hurry outside to look at a rainbow. Once after a late snow a multicoloured arc stretched across two snowy hills beyond Mosset, appearing to land right in the village. This one really did seem to end in the road opposite, and Theo wanted to try to find the end of the rainbow. Polly had told him that she had once driven right through the colours of a rainbow, and we have argued ever since about whether this is actually possible. If it is a visual phenomenon, how can you be in it? Surely you can only see it from a distance. Whatever, we tried anyway, and I drove Theo to school that day, taking the long way round the valley, but the rainbow had gone.

Chasing rainbows is an obvious cliché but somehow appropriate here often enough. I savoured the moment, knowing it could not last. I was as happy as I had ever been. All these new pleasures, new discoveries, would become familiar, though it was hard to imagine they would ever pall. But it would soon get cold, which I dreaded.

Autumn is what the locals call the *arrière-saison*, when all the tourists have gone home and the land reverts to its true owners. It is calm and golden, still very warm, with long peaceful days. The vine by the door was heavy with grapes, the hay baled. We gathered rich, sweet black figs from a gnarled old tree on one of the lower terraces. I found apples – small, hard, but our own – growing beside the peach field. I made apple jelly, inserting springs of tarragon, rosemary and thyme into the jars with the clear green jelly. It looked so pretty lined up on the windowsill with the view of the garden beyond, it could have been a picture in *Country Living* magazine. I took a few cuttings of rosemary, lavender and thyme, stripping the leaves at the cut end and nipping off the new growth at the tops – the most susceptible to disease. Then I stuck them in jars of water, checking daily to see if roots had appeared.

*　　*　　*

Theo went back to school, the great French *rentrée* when the shops are full of new *cartables* (satchels), pencils, pens and notebooks. His French was improving, though he swore to me he didn't know anything, but he visited our new neighbours with three children quite happily for the afternoon, and they said he spoke French well.

Once the schoolchildren can read, normally at about age six or seven, they moved into the *salle de classe* next door, where they were organized into small teams, each with a mix of younger and older children. The *maître*, Theo's new teacher, was a reserved, self-possessed young man whose little ponytail and computer skills seemed somehow at odds with this remote mountain school, but his commitment was clear.

The atmosphere in the *salle de classe* was relaxed and casual; in common with most schools in France, there is no school uniform and the teacher himself wore jeans and espadrilles. Nevertheless Maître was treated with deference; children in France generally still have great respect for education and for their teachers.

Although the French school system has a reputation for being highly regulated and lacking creativity, in practice the school in Mosset combined the basic curriculum with a considerable amount of freedom and alternative activities. The French national curriculum (*instructions officielles*) is followed by every state school. This may be strictly observed using traditional teaching methods, but, especially in primary schools, the teachers have considerable autonomy. In France Church and State are firmly separate, so French state schools are *laique* ('lay') and there is no religious education. Education in France is all about learning to be a good citizen, and this includes sex education; the permission of parents is not considered relevant.

Maître favoured a co-operative and non-authoritarian

method of teaching, based on the theories of the progressive French educationalist Célestin Freinet, trying to instil a sense of self-determination and responsibility in the children. Every week they had to make their own *plan de travaile*, scheduling the work they proposed to accomplish. The school had its own market every Saturday morning, an exercise in real-life economy that was supposed to teach them the value of money and the use of arithmetic. The children brought toys to sell, spending *mossetos*, as the school currency was called. In theory they earned *mossetos* for doing extra-curricular school work, but a thriving black market appeared to exist and children had been known to try to spend their *mossetos* in Yvette's village shop. They got short shrift.

The educational philosophy was based on learning from real life, and the school went to see farms, wildlife reserves and historic buildings. The children visited old people in the village to hear and tape their memories, and discussed the war from the perspective of their own families' involvement. Theo took in a Remembrance Day poppy, an English tradition with which the French here were unfamiliar. They wrote up all their adventures in painstaking French script, the best of which were included in the school newspaper, or posted on their new Website.

They often went off tramping into the mountains, and Theo came home one day with spectacularly muddy boots. He explained: 'We went for a walk, and hid in some bushes, then we put down some bread and had to be really quiet while we waited for birds to eat it.' Bird-watching, I figured, though Theo seemed even more excited at having identified wild boar poo. He became very knowledgeable about poisonous mushrooms and, even more important, like any good French child he knew which ones are good to eat.

Learning about food was a serious matter. One of Theo's French homework exercises entailed identifying five different types of bread – *baguette*, *brioche*, *ficelle*, *épi* and *pain de campagne* – from the shapes on the page alone. Another writing assignment involved composing a favourite menu, and he was once asked to write his favourite recipe. That night, as it happened, Miles was making stuffed squid, one of Theo's favourite dishes, so Miles took him through all the stages: frying the chopped tentacles with garlic and parsley, adding breadcrumbs, then stuffing it all back into the squid – the bit Theo liked best – and securing the ends with wooden skewers. I hope the teacher enjoyed the recipe as much as we did.

I joined the class once on a trip with another school, and was puzzled by the large rucksack Maître had been carrying all the time; the mystery was solved when we sat down to a picnic lunch with the other teachers and parents. From his bag he produced a bottle of Banyuls, the local aperitif, and a bottle of good local red wine, which we drank with our meal.

The *maître* was passionately Catalan and keen to teach the children both the language and history of Catalonia. Theo learnt about all the Catalan-speaking countries, the glorious history of the Catalan nation, even Catalan playing cards. I felt ambivalent about the children learning Catalan, since after all Spanish (or, of course, English) would be a great deal more useful for most of them, however understandable was the desire to preserve a rich culture and language. But at least it is not like Spanish Catalonia, where since Franco died and the Catalans have reclaimed their culture Catalan is the first language in schools and Castilian Spanish is frowned on.

We were intrigued to hear from Theo that the founder of the Catalan nation, Wilfred the Hairy, came from Ria, a little village just the other side of Prades in what was then part of the Spanish March (Roussillon, Cerdagne and what is now Spanish Catalonia.) Theo did a series of drawings to illustrate an account of the story in Catalan, which he loved to recite, revelling in the gruesome details. During the ninth century the Catalans and the Franks, under Charles the Bald, joined forces to drive out the Moors from Spain. Wilfred the Hairy (Guifré el Pilôs in Catalan), a minor lord, was wounded in the fighting, and the Frankish king honoured his bravery with stripes on his shield. 'So he put his fingers in Wilfred's wound, and drew four stripes of red blood across his golden shield,' Theo explained. Thus the red-and-yellow-striped Catalan flag was born, and Wilfred went on to become Count of Barcelona, liberate Catalonia from the Moors and unite the region under his rule.

For us, learning about Catalonia added to the rich *mélange* of cultures we had discovered living in a border-land and reinforced the idea of a future Europe of identities defined by language and culture rather than physical boundaries.

A few weeks after returning to school Theo broke his arm. He just tripped over in the school playground and fell badly on his elbow. The treatment he received was excellent. After a visit to the doctor he was sent for an immediate X-ray in the same building. We were shown (and then kept) the X-rays and went straight round to the hospital, where the arm was put in plaster. It all took only a few hours and I was impressed that such facilities were available in a small mountain town like Prades with a population of 10,000. Theo was in plaster for six weeks, but he was remarkably sanguine about it. In a way it gave him status, a glamorous quality in the context of the tiny school. He told me the plaster was especially useful for cracking nuts. He had sat under the walnut tree outside the school smashing the nuts for the other children with the weight of his plaster.

Miles and I both had work to do. He had completed his biography of Paul McCartney, an old friend, and needed to travel to Britain and the USA to promote it. I had a guide to France to write, which had been originally proposed by the publisher as a selection of the best of France, with a personal voice. Then the designers moved in and decided each place, whatever its importance or lack of it, must fit one page. This meant that every entry had to be exactly 370 words long, so it became a gruelling formulaic task. Still, it meant there was a small budget to travel, including a trip to Provence to visit art museums.

We seemed to have arrived at a tolerable balance of time apart. I had always wanted lots more time to myself, had craved it ever since Theo was born, and I was mostly content to be alone and see the few friends we had in Mosset. Miles liked to travel, needed the stimulus of the city, and certainly to get away, and was psychologically rooted in London. At best it meant that our time together was enriched by the different experiences we both had. I told him I missed him for my morning cups of tea and sharpening the knives. I needed that everyday ritual of care, and I needed him to keep me sharp, honed, like the knives. After a while I became dull and there was always the danger of losing perspective if I was here too long. Miles kept me from getting too sentimental, was always questioning, never satisfied with the obvious answer. For Theo, Miles's absences were fairly normal, although he did miss him, but he too was making friends. And there were always other adults around, other role models for him – Bob the artist, Paul the builder, Jacques the farmer, Rose the photographer.

By the time we got back from our various travels winter was almost upon us. The leaves had fallen, smoke was rising from the neighbour's chimneys again, the buzzards were circling in the winter sky. The cows were back from their summer on the mountain pastures. 'So many cowbells,' said Miles. 'It sounds like *Wagon Train*.' Suddenly after the summer, when the state of the house

211

did not seem so pressing, we become aware of all the problems again. We stuffed newspapers once more into every possible hole in the walls to curb the draughts. Finally I hung curtains in the French windows downstairs, plain cream heavy cotton, making loops from the hems I cut, to tie them back. The store cupboard was gratifyingly full of cherry jam, pickled peaches and fig jam from Martha – hardly a sustaining winter diet, but, hey, I'm doing this for fun. The apple jelly turned out to be disgustingly sweet, but I left it looking pretty for a while before I chucked it in the bin.

The farmers warned us that the exposed pipes outside needed to be protected against frost. To their bemusement, instead of the traditional straw Miles used bubble wrap, left over from our packing.

Finally we confronted the wood-fire problem and bought a very expensive wood-burning stove, a Godin, the Rolls Royce of French stoves. As I wrote out the cheque (well over a thousand pounds, including installation and chimney cleaning) I told myself that it was about the price of a Chanel suit. Not that I've ever bought a Chanel suit, or am ever likely to now, but it seemed a suitably frivolous alternative at the time. The stove was brilliant, black cast-iron with brass knobs, a big glass window through which to see the flames, and a nifty side door for the logs so you don't have to open the front door.

We installed it in the upstairs library, which was still our winter living quarters. Downstairs was impossible as too much of the space still needed to be renovated and there was simply nowhere permanent enough to install a stove and chimney. Apart from the crumbling ceiling, to be torn out at a later stage of building, the library was what we always wanted. The walls were completely lined with books, fortuitous since without them they were still stained with mysterious brown patches, despite the endless coats of white paint I had applied. The shelves were already overflowing again onto the floor. However many bookshelves we buy or build there are always more unaccommodated piles of books on the floor. (Basic plant, says Miles, ordering another boxful from Amazon.com.) We had found an old worn red-leather sofa and chairs in a second-hand furniture store and spread several brightly woven Persian kelims on the floor.

As commune householders we were entitled to firewood culled from the commune forest which stretches halfway up the mountainside. This was the autumn *affouage* (woodcutting), when lots were cast for your quota, so it was a matter of chance how accessible it was. You drive up the mountain, along incredibly bumpy potholed dirt tracks, deep into the forest, seek out your lot, look with bemusement at several marked trees waiting to be cut down, and hire somebody else to do it for you. The wood needs to be seasoned for at least a year, so that year's wood had to be stored. M. Fons, who cut the wood for us, simply dumped it out of the back of his truck in great logs right outside the chapel door, and then vanished. He said he would come back to chop it, but he never did, though neither did he come back to be paid. In fact it wasn't till the following August that his teenage daughter turned up and asked for the 800 francs I owed him.

So that first year we had the stove I had to go and buy more wood. After a few attempts I found the wood supplier in his timber yard surrounded by bewildering stacks of different woods. We agreed on a mixture of pine and oak, and I bought 4 *stères*, cubic metres. It was interesting trying to work out how many logs we might use, and I did underestimate but not by too much.

Next morning it was delivered, tipped out in a great heap from the back of a truck. As the last log hit the pile, snow began to fall. It rarely snows here, despite the fact that the village has constructed a small ski station only a

213

few kilometres higher up the mountain, but that morning it did. So it was all hands on deck, not excepting the central-heating lobby. Or the lobby who would rather be watching *Spiderman* on TV. It took the entire morning to carry them in, with flushed faces and cold fingers, but finally all was magnificently stacked, with Miles naturally in charge of the precise arrangement of logs so they would not immediately fall down like dominoes. Unfortunately when I tried to light the fire, it turned out that the logs were the wrong size and did not fit easily through the nifty little side door. They had to be loaded from the front, filling the room with smoke.

I had to recruit Pascal to cut them again, since I still had not mastered the axe. Miles was exempt since the wood-burning folly was entirely my indulgence. Wood here, I discovered, has an almost talismanic quality. I started to notice other people's wood piles and felt the stirrings of envy when I saw them smugly stacked by the end of summer. I too now think ahead, feeling a sense of re-assurance at the thought of a wood pile waiting for the next year, already planning where the wood will come from the year after that.

Until very recently, when mains electricity was installed in the village in 1960 and bottled gas became available, wood was the only source of fuel for heating and cooking. There are old photographs of village women burdened with great bundles of kindling on their backs as they return from the forest. Village history recounts many incidents of squabbles over wood rights and over people stealing wood from one another. In 1806 a murder resulted from a quarrel over wood stolen to make clogs, in those days the usual footwear for the peasants.

There is a pleasing symmetry that this is also the time of year to plant trees. St Catherine's Day on 25 November is the traditional day for tree planting, though I could never remember whether you are supposed to have everything planted before St Catherine's Day or wait till after St Catherine's Day. No doubt the monks would have known. Since you are also supposed to know the phases of the moon, and whether the sap is rising or not, I simply aim for an approximate time in November.

We recruited a gardener to plant cypresses as a windbreak for us, and to cut down the big old cypresses that had been planted too close to the chapel, so their roots were digging into the foundations and their branches damaging the apse roof. Miles hated anything growing anywhere near the building so all the planting had to be done away from it.

We are just about on the olive line, so although there are hundreds of old trees on the crumbling terraces lower down the valley there are very few any higher. Rose, though, had one in her garden, 100 metres higher than ours, albeit more sheltered. But we had heard of the terrible frost of 1956 that destroyed the olive crop of the entire region, and it is only now, several decades later, that people are daring to plant them again.

We planted the olives ourselves. When we went to buy them Miles looked at a fine old tree and we remembered a friend in St Tropez who had paid 5,000 francs for a 200-year-old olive to be planted in his designer-landscaped garden. There are plenty hereabouts of course and I did once see someone with a trailer loaded with an olive with a great tangle of roots and earth. But we bought modest-sized olive trees for 240 francs each. We wanted to plant them in the middle of the garden each side of a terrace, where we hoped eventually we could build some steps. Miles dug the holes while I spread out the roots, and then we filled the holes with earth and compost, staked them and watered them thoroughly. We knew it was an optimistic gesture, and Jacques the farmer, for one, shook his head in disapproval. 'Olives won't grow here.'

215

I liked the idea of planting two trees. I had seen marriage trees in American gardens, fully grown trees, which had been planted many years before by a newly espoused couple, and they were such a glorious metaphor for a relationship. I had always thought the best kind of relationship was like two trees, both with strong separate roots but intertwined branches. Slowly I found this was not enough, that many plants also need each other to pollinate, blossom, produce fruit. I may be thinking of courgettes here, which don't have quite the same grandeur as trees, but never mind. So for me the olives we planted became symbolic of our relationship. If the olives survived, so would we.

I went to gather walnuts one day from the trees I had discovered beside the river. Walnuts are best picked when they have just opened on the branch. Better still with a small boy up the tree to shake the branches. Once they fall to the ground they become black and oily, staining the fingers dark brown. I was struck by the distinct, slightly medicinal smell of the walnut tree as I stood beneath it. I had never realized before that trees had a particular smell. There was something glorious about that, the smell of trees.

It was almost Thanksgiving, an event I always loved in America, an occasion to give thanks that needed no particular religious belief to give it meaning. I wanted to celebrate it at Corbiac. I suppose I was seeking ritual too, as I began to respond to the seasonal rhythms of this place.

I invited new friends, Rose, Marianne, Lettie and Ludo, and Gerard, and tried to make a meal entirely of local produce. I bought *pintades*, guinea fowl, from the *ferme auberge*. Christmas was coming and their geese were very fat. They were being force-fed grain down funnels straight into their stomachs, to enlarge their livers to the point of bursting to make *foie gras*. I was warned not to go too close to the geese in case I surprised them and they died of a heart attack. This gave me pause, but my passion for *foie gras* outweighed my concern for animal rights.

I planned we would have a tart of walnuts and *cèpes*, followed by the guinea fowl served with some of the summer's pickled peaches, potatoes scattered with rosemary from the garden, followed by apple tart, or cherries in brandy, and the local *chèvre* and Yvette's well-matured Roquefort. A local Maury red wine, perhaps, with the guinea fowl, and sweet *muscat* with dessert. Then there was that very powerful *marc* we had been saving up.

All I lacked were the *cèpes*, and I knew it was the season. All of France is obsessed with mushrooms for months, and city-dwellers come out at weekends to scour the forests. The TV news always has items about food and every day will show some rustic scene of log chopping in the Vosges, mushroom gathering in the Auvergne, harvesting Breton oysters, or celebrating the Basque red-pepper harvest. The French themselves do as much as their tourists to foster the bucolic fantasy of rural France, where there are only happy cottagers and no high-rise estates or industry at all.

Weirdest of all is the fact that the TV always shows a meal being cooked in such extreme close-up that it is almost pornographic – much closer than the cook would ever see the food, as if the camera operator had climbed into the pan. Miles always liked to remark at this point in the broadcast that of course France was actually a highly polluted country still using lots of chemicals, with a disgracefully poor record of organic farming. France is in fact the second greatest user of agricultural chemicals and pesticides in the world, after the USA, and only 1 per cent of French food is organic compared with 8 per cent in the UK and 16 per cent in Sweden. So much for all that glorious market produce, and another reason to start the vegetable garden and compost heap.

In the village I had seen Henri the hunter, dressed in green camouflage and gaiters, clearly just returned from an early-morning foraging expedition. He discreetly showed the contents of a huge plastic bag to one of the good old boys sitting on the wall. Henri was known as *le roi des champignons* and the Pope of *cèpes*, so I guessed what must be in his bag. I asked to look and glimpsed a wondrous sight: several pounds of magnificent *cèpes*, fat and brown, the sturdy stalks with earth and grass still clinging to them. I could even smell that particularly pungent mulchy odour they have. But Henri snapped the bag shut quickly with a grin, touched his finger to the side of his nose and vanished into his little house overlooking the village square. I knew by now there was no point asking where he found the mushrooms, that indeed it would be extremely bad form even to ask. Trying to find anyone to *chercher les champignons* was no easy task. Reluctant to reveal their secrets, they would simply look shifty and embarrassed.

In the end I bought my *cèpes* and the dinner was a great success. Marianne entertained us with stories of her clients and their recent tendency to take mobile phones with them on donkey treks and call her up to ask which path they should take. Gerard described his efforts to plant trees on the land he owns on the mountain, and I decided he was like the shepherd in Jean Giono's *The Man who Planted Trees*, who planted a forest by scattering a few acorns every day. We all complained bitterly about the local farmers closing public footpaths and threatening tourists with their dogs and guns, still living off EEC subsidies and not realizing how much they needed tourism economically.

We discussed pottery, where to find the best local clay (Lettie liked to dig her own) and Ludo's efforts to make the perfect teapot. I was still trying to find the best pot to make *tisane* with large leaves of limeflower, sage or vervain, so I was full of opinions as to the correct length of spout, the size of strainer holes and the right kind of handle. Miles wanted to commission a teapot with the Corbiac crow on it. Theo meanwhile appeared to be speaking Dutch, and although the words were nonsense the Dutch speakers said he was making a convincing show of the rhythm and sound of the language.

The December light was nearer silver than gold. Autumn has the golden light, a soft mellow glory. In winter the light is sharper and the snow on the mountains adds a glittering definition. The wind dries the air, making it very clear. (Miles says that when there is water in the air it eliminates the red end of the spectrum and creates a bluish haze.) Sometimes it is as if one has put on a new pair of glasses, and can suddenly see clearly again. I am convinced that simply looking at mountains exercises the eyes, stretches the focus beyond any distance possible in a city. There is such beauty in winter and I began to understand why a Scottish artist who has lived here for twenty years says he prefers the winters now.

I was looking forward to our first Christmas at Corbiac, despite the cold and the inconvenience of the house. I had ordered the turkey, and our Christmas tree, cut from the village forest, found the Christmas-tree decorations among the boxes we still had not unpacked, brought mincemeat back from Fortnum & Mason. I invited friends for drinks and made mince pies, which filled the house with a pleasing nostalgic fragrance, and intrigued the French in particular. For years I had wanted to see the *pessebre*, the nativity play put on every year by the village on Christmas Eve, with live donkeys and the latest baby in the village in the crib.

We were invited to sing carols with the English expat community. Miles naturally passed on that one, but I like singing carols and I wanted Theo at least to know what an English carol was. We were instructed to bring food for a pot-luck buffet afterwards, and I guessed rightly this probably meant home-made cakes, mince pies and sausage rolls. The carol singing took place in a room full of horse brasses and family photos, on the top floor of a newish villa just outside Prades, dwarfed by a view of Canigou in the distance. Theo was the only child. Everyone else was retired, and the conversation was about where to buy mincemeat in Perpignan, the weakness of French tea, the best *pépinière* for roses, the infidy of French builders, the cheapest way back to Blighty, and how to get rid of garden moles. (The foolproof method for the latter, apparently, is a machine that you put on top of the molehill; it fires a blank cartridge, the shock waves of which kill the mole outright.)

Then everything fell apart for me. We had been invited to dinner with Paul the builder, and Polly, the first time we had been out together to dinner without Theo since we arrived here. Rose, who was baby-sitting, had settled down with Theo to play with his furry animals. It was about a half-hour drive, and it was dark and raining. Pulling out of a side road onto to the main highway I made a left turn. I could see a car approaching but it seemed far away. The road was on an incline, however, and I was too slow turning into it: my acceleration was inadequate to pick up speed quickly enough. The car behind was going fast and it crashed into the back of our car. I heard the squeal of brakes, the crash of glass, and then the car simply started spinning out of control. Miles and I threw our arms around each other instinctively, and just held on, the still point of a turning world. There was a precious moment of pure love in the middle of the crash which I will never forget. We came to a stop on a wide grass verge beside the road, where luckily there was no tree for us to crash into. The entire back of the car was staved in, and I saw with total horror that Theo's seat had folded in completely. He would have been dead had he been in the car. The other car was there and the young man driving was unhurt. For a few minutes I was calm and we crossed over the road to the *auberge* and phoned Paul, who came to rescue us. An ambulance came and took us to the local hospital, but I seemed to be merely bruised and shaken, and then Paul took us home. In the meantime the police had arrived at the accident, and then turned up at Corbiac about half an hour later, along with the other driver and his brother. They breathalysed me, and we signed the *constat* (the agreement between drivers detailing an accident), which I had completely forgotten about. I had had no alcohol, not even a stiff whisky when I got back, having elected instead for camomile tea.

The car was a write-off. When I went to collect my belongings several days later from the car pound, the scene was Dante-esque. There were several people round a table playing cards, like something out of purgatory, and a mournful-looking woman put out a cigarette in an overflowing ashtray and got up to help me find my car among the monstrous collection of wrecks over which she presided in the garage.

'This must be a hard job . . .' I ventured.

'*Oui*,' she replied brusquely, jerking her head at the horribly smashed-up convertible next to mine, '*Elle est morte.*'

It was an *annus horribilis*, as the Queen once put it in her Christmas speech. But at least Her Majesty had not brought it all on herself as I had. Christmas was a blur and I missed the *pessebre*. But Theo came home and described it, and I was consoled when he said, 'We had to replace the baby with a doll when it cried.' And I was thrilled he said 'we', that he felt he belonged.

221

12

The lie of the land

One day just before Christmas the peach farmers appeared in the garden, shouting up at the window for me. No-one ever uses the telephone, they always just turn up, and I am constantly interrupted, having to switch from a description of a château in the Loire, or writing the history of the Cathars in 200 words, to discussing the quantity of wood we will need the following year, or which branch of the pine tree the processional caterpillars are in, or to explain that the chapel is not open to the public. When I saw the farmers in smart Sunday clothes I knew something was up. Jacques had changed from his workwear and boots to his off-duty leisure wear of clean pressed jeans and zip-up tartan carpet slippers. Thérèse had exchanged her habitual pinafore and rubber boots for a dress and jacket and ruby ear studs. They waved a cardboard folder at me and said they needed to talk. My heart sank: another dossier. French bureaucracy is as good as its reputation, and every transaction here must have its dossier. Having come to understand this by now I happily construct my own for any project, whether it is complaining about a defunct oven or applying for grants.

Jacques announced that he intended to retire in a year's time, which came as rather a shock, but he assured us it was in our best interest to regain control of the land. '*C'est bien pour vous,*' he insisted, opening his hands wide. We had always assumed it would be a long time before we would have to take much responsibility for the two and half hectares of fields and woodland, sloping down to rivers on two sides, which surrounded the monastery. Jacques and Thérèse had firmly entrenched rights and their lease lasted a further nine years. Indeed they had advised us that we were fortunate they had no children since otherwise we would never get it back.

These were Jacques' fields and since we had quite enough to do with the house, and plenty of garden to worry about, we were content that he did as he pleased, though we had begun to look askance at the growing forest of brambles encroaching on all sides, and I had no desire for any more dealings with the wild horses that occasionally stuck their heads above the terrace wall.

In the first few months I had disgraced myself completely in an encounter with Faustine, the wild horse the farmers were grazing in the field. Theo and I had been down to the river and were clambering back up the hill to the house. The horse began cantering up and down the narrow path we were on. She was very frisky, rearing and neighing, and I was frankly terrified. The only thing I knew about horses was that you should always avoid getting behind them in case they kicked you. But what the hell are you supposed to do if they are running round you?

Shamefully I tried to hide behind a very small tree, while the horse stopped and sniffed curiously at Theo, who stood very still. He had of course been feeding her apples sometimes, so I suppose she knew him. It looked as if she was about to start munching his sneakers. After what

223

seemed an age she ran off, at which point I grabbed Theo and dragged him, stumbling and running, to the safety of the garden. He was pretty pleased with himself for not losing his cool, but I was still wondering if horses had ever been known to eat small boys or their clothes.

The following day the farmers announced they had been advised that they would be better off financially if they retired immediately. Would that be all right? Well, it wasn't at all all right as far as I was concerned, but I knew that trying to make Jacques farm peaches if he didn't want to was a non-starter. So we agreed. It is typical of the way the law is heavily weighted in favour of tenants that we would have the greatest difficulty in ever getting rid of them, yet they could leave us with only a day's notice.

We had to resolve this problem as quickly as possible. Realistically, there was no way we could farm the land ourselves and we could not decide the relative merits of all the local Catalan farmers. There were a few remaining peasants from Central Casting: an elderly fellow in blue overalls and beret who still cut his field of grass with a scythe, and an old couple we watched one day turning their hay with wooden pitchforks. There are a number like Jacques with vintage tractors and beaten-up old 2CV vans. But most of the farmers we only glimpsed in their sophisticated tractors, or behind the wheels of brand-new sports vehicles run on EEC-subsidized petrol. 'Our taxes,' as Miles was always keen to point out: 'France has more subsidies than anybody else in Europe.' He reckoned all the EEC-sponsored farmers should be obliged to wear berets and carry baguettes all the time.

Agriculture in the valley is divided between cows, for beef and milk, and fruit farmers, growing peaches, apricots, apples and cherries. There are also several fields of horses for breeding or riding, and a few EEC sheep, pigs and donkeys. Due to the Napoleonic Law of sharing inheritance between families, the land is all divided up into relatively small fields and one farmer will have plots of land dotted all over the place, instead of all in one place. This makes for constant arguments over territory.

All the farmers wrangled constantly over the fences, grazing rights, the *arrosage* quotas, who had blocked whose supply of water, and who had poisoned their dogs and chickens. One farmer famously took his revenge on another by putting his motorbike up in a tree. It was just as well they argued with each other, mind. United they would be formidable. Even Theo was aware of the feuds; eating dessert one day he said, 'Honey and yoghurt go so well together. It's a pity the people who make them are enemies. I saw them arguing the other day in the *épicerie*!'

Watching them drive up and down the fields all day, in high-tech tractors with enclosed cabins and massive shovels and ploughs attached that looked like they would be good for terraforming Mars, it struck me as a lonely life. There was little need for these farmers to work together any more, haymaking or threshing grain together in the village square. Despite all the technology, however, they had not mastered the land and were still ruled by the seasons. Their crops were dependent on the weather and a bad frost could destroy the peaches and cherries. They rose early, especially in summer, and stopped for a long break in the middle of the day. They worked incredibly hard, pruning peaches in damp spring mists, or calving on a bitterly cold night.

One day that spring I was hanging out the washing in the garden when I heard strange shouts. They sounded urgent, but somehow deliberate, with an ancient ring. Then I heard the cows, a great herd clattering up the valley road. It was the transhumance, with bells tinkling, people shouting and dogs barking, off to the summer pastures in the mountains, just as they had always done.

When we first arrived in early spring the year before, amazed at the numbers of cows around, we asked Jacques if they had changed their agricultural policy. He snorted with astonishment at our ignorance and pointed out that in the summer the cows were all taken to the mountain pastures, which was why we had never seen them. Even now the old tradition of summer and winter pastures is still largely observed, though it must be said with help again from the EEC, which subsidizes the transhumance as a way of maintaining the life of these mountains.

In the end we asked Jacques' advice about finding another farmer for our land. I still don't know how balanced it was or whether he was simply settling old scores. He advised against his great enemy, the horse farmer, for a start. We decided we wanted to continue with the peaches (the pink blossom looked so beautiful framing the chapel in springtime, and cows would have been so messy). At Jacques' suggestion another local fruit farmer was found, who agreed to look after the peaches on an informal basis for a year. He was a handsome, dark-haired Catalan who looked very dashing when he turned up on a motorbike one day, with his pretty wife with her long red hair and cowboy boots on the back. Young and friendly, they assured me that they would use the minimum of chemicals. Communication wasn't all that easy, since my French was still pretty poor, especially when it came to discussing peach pruning and land rights with a farmer with a strong Catalan accent.

Orchards covered less than half the land, leaving two fields to deal with. We didn't want to relinquish control over all the land we had just regained so we still had to figure out what to do with the rest. It was all making me very anxious, which was absurd. This is *la vie à la campagne*, I told myself – slow, free of urban stress; all that was going to happen was that the grass would grow. Which of course proved to be precisely the problem. The grass kept on growing, in particular the field of *luzerne* (alfalfa: animal feed) that Jacques had planted when he had torn up half a field of peach trees a few years before. This field was very close to the house – convenient when everybody on the farm was digging potatoes, but less ideal for us – so I decided this was a good opportunity to reclaim a bit more land around the house and plant a vegetable garden. A neighbouring cow farmer offered to dig over the land for me with his tractor. I suggested he might like the *luzerne* in return. I was just learning how important it was that favours were returned: nobody ever wants to be indebted.

Then all hell broke loose. I seemed to have tapped straight into every sensitive issue, ancient and modern, and carefully trodden on every toe for miles around. Our field of *luzerne* was apparently already the focus of intense interest on the part of neighbouring farmers with animals. But because the fruit farmer had taken on responsibility for the peaches, it turned out it was also his to dispose of, since it was the same *parcelle* of land. I had naïvely presumed that, since his business was peaches, he wouldn't be interested.

As I dug away innocently in my new *potager*, the news that the cow farmer had been working on the land travelled like wildfire. He was trying to get the land! It was like the Milagro Beanfield Wars. The new peach farmer decided to avoid the issue by giving the *luzerne* to someone else entirely, whereupon the cow farmer stormed round and banged on our door and told me off. '*Ce n'est pas gentil*,' he yelled and stomped off. It seems now he should have known that the *luzerne* was not mine to dispose of, but I didn't realize that then.

Once Jacques had gone we were invaded by hunters; his fearsome reputation had kept them at bay till then, and he had after all been the *chef de chasse* himself. I was on the terrace early one morning when a shot bounced off close to my ear. Then the following week we saw a hunter in full camouflage striding across the overgrown field below, gun aloft, his dog yelping after him. Miles yelled rude words at him in English and I had to restrain him from going down there to tackle the intruder. Not for the first time Miles lamented the fact that he didn't have a gun. He was, rather surprisingly, a good shot, though I had only seen him demonstrate once. (He also tells me he is good with a lasso, but I've yet to verify that.)

Slowly we reclaimed our land and, equipped with machetes and shears, began to explore the woodland that rose up from the banks of the river and the little tributary which flowed into it, the Corbiac itself. It was a mess; the trees were covered in choking ivy, and barbed wire had been roughly tied round them, scarring and damaging the trunks. Miles began a major rescue operation of the trees, patiently sawing through the tenacious ivy and extracting the barbed wire embedded in the tree trunks. The river bank had been used as a dump for years and the rubbish still included the rusting hulk of an entire 1950s Citroën saloon car. Our task was often overwhelming. The land seemed a terrifying responsibility, and I sometimes wondered if we wouldn't be better off with a neat little front-garden patio and a gnome or two.

A priority was to burn off the brambles encroaching in a prickly tangle round the stone steps below the garden, a fairly typical peasant method of clearing undergrowth rapidly. Paul, the builder, offered to help, and set to with his cigarette lighter and a few scrunched-up bits of newspaper. He soon had a merry blaze going, and Theo stood importantly next to him, leaning on a stick almost as big as he was, as they watched the flames. I was terrified – it all looked medieval to me, like some grand torching of a castle, as if we were under siege. Once the fires had burned down it was a scene of total devastation, the earth scorched and burned (as was the poor pine tree over-hanging the terrace above as it later turned out). But it was interesting to be able to see the contours of the land for the first time. The terraces had been invisible before, covered with brambles, but now we saw how neglected the land had been, how the horses had toppled the old stone terraces and blocked the irrigation channels.

I was assured that the fires, still gently smouldering, were safe, and Paul left. But it had been a hot day and the Tramontane had got up, and as I was going to bed I noticed a great ring of fire on Canigou, like some sort of biblical warning sign. Fire was a constant risk especially in the spring, when people were clearing the land and it could turn unexpectedly hot and windy. Then I heard the sirens of the *pompiers* and saw there was yet another fire licking its way down the hill to the north of us, the other side of the road. There were no roads up to it, so the *pompiers'* fire engines were excitedly driving up and down the road and struggling to get up the hillside via small cart tracks. The fire seemed to be getting closer and closer and I grew very scared. I called Rose, who was watching too from her different vantage point higher up, and we both stood with our cordless phones watching and commentating with horror as the fire crept down the hill. At least there was a narrow *arrosage* canal in between the fire and us, and then the road. For good measure I belted my dressing gown round me more tightly, put on my wellingtons, filled both watering cans and went down to extinguish the last of the smouldering fires on our own land.

I started planning how we would escape from a burning building. Could we leap from the upstairs windows, and what should I rescue in case of evacuation? In the end it wasn't really very much. Some jewellery, my journals, my work discs, a few books and pictures. I wondered whether, if I piled all our computers, precious books and discs in the middle of the stone chapel, that would be safe enough. What was most unnerving was simply not knowing, not being able to assess the level of danger.

When I called Miles later, he pointed out that the monastery was built of stone and had been there for almost eight centuries. 'Why should it suddenly burn down now?' he asked. 'Well, I thought it is just the kind of thing that would happen to me,' I said. We both remembered the experience of Aldous Huxley: he and his wife simply watched their house burn down with everything in it, including precious original manuscripts of which there were no copies, and made no effort at all to rescue anything. Huxley always said that afterwards he felt an awesome sense of liberation.

We still had not decided how to dispose of the remaining fields. The grass and weeds rose higher and higher as I agonized over the various merits of cows or horses or sheep, or even donkeys, and the varied reputations of their owners. Whoever you talked to seemed to have a vested interest and all the farmers warned me about all the others. Finally, despite Jacques' advice, we decided horses would look prettier (though not as pretty as lavender, I thought regretfully). My debt of the field of *luzerne* I had promised to the cow farmer remained outstanding and I felt guilty every time I saw him in his tractor. At least I avoided the experience of another Englishman who runs a bed-and-breakfast just outside the village. He lent out his field to two Dutchmen, apparently a couple, and they both grazed their horses there together. But then they quarrelled (and one of them got married, but that's another story). Our friend had to divide his field into two, with a half for each horse.

Having caused so much bother with my *potager* I now had to dig it, manure it and plant it, which I discovered was very hard work. Miles, of course, could have told me this. His parents were self-sufficient before I was born, growing all their own food, and the romanticism of tending vegetables escapes him. Miles sometimes recalls his parents' country ways. His mother apparently used to dig up dandelions with the bread knife. I tried it and broke the blade. His father knew how to deal with farmers: when one tried to enclose his favourite fishing bank he threatened to strangle him with the fence wire. I hoped Miles was not tempted to follow these tactics with the Catalans. He helped me, in any event, by constructing ingenious paths out of broken tiles and red brick, with a little stone bridge to go over the water channel, which looked like something out of a Japanese garden. He and Theo dug new channels for the *arrosage*, so that the water would flow around the new vegetable beds.

I was a complete novice, having tried to grow vegetables only once before in a hippie commune in Somerset. I attempted to make a herb garden then and never understood that the free-range chickens were immediately eating all the seeds. I wondered feebly about planting by the moon and stars, but in the event consulted the *Reader's Digest Gardening Annual*, moving everything forward a month or so for the more southern climate.

One of my most firmly extinguished fantasies was the idea that there would be a queue of friendly peasants, wooden pitchforks in hand, waiting to instruct me in the mysteries of gardening. One summer when we were still visiting from another planet, the farmers had planted the field with a row of peppers, aubergines and courgettes and it had all looked so easy. I eyed the neat *potagers* of the villagers with envy, trying to work out how they built their tomato tepees so skilfully. Hazel sticks were the answer, apparently, but at this point I didn't even know what hazel looked like. One day I saw Tonton Marcel, a toothless old fellow, who has his garden next to the school in Mosset. He was carrying a large bunch of parsley, and I wondered if I could ask him for advice, but in truth I can't understand a word of his Catalan accent. Anyway it seems that, far from passing on tips, the only thing gardeners want to tell you is what you have done wrong. They don't want to show you their gardens, they just want to criticize yours.

Gardening the *potagers*, the allotments around the village, has always been women's work; they used their gardens as a retreat, retiring to them to get a bit of peace. Incompetent as I am I love squatting down, crumbling the earth between my fingers, pressing it down round new seedlings, surveying a new row of plants and, best of all, seeing tiny seeds pop up. I planted tomatoes, cour- gettes, pepper and aubergines, carrots, onions, and more herbs: chives, chervil, tarragon, more thyme, hyssop. Once I had planted things I felt differently about the rain. I listened with satisfaction as it poured down outside, soaking into the soil and thereby saving me the labour of watering.

It was good to regain control of the land, we assured ourselves. We could try and take care of it better, improve the ecology, reduce or eliminate chemicals, encourage wildlife and wild flowers. I, naturally, had ambitious plans: perhaps we could have a swimming pool, one of those wonderful infinity pools where the water flows over the edge and the mountain starts. Or maybe a nice long lap pool, lined in grey slate. I could envisage parterres, flights of steps, statues, decorative vegetable gardens full of ornamental cabbages, bamboo plantations, terraces with rows of lemon trees in terracotta pots, a bed of antique roses, a pergola of twisting vines and grapes, a labyrinth perhaps.

I could plant an orchard of apricots, apples, almonds, pears and a fig. I wanted to grow every perfumed plant I had ever known – lilac, honeysuckle, mimosa, jasmine. I dreamed of monastery gardens, the chance to create spaces for work or meditation; the cloister garth with tinkling fountains, scented herbs and box hedges, the east and west paradises, gardens for peaceful contemplation

232

often cultivated at each end of the abbey church, St Bernard's arbour of sweet peas, a zen-meditation garden.

We could make a woodland garden, grow bluebells and plant daffodils. Miles fancied a small summer-house with a fridge full of wine in a shady spot by the river, and declared he wanted footpaths so he could conveniently walk anywhere with a glass of wine in his hand. Actually Miles would have been happy to cover it all in concrete, and his main horticultural contribution was to return from a trip to Arizona with lots of cactus seeds, one of which required a bat to plant it.

Since we had no money, and no full-time gardener, and had not had to think about the land until this moment, all this was going to have to wait a very long time. Meanwhile where the brambles had been burnt off, an entirely new species of giant thistles had sprouted, already waist-high and still growing. It was critical to plant the steep bank, to ensure no more of it eroded, and we trans-planted several acacia saplings as a start, along with a tilia I insisted on, and the mimosa I craved. In the event, that year there was a dramatic late frost, my tilia died, most of the cherries were frost-bitten, and there were no peaches at all for the new farmer to pick.

Our neighbour Sylvie arrived one day with armfuls of rose sage she had uprooted from her garden, and lots of tiny aloe plants, which are good for retaining the earth with their tenacious roots. She eyed our olives sceptically, and when I started to talk about purple bougainvillaea dripping over the stone terrace walls she intoned severely, 'Rosemary, ce n'est pas Provence ici.' This was, I admit, becoming a familiar refrain as I reluctantly began to accept that I was in the Pyrenees.

Sylvie gave me a tiny cutting from a passionflower she had taken from a little chapel high in the mountains on one of her horse rides. I had thought it was called a passionflower for *l'amour* but in fact it is named for the

233

passion of Christ, because of the shape of the cross made by the stamens in the centre of the flower. Surprisingly it took, found water where I had haphazardly planted it, and now looks amazingly exotic, the curious yellow-and-blue flowers climbing right up the high stone terrace wall, perfuming the air.

One day we went to pick a salad for lunch from the new vegetable garden – small pale-green lettuces, a few leaves of mineral-green sorrel, tiny crisp radishes and peppery leaves of rocket. We speculated how the monks had arranged the land. They would have cleared the woodland to make pastures for sheep and cows, kept a pig perhaps, a goat, and certainly chickens. Perhaps they had a fishpond, though we can find no evidence, so maybe it was enough to fish trout from the river. Since the Trinitarians used donkeys when they travelled on their rescue missions, there may have been a field for donkeys.

The air was still and we heard the sound of the church bell in Campôme, tolling midday, still the signal for most of France to stop for lunch. I could see our own *clocher*, the red-brick tower, silhouetted against the sky, silent and empty of its bells. For centuries the bells of Corbiac would have tolled in the valley, signalling the prayers of the monks, and marking the natural rhythms of the day and the seasons.

The Angelus announced the main points of the day: daybreak, the midday meal and dusk. For a country community such as this one, it would summon the workers in the surrounding fields and pastures to break for lunch, or head home to supper and bed. Mountainous terrain like this called for both a loud bell and early announcements, and people were always complaining about the failure of bells to carry.

Until the French Revolution the whole country rang constantly with bells; every village had at least one bell, often several, and the towns and cities had dozens, even hundreds. Added to these were the abbeys and the monasteries strung across the countryside, all of whom depended on their bells. There being no clocks, bells were the main means of marking the passage of time. They were also an essential method of communication, rung to announce a declaration of war, a defeat or the death of the sovereign. Most of all they were a summons, and every event had its own special peal, its own language, understood by all. They summoned the people to mass, told them when the market had opened, when the tax collector had arrived, when the flock had set off for the mountains, or when the wine harvest was declared. The bells also sounded rites of passage, a birth, a death, with different peals for men and women. The bell would be tolled while someone was dying – the death knell – as well as later for the burial. During the plague years the death agony bells were silenced, since they brought further despair to those who were still suffering.

Exactly how the bells were rung was of critical importance. To toll the bell was to ring the clapper directly against only one side, or even simply to hit it with a mallet. Pealing the bell meant striking each side of the bell in turn with the clapper. Playing a carillon required at least four bells to create a melody. The tocsin was the most feared bell, since it announced danger or disaster – the arrival of bandits, say, or the threat of war or massacre. An irregular, hurried, intermittent jangle, designed to spread alarm, it rang throughout some of the worst massacres in Paris, after the Revolution, spreading fear and encouraging the mayhem.

People fervently believed the bells had supernatural properties, that they could summon angels and drive away evil. On the eve of All Souls the bells would be rung continually for several hours, sometimes throughout the night, to keep the evil spirits at bay. They were considered particularly efficacious for counteracting thunderstorms.

It was believed they would drive away thunder and cleanse the air. As soon as a storm threatened, the bell ringer would hurry to the church to start ringing and then keep up his pealing till the storm had passed. They were also used to try to drive away the dreaded springtime frosts, which threatened the tender new growth of fruit and vines. Widely believed to have other therapeutic properties, it was said you could cure warts if they were washed in mud while the death knell was tolling. Once the evening Angelus had tolled, it was advisable to stay snug at home, and never to leave the stable door open once the bell had rung, lest the animals come to harm. Nor were you supposed to take milk outside after the bell, since it might be vulnerable to witches, turn black and spoil.

In 1790, a year after the fall of the Bastille, all the bells in the country were pealed simultaneously in a national expression of collective joy. But such volume and intensity of ringing was never to be heard again. Shortly after, the bells were requisitioned to be melted down for cannon, to defend the new republic. Then as the Revolutionaries tried to tighten their grip and stamp out religious observance, all ringing of bells was banned. It was a measure that was fought bitterly: bells were taken down and hidden away and people protested by breaking into their bell towers and ringing the bells themselves.

For the monks of Corbiac the bells rang for the offices, starting with matins at 2 or 3 a.m. The bell would be rung until the monks had risen and taken their places in choir. This was the most important bell for them, signifying the resurrection, and the new dawn. I remember the church bell in Dinnington was always tolled nine times as my brother raised the host for mass. It was always the most solemn, effective moment of the drama.

13

Instructions for hermits

I had always cherished the idea of the hermit of Corbiac, but I didn't realize how like a hermit I might be tempted to become myself. It was easy to remain enclosed here – *enfermé* – outside the village, with a large house and garden, supplies of books, food and wine, and remain in our own little world. It had been a bit like entering a monastery, this life, detaching the familiar supports, divesting ourselves of so many of the worldly things on which we usually depended. The absence of a familiar language was the most significant. My French was not too bad and I could manage to do shopping, deal with plumbers and electricians, and even hold simple conversations, but I was not constantly bombarded with language as I would be with English. It was curiously relaxing, not to have my mind cluttered all the time with the ubiquitous English text I would absorb unconsciously, reading everything from cereal packets to roadside advertisements. Unless I made a conscious effort, other people's conversations, TV and radio flowed by without my really understanding. It was like the Rule of Silence for the monks, which in most monastic orders limited them to necessary communication; only the austere Cistercian Trappists were really forbidden to speak at all. I could understand now how it would have helped them to focus on their worship, how it could help me to explore my own resources, what my brother Simon liked to call the 'well within'. I wanted to know what I would find in my own heart when everything else was taken away.

There were so many things we lacked that first year or so. This was in part deliberate, because I wanted to see what we really needed; I suppose I was trying to down-shift, though it wasn't called that then. It was like one of those denial diets recommended to find out what might be causing a food allergy. You take everything away and then 'challenge' the body with individual foodstuffs such as wheat or milk to test the reaction. In our case at first we had no stove, only a two-burner gas hob, no curtains, no iron, no proper bath, no English TV, no satellite dish. Slowly we discovered our needs: curtains appeared slowly, the iron took over a year, but finally my craving to wear crisp white linen in the summer, however im-practical, triumphed.

Curious to know more about the austerities of monastic life today, I wrote to the abbot of St Michel de Cuxa, who graciously invited me to visit. It was raining when I got there but the monastery still looked beautiful. Its setting is so magnificent that no weather could make it look otherwise. Stormy clouds obscured the mountains but the greyness made the colours of wisteria and lilac in the garden more vibrant, and the pink marble of the cloister columns glistened in the rain.

Père Oleguer looked quite severe when he opened the door of the monks' quarters, but his handshake was warm and when we settled down to talk in a small visitors' room with a carved wooden bench, an eighteenth-century statue of St Michel killing a devil, and several modern paintings of the abbey, he smiled comfortably and his face was transformed. His smile has made by far the deepest lines in his face and his forehead was crosshatched by thinking lines. He smiled a lot, and I wondered how so much prayer could make anyone smile so much. My father was usually frowning with his head in his hands when deep in prayer.

The abbot explained the life of the monastery to me – the daily round of the remaining four monks, their primary objective, 'to seek God above all, all the time', through prayer seven times a day beginning with morning office at 4 a.m. They observed the rule of silence except at mealtimes, which was their opportunity to communicate. They worked on the land, growing fruit trees, and made pottery to earn their living.

I was a bit disappointed that instead of the traditional habit I expected he was dressed in ordinary clothes: grey trousers and a zip-up blue jerkin. He looked just like all the other old men around. That, he explained gently, was exactly the point. Although they still wear their habits for the offices at St Michel de Cuxa, St Benedict's original idea was that monks should dress in simple peasant wear. At the time he prescribed rough woollen gowns, hoods and rope belts, that was what everyone wore. He had never intended the monastic habit to set them apart with an aura of mystery and otherness.

This real flesh-and-blood monk somehow made sense of my imagined monks. He asked me to guess his age and was pleased when I got it wrong and he had to tell me he was over seventy-five. Despite his hands twisted by arthritis, and his hampered gait, his shining face made it all seem very simple. I asked him a question that had been vexing me: 'How did medieval monks know the time to say the offices at night?' He looked surprised. 'By the stars, of course,' he replied.

In Mosset some of the older peasants still dressed traditionally, the men in blue trousers and black sweaters, the women always in black, sometimes with a black kerchief even in summer. They even used to get married in black, but at least the bride-to-be always had a trousseau. Now I searched in *brocante* shops and markets for their exquisitely embroidered creamy linen nightgowns and white lawn nightshirts, the initials of the new couple embroidered on the breast of each garment. With their delicate hand-stitching and natural fabrics they are wonderful to sleep in. I wondered why so often they seem new. Perhaps it is because some of the fiancés never came back from the war.

All my own clothes have acquired a somewhat faded quality. It fits the building, I suppose. I suspect I will become like some other women here – you can almost date the year they arrived by the clothes they are still wearing: the cut of the trousers, the length of the skirt, the shape of the collar. But more and more I liked getting out my old clothes, cherishing them. I have even taken up mending again, stitching a vintage silk skirt back to life, patching a loved linen jacket, finding a cache of mother-of-pearl buttons to add to a cotton shirt, patching Theo's denim jeans.

Each summer I take out my favourite sarongs, the faded black *kikois* from Africa, with striped coloured borders, the soft pink-and-blue ikat from Indonesia. These have become my summer uniform, wrapped and tied around the waist over a T-shirt or swimsuit. I craved comfort, rejecting garments that are too tight or badly cut. My rings felt too small since my hands must have developed more muscles from physical work. I bought shoes that were too small, only gradually realizing that after years

240

of wearing only flat shoes, sandals and wellingtons they must have expanded, or simply relaxed to a natural shape. I remembered the hippie friend who spent so many years barefoot in India she could never wear anything but wellington boots once she returned to Britain. Eventually she went back to India and was last heard of living under a banyan tree.

My friend at *Vogue* tried to keep me up-to-date, bringing red lipstick, finding me bargains in the Ghost sale, and sending me the latest anti-wrinkle creams . . . But I knew I was losing the plot when I returned to the UK after a long time away and spent a happy hour in the bath reading that month's *Vogue*, only to discover later that it was from the previous year.

Fortunately our reclusive existence was regularly inter- rupted, and when guests came I switched roles from hermit to guestmaster. His task, according to the mon- astic customaries, was to make everything ready for monastery guests; to clean and sweep, provide new rushes for the floor, dust, attend to a fire if necessary and ensure that writing materials and candles were in ready supply. Any guest had to be entertained for two days and nights without question. After the guest had left, the guestmaster had to check the chambers to see nothing had been left behind such as a sword or a knife, and nothing taken off by mistake, before wishing them Godspeed.

English friends came with families for summer holidays or for Christmas. My family visited, especially Mother, who enjoyed the mountain view from our terrace so much that she said she would like her ashes scattered there. But for a lot of English people the Pyrenees seemed to be just too far away. They got as far as the Dordogne or the Lot, hit the wine and fell asleep. Someone once said that the English used the cost of wine in France as their bench- mark. Miles used the cost of lunches in the Groucho club, so everything seemed cheap. Actually a few Groucho chums did make it, and we had long, inebriated lunches in the garden instead of Soho, gossiping about London artists, writers' advances, which editors had moved where.

I liked it when there were lots of different nationalities here. I wanted to create a rainbow tribe of our own. Spanish friends came, Italians from Bologna, Australians, Russians and Dutch. Martha contributed Swiss, Austrian and German friends. Sometimes there were several different languages spoken at once, sometimes by people who had no language in common. Mostly, in the event, it was Americans who came, from New York, California, Arizona, Texas. Once they got to Europe, to them nowhere was far away. They simply dropped by, from Paris, Nice, London, Spain, wherever. Gracious, courteous Americans, the perfect guests.

The best visitors were those who understood why I was here, who did not think I was mad. It has always made me sad that Simon never came. Some arrived and succumbed immediately to terrace and mountains, painting pictures that now adorn our staircase, or took wonderful photos. Some just lay in the hammock and listened to birdsong. Some took mountain walks, swam in waterfalls and hot springs, or came with us to visit Romanesque churches. Some went sledging or rolled in the snow. Some with greener fingers than I bought us plants that now flourish in the garden; one planted a whole row of little pine trees, hauling bucket after bucket of water for them. An old friend of Miles helped me plant the vegetable garden one year. He lived in Seattle but still planted the raised beds the old Yorkshire way he had known as a boy. Another brought us special seeds, *nicotiana*, and poppies, which pop up in the most surprising places, did *t'ai chi* in the garden and drove us to visit the amazing cave paintings at Niaux in the Ariège.

Some responded immediately to the spirit of the place.

242

Clara, for example, is Spanish and even more emotional than I am. 'It is so beautiful,' she whispered with tears in her eyes, the first time she came. When she went into the chapel, then still a dingy tangle of old tools, paint pots and bags of rubbish, she immediately began to sing, a Spanish hymn from her childhood that just poured forth and rose to the cobwebbed vault above. She said she envied me but with *envidia sana*, literally: 'healthy envy', envy that takes pleasure in the other's good fortune. The opposite of *schadenfreude*, I reflected, the German word meaning 'to take pleasure in another's misfortune'. What a pity *schadenfreude* has been incorporated in the English lexicon but not *envidia sana*.

There was Ilona, a Russian artist, a typical White Russian with pale-blonde hair and blue eyes, always dressed in a poetic combination of antique lace, velvets and designer cast-offs. She arrived with almost no luggage except a collection of large handmade puppets for Theo, for me her Nicole Farhi jacket I had particularly coveted, her Bible, a copy of Pushkin to read to the children and pots of lapis lazuli and silver, with which she hoped to paint the sundial. Since this was not a priority, instead she painted delicate botanically detailed flowers on the whitewashed kitchen walls. Ilona, happy to believe in our hermit's cave, suggested we get a hermit of our own, like English landed gentry in the eighteenth century, who embellished their gardens with follies and *faux* ruins, and hermits became a fashionable accessory.

The Desert Fathers, the hermits of the Egyptian desert, were the founders of the western Monastic movement in the third century AD. They escaped the wealth and decadence of the Roman empire, which by then included the Roman Christian church, for a simple life in the remote wilderness of the desert. The desire for spiritual adventure inspired many, both rich and poor alike; even Arsenius, the confidant of Theodosius, the last Roman emperor, left

243

the luxury of the imperial palace to go to live in a reed-thatched cell with a shepherd in Egypt. The Christian bishops at first disapproved of what they called this 'new enchantment', but adapted soon enough when it proved a success.

At first the ascetics were simply groups of solitary hermits, living spectacularly austere lives. They competed in their privations, going without food or drink, suffering gladly, sometimes not emerging from their caves for months or even years. Their asceticism and wisdom attracted followers and sightseers, even biographers. They were the celebrities of their time. Gradually more organized communities were formed, and even in those early days there was a recognizable regime of prayer, which required rising at midnight and cockcrow, and marked daybreak, bedtime and the hours of Christ's passion.

Most bizarre were the stylites, hermits who lived on pillars. Most famous of all was St Symeon Stylites who lived for the final forty years of his life on top of a tall pillar in Antioch. A monastery was built around him, but he died on his column in 459. As one of the Lives of the Saints puts it, 'there he stood, snowed-on, rained-on and sun-shrivelled, and many came unto him'.

Skall was our local hermit, an Austrian ex-punk trying to live a self-sufficient life in Gerard's *cortal*, high on the hills above Mosset. Gerard, who had moved down to the village and was busily creating a garden for the newly built *mairie*, was owner of fifty hectares of wild *garrigue*, once used for pasture and growing barley but now abandoned, and a stone barn and one-roomed shack where Skall was now ensconced.

Theo and I went with Gerard one day to visit him. The path had become overgrown with cistus and broom, and Gerard automatically snapped away at branches to clear it as we went along. This was the old road to Sournia, he explained, up and over the crest of the hill across the plateau to the Fenouilledes. The path was deeply eroded from centuries of use, the flat stones with which it was once paved now upturned and scattered. A few decades ago oxen would have descended this path, dragging swaying carts of grain for the winter. In one or two places the stone had been replaced by Gerard, an impossible Herculean task of restoring the road. At one particularly steep turn of the track was a ceramic sink. Gerard regarded it regretfully. 'That is as far as we could get it, even with two people.' It was after all a double sink.

We paused for breath on a little promontory overlooking the terracotta roofs of Mosset below, where the shape of the village curved snugly round what remained of the château. Beside the château, against the hill that rises above it, was a broad green terrace, where once, Gerard suggested, the château had its orangerie and its vegetable garden.

Gerard pointed out serpent eagles, the song of a nightingale, a viper, the tumbled walls of a stone *cortal*, and a natural stone menhir about ten feet tall, a sacred place many millenniums ago for the neolithic folk that were then denizens of the valley. Suddenly Gerard veered off the path to show us a neolithic grave, stone slabs on three sides of a tiny tomb perhaps 4,000 years old. He crouched down with his hands round his knees to show us how the bodies were buried. Beyond, perhaps, were more tombs, but tangled gorse and brambles made it inaccessible. I looked round, at the blue mountains in the distance, the wide sky above, and thought it not a bad place to be buried. Then I saw the horse's skull, carefully strung with cord, a feather attached, hanging from a tree above the grave. It looked like powerful Indian magic, a protective talisman. 'It must be Skall,' said Gerard.

Gerard's cortal was named La Perelada, the place of flat stones, referring to the dolmen – a grave with stone sides and a flat stone on top like a table – of which there is evidence. There was a Stone Age domestic quality about it all, cosily enclosed by huge smooth boulders on which Gerard had perched small bronze balls. A basic stone-wall terrace was flanked by a barn for the animals and a much smaller stone shack for the human. Two horses and a white goat poked their heads enquiringly over the weather-beaten wooden door of the barn, chickens wandered across the grass, and a dog barked from inside the little stone house.

The *cortals*, which had always been very basic, were built near a stream for water, roofed in *ardoise* (slate) tiles and divided into stables and living quarters. Cooking was over a fire with a basic chimney, and furniture consisted of rough plank tables and benches, and straw mattresses. For light some might have oil lamps or candles, but since these were expensive the resinous root of the pine tree, which gave a dim but adequate light, was a useful alternative.

La Perelada was in the same tradition. On the terrace was a table of wooden planks, and in the corner a rudimentary fireplace, with a large black pot hanging over it. Along the wall beside the little house was a stainless-steel (double) sink, with a pipe and tap, and pots and pans ranged neatly underneath. 'Stainless steel', explained Gerard, 'was lighter to carry.'

Gerard had originally retreated to La Perelada after giving up his horse-riding enterprise. He explained that, since beyond his fifty hectares there is only more abandoned land, it as if his estate spread for miles and miles. 'I feel like the Marquis of Carabosse' (the cat in *Dick Whittington* who invents the vast estates of his master to impress the king) he said.

Then Skall himself appeared between the rocks, leading a young goat on a piece of rope. He could have walked straight out of a Russian fairy tale, dressed in a waistcoat of home-cured rabbit skins with buttons of boar's teeth, jeans that have been almost completely renewed with leather, a leather tobacco pouch and a knife sheath round his waist. When I asked permission to describe him he said I must be sure not to forget his purse, a furry white pouch, which he pulled out of his back pocket. 'Made from sheep's bollocks,' he said proudly. 'I cured it myself.'

The goat, which he had found wandering in the forest, was only three months old, had a chestnut coat with a dark streak down the backbone, an elegant, heart-shaped face and two tough little horns. It met the other, white, billy goat and they began butting each other in what we guessed was some sort of friendly standoff.

Skall made us tea in a pot over a few twigs on the fire, using a very fine mix of Earl Grey, which put my tea bags to shame. He is a tea connoisseur, up here in his wilderness. He described his quest for a particular favourite, Tibetan silver tips, which I had never heard of, and have to be convinced it is really tea and not an exotic drug. Theo was most impressed when Skall lit his roll-up using a magnifying glass and the sun. (When we told Miles about this feat later, he commented sceptically, 'So he can only smoke when it's sunny, then?')

Skall had been there only a few weeks but was determined to try and live completely self-sufficiently. Previously he had worked as a *berger*, a shepherd, looking after a flock of sheep on the Col de Jau. But then one day he decided that although he might be living a pure, simple life looking after the animals, they were still being taken off to the abbatoir to be slaughtered. He explained he wanted to live in harmony with the planet, as close to the land as he could. He used to like cities but not any more. He had lived in London: 'I was for a few years living in Peckham,' he said. 'I was in a squat, but it was all too violent, too many crackheads.'

He showed us his rudimentary accommodation, one

small room with a wood stove, a table, a chair, a candle, a mattress, and sheepskin rugs he had made himself. There was no electricity – a small solar panel sometimes supplied enough energy for a light-bulb – and no phone connection. The book shelf held an extraordinary mixture of books, left by Gerard, which included Roland Barthes in French, Aldous Huxley in English, an English guide to horse breeding, a German tome on raising goats and a Spanish phrase book (into Dutch, I think).

Keen to grow his own food, Skall had planted a potato patch and had tomatoes and pumpkins growing from seed in little pots. Gerard asked how he would manage for money. 'I can make good money out of juggling, and I make leather goods,' he said, showing us his handsome tobacco pouch with an inset slice of agate. After tea we walked further into the forest to see the neolithic settlement Gerard had discovered, with remains of pottery and axe heads. Skall pointed out the edible plants he had identified, including a specially succulent round green leaf called, Skall informed me, 'Venus's navel'. It tasted a bit like lettuce. Skall recommended it with vinaigrette.

Our little band had now grown like the Pied Piper's; we were accompanied by three dogs and the goat, who was climbing the rocks with sure-footed ease. She leapt from stone to stone so delicately, so lightly. Poised on a crag she looked magnificent, her bone structure clearly etched, a living sculpture. You understood why Picasso was so inspired by drawing goats. I wanted a rock and a goat for my garden, and Skall told me you can get miniature goats for gardens. I was very tempted.

'Don't you ever get lonely?' I asked, thinking of the long nights with only the sound of the river, the wind in the trees, owls hooting. 'I have the animals,' he said. 'Like Kathy,' he reminded me. People always spoke of Kathy with such a mixture of awe and disbelief in these parts. I had been to see her once up on the windswept plateau

248

further up the mountain north of Mosset, where she lives alone without electricity or running water, in a rudimentary dwelling adjacent to a great barnful of animals. She is about my age, mid-forties, tough and weather-hardened, her skin as sunburned as a South American Indian, her springy dark hair thickly streaked with grey. Kathy always has a wide smile on her face, and her speech is punctuated by peals of laughter. She cares for an entire sanctuary of animals: over forty horses, which roam the rock-strewn plateau, goats, sheep, chickens and a pig of enormous size because it has been allowed to live so long. Over the years she has rescued dozens of stray or abandoned animals including dogs, of which she has at least half a dozen, in all shapes and sizes.

No other human habitation is visible from her plateau, surrounded by mountains on every side, and visitors are few. She seems happy alone in the wilderness with just the sky as her boundary. It is a solipsistic existence, perhaps, and she certainly takes a gloomy view of the planet, seeing no hope for the environment, damaged beyond saving. Exploited animals receive her greatest sympathy.

I was tempted by these lives, after our visit to Skall, and when I returned to Corbiac it felt too enclosed, the few habitations around seemed like a crowd, the occasional vehicle a horrible invasion. I dreamt of a tiny cabin high up in the woods, a river running by, gathering herbs and leaves to eat, letting the birds feed from my hand like St Francis. But I was soon consoled by the chilled white wine in the fridge, the smell of roast chicken, the dishwasher, the white linen sheets on the bed. I postponed the goat. But I like it that our hills are being colonized by these new hermits, these self-appointed guardians of the planet, struggling to live good lives, rescuing lost goats and dogs, dancing by the light of the moon.

14

From cowshed to Côte Sud

Autumn returned. It was the *arrière-saison* again and the light seemed to go gold on the first of September. The shops sold off all the summer tables, parasols and hammocks, and suddenly there were wood stoves, log baskets and wheelbarrows again. Hay wains and lorries loaded with winter fodder passed us by. The fields were cut to get in another crop of hay. The smoke from bonfires scented the still air. Friends left us apples and late figs, and down on the plain there was the ripe scent of fermenting wine in the air as the first of the wine carts carried the grapes to be pressed.

In the garden the pumpkins swelled and ripened further in the sun, great yellow and orange globes, and I nestled them in straw to stop them rotting on the ground. They were heavy and smooth-skinned, good to grasp in both hands. I anticipated delicious smooth pumpkin soup scented with oregano; pumpkin pie; and pumpkin lanterns with rows of teeth and slit eyes for Halloween and Theo's birthday. There were still lots of tomatoes to be made into soup and sauce for the freezer, a few more courgettes, aubergines and peppers still reddening. My store cupboard was full of apricot jam and liqueur, pickled peaches, cherry jam, cherries in port, and dried mushrooms.

Those September days were slow, calm, the sky bluer than in summer. The cicadas chirped on. There was no wind, so we could hear the church bells, the cowbells too, signalling the cattle's return from summer pastures. The sunlight was tawny on the stone walls as I opened the door each morning and as I turned the corner into the garden a great flock of little brown sparrows would rise, chattering, from the tree beside the house. The nights were clear too, with bright stars. With the aid of binoculars we could see the Sea of Tranquillity on the surface of the moon.

We went up to the Col de Jau to find the Roman road we had heard about. The autumn colours – 'real eyeball kicks', as poet Allen Ginsberg put it – were just beginning. Myriad hues of red, gold and yellow were appearing on the trees as the leaves of chestnuts, ash and beech all turned colour slowly, and the bracken was bright orange beneath them.

There was not much left of the Roman road, we discovered, once we had found it, but it had clearly been paved at one stage and had probably led to an iron-ore mine. We quickly lost it in the forest. There had been considerable rain so the road was more of a river than a path. Theo leapt happily from stone to stone, instructing me where to put my feet. The forest was cool, the trees mostly pine sheltering delicate ferns and grasses, mossy boulders, bushes dotted with berries, a few sinister mushrooms – some red with white spots that looked like illustrations from a fairy story. There was the distant sound of a chainsaw as wood was gathered for the winter. We sat on a rock in a shaft of sunlight and ate apples, while Theo played industriously in the stream with what Nietsche called 'the seriousness of a child at play'.

Theo went back to school and was embraced again by the daily rhythm: the school bus, the lunches in the café, lessons with the *maître*, rooting out abandoned toys for the *marché*. He began to sign his name with an acute accent over the 'e' in the French style and practised his flourishing French handwriting until he had a signature he liked. He learned poems and songs in Catalan and Spanish as well as French. Asked to volunteer a song of his own, though, he tried to write down an English song he had learned from the Narnia stories, Reepicheep's song. The *maître* had a hard time trying to understand the English as it was written phonetically by Theo, and nor was it easy to translate. Theo worked hardest at researching his projects, always further complicated for him since most of the information we had – whether it was on crocodiles, Mars or the Pont du Gard – was in English. Theo's task was therefore two-fold: he had both to research it and to translate it into French. We learnt a lot too.

He went to do a pottery class at La Coume, the school founded by German refugee Pitt Kruger, now an educational foundation. Surrounded by mountain peaks, but sheltered in a cradle of woodland with a river cascading through it, lies a complex of houses and dormitories around the original farmhouse. La Coume is run now by Olivier Betoin, eldest son of one of the original group of volunteers who ran it with the Krugers as a centre for Spanish and Jewish refugee children during the Second World War. Olivier and his Catalan wife, Martha, offer holiday courses in art, pottery, music and skiing, and still run the centre according to the original ideals of communal living, co-operation and education through practical experience.

Theo particularly liked the log *cabane* they had built in the woods where the children could camp out and live outdoors, cooking their own food on an open fire. He returned full of enthusiasm to build himself a *cabane*. The tools were the thing, and he demanded his own hammer and nails. He said he wants the *cabane* he builds to be there for his own children.

For the first time I entertained the idea of grand-children, indulged in remembering the sensuality of a baby, the intimacy of breast-feeding, and thought about a brother or sister for Theo. But grandchildren might be better: all the pleasure and no responsibility. I suppose for most people, especially in a community like this, it is a quite natural progression, to expect the next generation to come along before you go. But to me it feels odd, almost wrong, tempting fate; there is a sense of the forbidden. I don't feel I can take a next generation for granted the way people here do. Perhaps Theo will be gay or celibate or childless. Having children is after all a privilege, not a right.

I like that Theo has a sense of place, of his home as a place. He feels part of the village too now. He leaps the fire with the other boys at the Fête de St-Jean (checking first to see if his clothes are fire-retardant). Now I am the mother who explains to another anxious parent that the fire-leaping is traditional.

I suppose we will have to introduce him to the 'real world' one day. It is as if we have extended his childhood by being here. In some ways he is less sophisticated than his English friends. Perhaps he is more dependent on his parents. That was certainly true at the beginning, when he had no French and no friends, but in other ways he has had to develop more independence. He has had to cope with French without as much support as he would get if it were our first language. He has forged his own identity in French, less mediated by his parents than it would be in English. Indeed, he has to support us, which alters the balance of power considerably and gives him confidence.

He speaks English well but his writing in English is not up to the same level as his French. He tried to write a story in English one day. 'How do you spell "once", Mum?' 'How do you spell "upon"?' So he gave up and wrote it in French instead. He and his friend Clément played chess together, exchanging the French and English names of the pieces. I was amused to learn that in French the bishop becomes *le fou*, the jester.

Theo liked to help me with French, and he was a good teacher. 'No, Mum, use your tongue like this,' he would demonstrate. He agonized over my pronunciation and tried to get me to lift and chop off the word at the end. Then he imitated with glee the English speaking French. He explained that although the French do not pronounce 'h' the words beginning with that letter do still have a hint of it, such as *hiboux* (he was learning a poem about *hiboux*, owls), and he breathed on my hand to show me how gentle a hint it was.

We spent a couple of weeks in Britain that autumn. Sometimes I missed it. On one occasion, standing in the rain waiting for the school bus with Theo, I watched water trickle down the leaves on the stone wall and felt overwhelmed by nostalgia for the dripping green of England. Listening to Frank Zappa's 'Peaches in Regalia', one of Miles's old favourites, I felt regret for a former life. Sometimes I felt frustrated at always being a foreigner, never properly understood, an outsider. On the train journey from Stansted airport to London, I found myself utterly enthralled by the clouds. I simply gazed and gazed, finally understanding and appreciating as never before the shifting complexity of the clouds in the paintings of Constable or Turner.

Things had changed in the two years since we left. There was a Labour government and everybody had the

Internet now; instead of being ahead of the game we were behind. The celebrity cult was burgeoning. Half the people on the street seemed to have mobile phones (and be talking to their mother. No wonder Italians have nicknamed mobiles *Ciao, mammas*). Theo and I giggled together whenever we heard someone say, 'I'm on the train.' Women were wearing high heels again, in retreat from the liberated life they found so hard. There was something I read about in *Vogue* called Botox, a newly fashionable kind of plastic surgery.

I found myself behaving inappropriately for city life, saying hello to people on my street, smiling at strangers. I tried to talk to people on the Tube and they thought I was mad. It took me a little while to re-gird myself, retreat behind a suitable shell of armour.

We talked about coming back. I thought about how we would all squeeze into the London flat. Anyway, we still wanted to turn the cowshed into Côte Sud. We knew it would be crazy to sell at this stage even if we wanted to. Our dream remained intact. We wanted to restore the monastery to the way it was before the farmers took over, to rewind the tape and restore the integrity of its original proportions. It was like a jigsaw puzzle we had started and had to finish.

We knew we had to do something soon. We had never expected our temporary shoring up of the ruin to last very long and now it was crumbling round us. We had done a bit – rebuilt an arch that was on the verge of collapse; tied together with wooden beams two walls that looked as if they might soon fall down – but our dream conversion was still looking very remote and our finances were as dodgy as ever. We needed to find a way to restore it and be able to use it functionally, and we had endless discussions about how to do it and how to fit in such mundane essentials as bathrooms, fridges and washing machines in a building that had never had them.

For years we had made mental notes as we visited other houses, such as the Provençal *mas* we first stayed in all those years ago on my first trip to the South of France; surrounded by lavender fields, it was a long low *mas* with stone floors and white plaster walls. Then there was the house of Christine Picasso high up in the Luberon, with one bedroom and two swimming pools. We visited a château in Gascony, which embodied all our ideas. Renaud Camus, the owner, was a writer and used the château for modern art exhibitions. We saw Joseph Albers' paintings, amazing simple squares of colour, reds and yellows, shades of white and deep rich blacks and browns, all perfectly set off within austere, solid Romanesque arches.

I bought *Côte Sud* magazine and fantasized about the perfect house, with old linen, antique furniture, oak chests, well-worn tiles. I lingered over pictures of Provençal *mas* with blue shutters, stone walls, and cool stone-floored kitchens, cream linen curtains in a shady room with sea-grass matting on the floor, a few frescos perhaps, bowls of artistically placed fruit, sculpted moulded fireplaces, geometric stacks of logs, modern furniture in old rooms, chandeliers, *chaises longues*, marquetry marble tables, old masters, Picassos . . .

It was all wildly beyond our purse, if not our imaginations, and we knew that even if we could get together another mortgage to restore part of the building it would barely pay for the stones, let alone furniture. Best of all anyway I liked the idea of the sheik's desert room in a story told by Lawrence of Arabia. He visited the ideal palace of an Arab sheik with a magnificent courtyard, full of fountains and flowers, and seven opulent rooms, each with different hangings and furnishings, each with amazing views. But the last and most valued room of all was white and bare and open to the desert.

Another inspiration was the house of Salvador Dali in

Port Lligat, a tiny fishing harbour in a rocky cove across the peninsula from the Catalan fishing port of Cadaqués, in Spain, where Dali spent his childhood holidays. He always loved to paint there, inspired by the hallucinatory rock formations of Cap de Creus, 'exactly the epic spot where the mountains of the Pyrenees come down into the sea, in a grandiose geological delirium', as Dali put it, the rocks scoured and sculpted by the fierce Tramontane wind.

We went to see it on my birthday weekend in October, driving along the winding coast road to Spain, stopping for lunch in the fishing port of Banyuls and sitting on the shore to eat piles of fresh sardines with lashings of *aïoli*. Once across the border and into Spain we made a detour, a winding precipitous drive up to St Père de Rodes, a ruined monastery that was being restored with great Catalan boldness, confidently blending old and new: entire replacement pillars in the cloister, new arches of cement, glass cut to fit stone walls, an iron balcony looking into the church with views of the capitals high above.

In Port de la Selva, near Cadaqués, we found a hotel – a double room for us and tiny room for Theo. He was excited to find he had his own wardrobe at last, and carefully hung up all his clothes, stretching his little T-shirts and pants to fit onto the hangers, though because the rail was so high he had to climb into the wardrobe to hang them up. We walked around the rocky cap at the end of the bay to a sea of strong waves and many blues. On the beach Theo skimmed flat stones over the water and said he had a dream of skimming a stone right around the world.

Cadaqués, like Ceret and Collioure, was a favourite retreat for artists. Picasso and André Derain came in 1910, invited by Ramon Pinchot, the Catalan Impressionist artist. A proto-Surrealist, Pinchot and his family's diversion on a moonlit night with a calm sea was to take out a grand piano in a wide-bottomed boat, to be played by musicians in full evening dress, with tame swans floating by. Both pianos and swans became key symbols for Dali. Lobsters were another, not surprisingly, since the equally surrealist fishermen of Cadaqués held a traditional service in honour of their saint in which they tied live lobsters to the altar and watched their claws dance slowly to the music by the light of the church candles.

The house the Dalis created sits like a magic fortress on the rocky shore of Portlligat, a ziggurat of wedding-cake white walls and burnished terracotta roofs stepped down to the sea. Giant white alabaster eggs adorn the roof, dark-green cypresses stand sentinel, and at rest on the shore are gaily painted fishing boats. The house is totally idiosyncratic, reflecting a playful, cosy side of Dali and his wife Gala, strangely at odds with their decadent image. It is hard to think of any other painter's house that illuminates so effectively the machinations of the artist's mind. Inside it was like walking into an Escher drawing. What began as a tiny fishing shack mushroomed into a bizarre labyrinth of white rooms with balconies, mezzanine floors, twisting passages and secret stairways, a physical manifestation of Dali's dreams. I was inspired by the windows, cut into the walls at whimsical angles, which suddenly revealed postcard views of blue sea and rocky hillsides and wondered if we could create a terrace wall with windows like that framing mountain views.

We liked the way the Dalis had always used local materials: terracotta tiles on the floor and locally woven esparto matting (originally used on the roads for carriages) to cover the floors. Slices of local slate were used for steps and shelves, the grey of the stone in dramatic contrast to the whitewashed walls; until then I had resisted the idea of using slate, which I associated with the grim north, but now in a Mediterranean setting I could see its potential. The fireplace in the dining room was carved out of the bare rock, with niches for the fire and logs of wood, and windows framing dramatic views of hills and sea. In the bedroom Dali positioned a mirror so he could see the dawn from his bed and thus be the first person in the country to see the sun rise, since the Cap is the easternmost point of Spain.

From the olive terraces above the house, edged with the dry-slate walls that are typical of Cadaqués, the Dalis created a sublime garden, like a mythical Greek hillside under a deep-blue sky. The entire glorious place inspired the imagination and it was clear that what they had created together was an expression of their relationship. It had resulted from a profound appreciation of the surrounding landscape, using local forms and material so that it seemed to have grown there organically. On the way home, I picked bunches of yellow everlasting flowers from the clifftops and arranged them, as Gala had done, along the top of the *armoire* in the kitchen.

Back at the ranch it was winter. We woke to howling winds, and snow drifting on the fields across the valley, casting the terraces into relief. It was hard to get up, hard to wake Theo for school. He looked so warm and snug in bed, curled up with the new ginger kitten. Tom had turned up at the door in a shopping bag, kidnapped by two little girls who were moving to Paris the following day and forbidden to keep it. One look at the tiny, tawny face and I knew this was Theo's promised pet. Tom turned out to be female – 'Ce n'est pas un chat, madame, c'est une *chatte*', sniffed the vet – but the name stuck. Tom had been taken too early from her mother and failed to learn the basics, such as fear, or even that she was a cat at all. I reckoned she simply reflected whatever creature she was with; she chased dogs, even cars, tried to play with the donkeys, and followed Theo wherever he went.

As I pulled back the bed covers, the cat and his boy both blinked sleepily.

Still, I opened the outside door straightaway, and despite the snow and wind there was enough sun to make a beautiful mother-of-pearl light, soft mauve, pink and white swirling in the weak light of the sun, like the inside of a shell. The wind soon blew the clouds away and Canigou reappeared, its flanks veined with snow. Miles, though, was shivering, and the prospect of a second winter with all our holes and draughts was ominous.

Christmas that year arrived with the *pompiers*, several of whom turned up at the French windows with their annual calendar. Theo shouted for me to come – at first, he said, thinking it was a fire. The *pompiers* (literally 'pumpers') attend not just fires but all sorts of emergencies. In a place like this they are usually the first people to call, so it wouldn't do to be parsimonious and I gave them 100 francs. The calendar was very strange, featuring pictures of the accidents they had attended throughout the year. The *facteur* (post lady) also proffers an annual calendar, with a more soothing choice of kittens or blossoms on the cover, and packed out with useful information such as all the name days for birthdays and the phases of the moon.

I had already made my first Christmas cake, and had ambitious ideas how to decorate it. 'How about a model of Canigou?' I hazarded to Miles. I had a vague idea of modelling the peak we could see from our garden, but once I recruited Miles the enterprise became more serious. He spread out the large-scale survey maps on the kitchen table and studied them carefully. It was going to have to be an accurate rendering of the topography: no one-sided views for him. Theo studied the map with him and got a lesson in map-reading. Miles succeeded in constructing the correct shape of the peak and its surrounding valleys out of dried apricots and I then poured white icing all over and decorated it with a plastic monk and a Virgin Mary in the snow. We asked Paul, the builder, what he thought it was. 'It's Canigou, of course,' he said gruffly.

We went up to the Col de Jau to find holly. There had already been a fall of snow up there, and it was a bright sunny day with blue sky. We passed a hunting lodge beside the road, just a little shack really, but outside was a group of hunters who were roasting their prey, an entire wild boar, on a spit. Once I saw a hunter running along the roadside on the way to Perpignan with the head of a boar skewered on a stick.

We stopped in the pine woods before the top of the Col to look for holly. It was so quiet and the air was as fresh and stimulating as chilled Perrier, the snow deep, with a crisp crust. There was a stream where icicles hung in frozen drips from mossy stones, as artful as Andy Goldsworthy sculptures. I had interviewed him once, and he had shown me his wood in Scotland, pointing out the carefully arranged twigs along the way, the patterns of flower heads, the woven leaves and grasses, a delicate ice sculpture on the rocks in the river. In the end you didn't know which was his work and which was nature. You looked at it all with new eyes. Ever after, part of me has been looking for the art in nature, for the Goldsworthys all around us. Like the best art it opened my eyes permanently, gave me a new vision of something I had always taken for granted.

We made our own Christmas cards, decorating the postcards of Corbiac and the statue of Notre Dame de Corbiac with stars and glitter, and made present tags, cutting out pictures from the cards we were sent the previous year. The French did not seem to be very big on Christmas cards; in fact Christmas altogether is very low-key compared with our experience of living for years near Oxford Street, which was always hung with dowdy decorations from November on, and heaving

261

with harassed shoppers and killer pushchairs for weeks.

Prades usually has a few desultory decorations, and in Mosset a star is perched on top of the village church and a Christmas tree is erected in the square. Traditionally on Christmas Eve children put out their shoes instead of stockings and they open their presents on Christmas Eve. There is a special Christmas Eve meal but people also have a traditional lunch on Christmas Day. The day after that, everyone goes back to work. Boxing Day is unheard of.

I was so used to England, where everything shuts down for several days over Christmas and you have to do the most enormous amount of shopping beforehand, I enquired in the supermarket what days they would close. '*C'est comme d'habitude*,' they replied, and I said, 'But it's Christmas.' They hesitated, puzzled, clearly having forgotten. '*Mais oui*, we will be closed on Christmas Day, but that's all.'

When I asked the butcher the reply was the same. Yes, he conceded, they would be closed after lunch on Christmas Day, but they would be open in the morning. It was the same with the *boulangerie*. How else would people get their food fresh? The gastronomic aspect of the festival is the most important one for the French.

Peter and Leslie and seven-year-old Audrey were coming all the way from Los Angeles again, prepared to brave our primitive conditions for a second Christmas in the Pyrenees. I ordered duck and *foie gras* from the *ferme auberge* next door and a goose from the butcher in the market. A *chapon* is the most popular bird for Christmas, but too large for us, and I was disappointed not to have the chance to serve a castrated cock to our Freudian friends.

The weather those days in mid-December became very mild, with the warm wind from the south, the sirocco, which seemed to carry the very scent of the desert: you could almost smell oranges and dates. Nature itself

262

looked festive as the persimmon trees lost their leaves, leaving fiery balls of orange fruit like Christmas-tree baubles. We ate meals outside on the terrace, *tortellini* with parmesan and fresh sage from the garden, salad of rocket and sorrel, with walnuts from our trees.

We left the doors open in the warmth and a robin flew into the house and perched on the kitchen sink, as though in search of a Christmas tree to pose on. Just before Christmas it snowed, and for a few hours the village was inaccessible. Twenty tonnes of salt and sand were needed to clear the road. On Christmas Eve there was still snow, and the village was magical, a perfect setting for the annual *pessebre* (nativity play) with the star glittering on the roof of the church, illuminating the coverlet of snow on other rooftops, lanterns glowing in dark streets and the gentle muffled stillness only snow can give.

The *pessebre* of Mosset, introduced by the poet, Michel Perpigna (brother of the honey maker), who had first come to Mosset as a child during the war, is famous. Rather than a mere tableau of Christ's nativity, it is a performance of the Christmas story, a living crèche (*pessebre* means cradle) by local farmers and shepherds, with singing and live animals, in the Catalan tradition. At Perpigna's suggestion, the village had formed a choir, and the first *pessebre* was performed in 1983. The children of the village participated, with Isabelle Mestres in the role of Mary riding on a donkey, Pascal as one of the shepherds, and pigs, chickens and goats all brought to the cradle in front of the altar. Perhaps that was when the fortunes of Mosset changed. In 1986 they even performed the Mosset *pessebre* in Paris, at the church of La Madeleine in front of 2,000 people.

Fifteen years on, the cast had changed, with roles passed on to brothers, sisters and cousins. But the story was the same. The public crier, in traditional Catalan garb – sheepskin jacket, red bonnet and espadrilles – rang his

263

bell to announce the good news, shepherds came with sheepskins to warm the babe, the woodcutter brought wood, the *sabotier* offered little wooden clogs of olive wood, the gypsies brought oranges, the hunter pulled a rabbit out of his bag, and there was even a live chicken in a basket. Theo's friend Maxime, dressed as the devil all in red with a tail and a toasting fork, looked as if he had leapt out of a Brueghel painting. The carols sang of peasant offerings: simple gifts of wine, bread, almonds and cheese. In Catalan they sang of Canigou and Roussillon, sometimes called 'the garden of Mary'. An innovation was 'Swing low, sweet chariot', sung in Catalan. The foreigners too participated: the Dutch proffered Edam and tulips, and Marianne in a little white coiffed headdress, white apron and clogs, led the donkey (somebody stood by with a large spade for the manure, just in case); the English were represented by Bob, with a bowler hat and a stick, singing an English hymn. I tentatively joined in his rendering of 'In the bleak midwinter'.

The carols were so familiar that even in Catalan we could all sing, 'Silent night, holy night . . . *Santa nit, placida nit, els Pastor, placida nit.*'

That Christmas succeeded in being sunny, warm and snowy all at once. We ate lunch outside, with snow still on the ground, shelling dozens of oysters we had bought in a crate in the market. Miles followed a Catalan recipe for Christmas goose with quince and a *picada* sauce of garlic, pine nuts, sweet Maury wine and bitter chocolate, and then we moved on to our Canigou Christmas cake.

15

The noonday demon

But then came my time in the wilderness. Miles was away for a long time, a month in the baking heat of Phoenix, Arizona, to work on a William Burroughs project. So I was alone with Theo in February. Nobody came. Clouds descended round us, a damp grey mist that lasted for several days. We could barely see beyond the garden wall, and the other side of the valley was lost completely.

Then the wind came and we felt the full force of the Tramontane pounding us for an unprecedented ten days. It blew away the clouds all right, it blew away everything, but it was so exhausting. Any words to describe it were simply blown away. It scoured the brain. From rain one can shelter, from the sun take shade, but the wind sneaks through every crack and is impossible to escape. Outside it was impossible to stand up straight; the wind got inside your clothes and whipped them open, made your eyes water, streaked tears across your cheeks. Umbrellas were turned inside out. The dustbin was constantly blown around. I couldn't put out the washing, as the pegs were

265

scattered hither and thither. The poor olive trees were bent almost double despite their stakes. The wooden bench in the wood blew over and the seat broke. The cats' fur was blown fiercely backwards as soon as they ventured outside, and only little Tom kitten seemed to enjoy it as she leapt into the airy gusts and was blown along like a leaf.

A Roman historian wrote of the wind that it would force your mouth open wider when you spoke, and blew chariots and soldiers to the ground. Spanish soldiers stationed at Portbou had special permission when the Tramontane was blowing to ascend the steps to the garrison on their knees. Like the Mistral it was reputed to drive people mad, most particularly in the Ampurdan further south in Spanish Catalonia, where psychoanalysts in Figuères had named the psychosis *Dalinienne*, citing its effect on Dali and his bizarre paintings. These winds reached 100 k.p.h. in Perpignan, and 137 k.p.h. on the coast; roofs were blown off, cars swept off roads, and huge waves smashed beach houses and destroyed sea walls.

It was, moreover, Lent. Did the monks have to put up with this when they were also on short rations for Lent? How grim. Perhaps it was necessary, this time in the wilderness. Perhaps this was what the monks called the noonday demon, or accidie, the worst sin for a monk: the sin of not caring, of despair. The word comes from the Greek *akēdia* meaning indifference, the absence of care: what is now called depression. It was called the noonday demon, perhaps from the time of day when the sun beat down most mercilessly on the desert monks, the time when Jesus gave up his spirit on the cross, crying 'My God, my God, why hast thou forsaken me?' – perhaps the time when he most fully experienced the human condition. Noon then meant a period of time rather than an exact hour; the word 'noon' comes from the Latin *nones*, for nine, and originally meant the ninth hour of the day, about 3 p.m., nine hours after sunrise.

Finally the wind dropped. I opened the shutters in the bedroom. The landscape was scoriated, every dry twig and dead leaf stripped from the trees, the impurities blown away, the air pure and fresh. My brain felt like that too. Cleaned out. Purged. One day there were two layers of sky: above, sun and blue sky; below, horizontal rain and wind coming through. I decided to go for the other side, literally to rise above the gloom.

I went into the church to gather kindling from where it was stored beneath the apse. The sound of cowbells sounded liturgical, like church music, and I realized that there was light coming through the cracks in the bricks and stones that blocked the narrow stone lancet window high up in the curve of the apse. A beam of light was cast at an angle through the church. Yellow splashes high-lighted the dust. I wanted to know where the light would fall at different times of year. There must be a moment when it shone straight through the church at sunrise, a moment the monks must have celebrated. I wanted to climb up and knock out the bricks and open up the window again.

In the cold sunshine one day I walked to the far end of the field to the east. The peach trees here had been uprooted and low-growing alfalfa planted instead, so there was a good view of the monastery. I tried to take a picture of the entire ensemble of the building, but the sun was too bright. There were no shadows. The building looked strangely naked. When we came it was romanti-cally cloaked in ivy, with cypress trees growing up against the ancient walls of the church, their roots digging into the foundations. We have systematically stripped back all this vegetation. The ivy has been ripped away and the trees cut down. The lovely mossy slate tiles on the chapel roof are partly obscured by black car tyres, holding down a tarpaulin – ugly, and often criticized, but, we try to explain, better than the roof falling in while we figure out how to restore it and pay for it.

I had wanted to live in the country, somewhere beautiful, with a view of mountains perhaps, a garden certainly, a log fire, and, above all, space. An old building, with shutters and old stones. This much, however, I had not anticipated and I have had to learn to appreciate its beauty, its value as an old building. It is treasured, part of the *patrimoine*, that word the French love so much and invoke constantly. It means more than 'heritage', which has a cold, queenly sound to it. *Patrimoine* also includes a sense of common ownership, and our own desire to renovate the monastery combined with an increasing sense of responsibility for the building.

It was then that I began to write this book about it all. I had been keeping journals for years, but now I realized I wanted consciously to shape a story, find out more about the building and the monks who lived here. From then on even the disasters held consolation: they were always good copy. In the process of writing I began to articulate my own feelings, about what I was seeking, what I hoped to achieve by living here. I think it was only by writing that I found what was in my heart.

Hot thermal baths were the best way to relax in winter, and for respite we went with Rose one day to the hot springs at St Thomas-les-Bains, open-air baths where you float in steaming water surrounded by pine trees and snow. The warmth of the water, so hot when it comes out of the ground it must be cooled down for the baths, is a delicious contrast to the cool wind blowing on your face. It was profoundly relaxing.

For Theo winter held one major attraction: skiing. Corbiac is just above the snow line at 2000 feet, and usually we get one or two sprinklings a year, with the occasional heavy frost. Once or twice, though, it really snowed. That year Theo and I were even trapped for a few hours until the snow plough passed along the road. Theo was very pleased because he couldn't get to school. I as usual was anxious, not knowing how long it would last, and not sure I could drive without chains on the car, but extremely reluctant to get them, since then I would have to struggle to put them on in the snow. I went and counted the tins and supplies in the larder, which Miles, responding to some leftover primeval instinct, likes to keep well stocked. There were tins of *petits pois*, several large tins of *cassoulet*, and dozens of jars of stuffed mussels and squid. The snow only lasted a few hours, in the event, and by lunchtime the snow plough had cleared the road, the sun had come out and the snowman Theo built had already begun to melt.

Each morning, everyone observed with trained eyes the snow that cloaked the mountains. Would there be enough snow to ski? Mosset has a small ski station – well, really just one piste and an antique-looking ski lift. It claims to be the smallest ski station in the world. Without doubt it is the scruffiest. As it is located a few feet below the pass over the Col de Jau, not every year is there really enough snow to justify opening it. When it does open the village decamps *en masse*. The school kits out the children in a jumble of shabby hand-me-down salopettes and teaches them to ski. Theo had started to learn downhill skiing the previous year and was immediately boasting of impossible exploits. He described one day out in the forest with the *maître*, learning ski *de fond* and skating on frozen rivers.

This time I resolved to take him up to the ski station myself. The day dawned bright and sunny, even warm, and the snow seemed very distant, but we packed egg sandwiches and apples, and set out for the day. Anxious as ever about the snow conditions, I put Puccini on the car stereo and gritted my teeth.

The drive up the Col is always a challenge. As you mount higher and higher, the narrow road twists alarmingly and there is often a steep drop below. Sometimes there are cows wandering happily across the road, sometimes a few silly, woolly sheep; once, a horse confronted me right in the middle of the road as I turned a bend. It crossed slowly, unconcerned, pausing to nibble some grass before it disappeared down the hillside.

The snow deepened as we mounted higher and soon was stacked each side of the road in substantial drifts. The peaks ahead loomed majestically and Theo hugged himself in anticipation. The leafless trees of winter revealed much more of the landscape. There was something more austere, pared down, dramatic, in being able to see all the forms. There were houses and farms normally obscured by thick greenery, places I had thought derelict, with roofs full of gaping holes in the tiles, shutters hanging off, yards full of rusting machinery and broken-down chicken coops. But, with smoke coming out of the chimneys, they were clearly inhabited after all. We passed the desolate walls of the Monastère de Jau, snow capping its one surviving arch and cows wandering over the littered stones. A former Cistercian foundation, it looked as if it would suit the most austere Trappist, so wild and lonely is it, with just the wind and snow for company. A hawk coasted low over us and I could see its wingspan clearly as it wheeled off silhouetted against the snowy hillside.

At the ski station it looked as if all of Mosset were there, including those who habitually propped up the bar, and the dogs from the square. Several familiar characters were leaning over the small wooden veranda, smoking roll-ups and watching the skiers, but clearly with no intention of skiing themselves. Others sat around on hay bales, swopping babies and gossiping.

The ski station is a corrugated-iron hut, painted a shade

of pale blue that was probably always dirty. The interior looks exactly as it must have done when it was first put up with some vague notion of décor in mind: thin wooden panelling on the walls, with dog-eared posters promoting the pleasures of skiing in the Pyrenees, annotated maps of the ski pistes, old scarves and abandoned woollies hanging from rudimentary hooks. A smelly oil stove created a warm fug for the skiers gathered round plain wooden tables, their skis and boots leaning against the walls.

Alain, the village chef from Marseilles, thin, whippy, with a cleft chin, whistled Charles Aznavour songs as he served coffee, and crèpes whipped out on a butane-fuelled stove. At lunchtime a grill was lit outside and sausages were cooked on it.

The hard-core Mossetans were the ones without ski gear. A sort of anti-chic prevailed, with young men skiing in jeans and leather jackets, as often as not with a cigarette hanging out of their mouths, and the girls in jeans and woolly sweaters, long hair loose and flying behind them. One old chap had turned up in his wellington boots. Charles, our soldier neighbour, a colonel in the French army, swept smartly down the piste, looking like Action Man by contrast in his smart candy-coloured kit.

The previous year Theo had only been skiing once with the school and he was still a novice. Since I had even less idea, he staggered outside with skis far too big and promptly fell over. But everyone helped. As far as they were concerned Theo too was a child of the village, one of theirs. Kind José spotted him falling over and insisted he swapped his skis with another, bigger child. Pascal spent over an hour teaching him, coasting backwards down the piste ahead of Theo to help him get his balance. I know I should try myself, but there is enough pleasure in seeing Theo flying fearlessly down the piste, his jacket open, cheeks flushed pink. As Miles, the world's most unsporty person, said, whoever thought I would have a child who could ski?

It seems to be a perfect sport for Theo, a solo activity but in the company of others, like swimming, with the potential for competitiveness included but not its *raison d'être*. And both skiing and swimming are sports that interact with the natural environment.

I walked beyond the piste where the forest descended and the shouts of children sledging were soon muffled. The snow was soft and I sank knee-deep. The trees were mainly beech, their thin, mottled silver trunks straight, their leafless branches a lacy fretwork against the blue sky above. They were interspersed with small pines, like Christmas trees frosted with snow. Granite boulders, scoured smooth by wind and rain and snow, rose out of the snow snug with outcrops of moss. The air was clean, unscented, and I breathed deeply.

But then snow started to fall again and I was anxious. The main advice offered about driving back down in the snow was not to use the brakes! Then someone said Monsieur Mestres once had to be rescued by helicopter after three metres of snow fell. In the end Alain, the chef, offered to lead the way in his Land Rover and I followed without mishap. There was no ice after all, only snow on the road. On the way back Theo recounted instructions for avalanches. Apparently in a deep snowdrift it is impossible to know which way is up. 'You can check gravity by letting the spit dribble out of your mouth,' he explained seriously. 'And you must punch a hole straight away so you can breathe while you try and bash your way out. You have to move fast before the snow becomes hard.' Then, with eyes shining, he told me about his dream: 'I dreamed of skiing all the way down to Mosset. I stopped at the school and then – whoosh – all the way to Corbiac!'

Most of all I wanted to stay now for Theo for at least a few more years. He had had such a struggle to adapt, had to try so hard with speaking French. He has been accepted as part of this community. I knew he had a better childhood here, though once he is a teenager his needs will be different. I knew we won't be able to palm him off forever with watching reruns of the *Railway Children* with Abigail, or swapping ancient GameBoy games with Guillaume. One day he will need to be part of a wider culture, and all the advantages this place has for a child will become disadvantages for a teenager. There isn't even a bus stop to hang around in Mosset. But for now I knew it was the right place for him. It was also the right place for me to be his mother, I reckoned, when friends from the UK visited us and I listened with growing dismay to the problems of finding a good school in London, the lengths people went to, even renting an apartment for a few months in the catchment area of the favoured school.

Not that it was particularly easy being an English mother of a French schoolboy, small and intimate as the school was. The *maître*, for all his progressive ideas, was shy and taciturn, and I found him very hard to talk to. It was only later that other parents said they found him difficult too; it was not simply my Englishness and imperfect grasp of French that was the problem. The system of work plans baffled me – and Theo – and he was always in trouble for forgetting his assignments and losing things. He had his *tête dans la lune*, his head in the moon, said the *maître*. He was put in charge of *objets trouvés*, which even the *maître* agreed, with a half-smile, was rather ironic. I was intrigued that in French they are merely 'found objects'; the language does not presume to identify them as actually lost by anyone.

I tried hard with the aid of large dictionaries to help Theo with his French grammar, which was becoming increasingly difficult. The mathematics were done in a different way too, using a different system for long division, for example. Fortunately, since I couldn't remember long division even in English, Miles succeeded in mastering the French method and could help him enough.

Sometimes the best lessons were out of school anyway. Driving over the Col one day on our way to a dinosaur museum in the Aude, the winter bareness made it possible to see all the contours of the mountains. It was as if the geology was still happening – you could see the way the mountain peaks had been pushed up millenniums ago, the glacier-hewed valley floors and gorges carved out by rivers. You half expected to see the boulders roll down the mountain as you passed. Even I listened as Miles patiently explained plate tectonics again. Living here gives you a real need for the basics, to go back to geology and the formation of the earth. Theo could understand that the dinosaurs were there even before the mountains, seventy million years ago.

Spring is cruel, so tantalizing. After a few days of warmth, applying sunscreen again (I had, foolishly, already been sunburned working in the garden without a hat), and watering plants, which seemed so dry, suddenly the Tramontane started up once more. It was really bitterly cold as the rain poured and the wind blew and finally it really, really snowed again. The newly minted green leaves of the trees were all covered in snow – tenderly furled new leaves, which were heartbreakingly soft and delicate. I couldn't believe they would survive, and a few ends of the new leaves of the honeysuckle were frost-bitten, with blackened edges as if they had been burnt. I had to go outside and shake the weight off the branches of newly planted trees and bushes.

Soon I could work in the garden again, plant out more little seedlings of rosemary, thyme and lavender and the pumpkin seeds I had saved from last year's yield. In truth, though, I was not a very competent gardener and as many plants died as grew. Bougainvillaea and plumbago, the

274

dazzling Mediterranean flowers I had always admired in Provence, could not withstand the wind, and slowly I learned to accept that their vibrant colours were as unsuitable as the sky-blue paint we originally chose for our shutters. We needed more subtle colours, the pale blue of rosemary, mauve and white lavender flowers, dark-purple irises, yellow roses, pink tamarisk, and, it turned out eventually, pale-green shutters.

I was beginning to despair and the enthusiasm that had compensated for lack of knowledge to begin with was flagging. A few months after I had planted my first wisteria, I noticed it going all brown at the edges and got very worried about it. I looked up the symptoms in my garden books and bought an insecticide to spray, in case the problem was a mysterious parasite. I was just about to call Sylvie for advice, when the truth dawned. It was autumn.

I clearly needed help so I was very pleased to meet Hans, who offered his services as a gardener. It transpired he didn't actually know much about gardening either, but he was very nice and his commitment to country life was as reassuringly theoretical as mine. I particularly liked the fact that he even wore clogs. He was another dreamer. A big, florid, red-faced Dutchman, Hans had arrived with his wife, Margriet, and eleven-year-old daughter Helena. Like Theo, Helena had started at the school without a word of French. They came to dinner one night and Theo and she spent the entire evening throwing toy animals around and happily comunicating in grunts and animal sounds. Happiest in riding boots, Helena was a lovely self-possessed young girl, with a tangle of curly hair. Hans' plans for his daughter included apprenticing her for a week or so to a shepherd.

Hans had always had a yearning for a country life, despite his work as a careers adviser in Holland. He had read that donkeys and pigs were highly intelligent animals, and decided to start work in a donkey sanctuary in Holland, thereafter becoming a passionate donkey lover.

Hans needed fields for his donkeys and it seemed logical to exchange my fields for his work in the garden. I liked the idea of donkeys at Corbiac again, remembering the monks as the *frères des ânes*. When I explained this to the horse farmer he did not see the logic as clearly as I and was furious with me. 'This is not how we do things here,' he said as he stormed off. I had offended yet another Catalan farmer. Hans, meanwhile, was talking about breeding a mule and repairing the ancient harrow we had rescued so he could work the field in the old way. No doubt the farmers would chuckle. But at least I had found a foothold in the local barter system, as Hans and I nego-tiated an arrangement where Miles and I would edit an English translation of the donkey brochure in exchange for a load of manure.

Discovering what was already growing on the land was often more pleasurable than struggling to grow things myself, so I was delighted to find our own mushrooms. One sunny morning after it had been raining I spotted someone picking in our field, and I was much more interested in what they had found than concerned that they were, technically, trespassing. The mushrooms were *cariolettes*, or *faux mousserons*, I was informed after I took them to the pharmacy and finally was given approval. '*Oui. Ils sont bons pour manger.*' In the end I had three names, Catalan, Latin (*marasmius oreades*) and French. In English they are called fairy-ring mushrooms. Theo and I gathered three basketsful of them and I sat on the terrace and cut their ends off and spread them on an old rush mat to dry. The sun was hot and they dried quickly, soon exuding that mysterious intense earthy smell. We ate them fresh, fried in garlic and butter, for lunch as the foraging trespasser had recommended. They were sweet and nutty, with a more elusive, delicate flavour than *cèpes*. We had plenty to fill several jars; being small they are quick to reconstitute with water and are wonderful for adding to soups, making pasta sauce with *crème fraîche*, and adding to sauces and stuffings for *pintade* or pigeon. I felt more at home with my own source of mushrooms.

Ironically, the irises Miles had transplanted in the autumn proved one of the great garden successes. Though their stalks were blasted and bent by the wind they had begun to flower, their long spears fleshy, purple and rich. We had found them growing on a heap of rubble that had once formed part of the defensive tower, and purple blooms began to force their way through the scattered stones and tiles. Irises are traditionally monastery flowers, planted about the doors of churches to ward off evil spirits. It seemed likely that these were the descendants of irises the monks planted.

Miles wanted to investigate the old stones in the pile of rubble so basically he transplanted the irises to get rid of them. But in his thorough way he researched the process on the Internet and decided they would be best planted on the bank below the terrace, where it slopes down to the river and where the earth needs to be retained by plants with strong roots. Much to my disgust, his methods seemed to work far better than mine, which sprang from ramshackle precipitate enthusiasm rather than calculation. I did my research too, though, and advised Miles: 'The Roman writer Pliny says that those who intend to dig up the iris root must first "offer a libation to please the earth. Then they draw three circles round it with the point of a sword, pull it up and raise it to the heavens. It is hot by nature, and when handled raises burn-like blisters. It is essential that those who gather it must be chaste."'

The poor olive trees, our marriage trees, had been bent almost double by the Tramontane, their stakes flailing uselessly. They had always looked a bit sickly, and I had considered them gloomily as a metaphor for our relationship trying to withstand the onslaughts of this experience. We decided to stake them more firmly, sawing two trunks from an ash tree as supports, and pruned them fiercely, removing branches that were crossing over each other, determined to make them root more firmly. Finally, for the first time the puny olives looked rock-steady and safe. If only human relationships could be so easily secured.

By the time the termites struck, in many ways the final straw, it was another crisis turned opportunity. Miles had only recently returned from his travels, and as we sat by the wood stove one night we heard distinct munching in the old rafters. The expert we called in told us we had capricorn beetles (it was they who were munching) and termites in the old beams. Miles looked them up on the Internet and recited his findings with a kind of gloomy satisfaction. Paul embellished his discoveries with descriptions of the nests, which could be up to half a kilometre away from the building, and how termites burrowed their way through stone and over roof tops.

Even after I bargained and reduced the price by about half, it was going to cost several thousand pounds to inject the building, to kill the present population of termites and protect it against further invasion. We had no money, so I decided to try to negotiate a loan with the French bank.

Looking back, I think we had reached a watershed. So many people, it seemed, gave up after two years. After one year it all still seems possible. It is only the first year after all. But then after you have been through it all again, and it all still appears difficult, your French seems no better, and the novelty, initial enthusiasm and adrenalin have worn off, that is when it is tempting to give up. But I was determined, because for me and for Theo the life still seemed to offer all we needed then. Miles, for his part, is tenacious. He likes to finish a job once he has started, whether it is mowing a lawn or writing a book, and he had started renovating a building he loved. Between us we could not give up. An estate agent came to see us, nodded gravely over the potential of the building, but pointed out that if we ever did want to sell it would be worth considerably more if we could reveal its potential, if at least some part of it looked the way it could. Not everyone had our imagination.

Friends who were less financially inept than we were talked about getting a French loan because the rates were low. For too long we and everyone else had said *petit à petit*, little by little, when we talked about the work that needed to be done. We had a sympathetic architect willing to advise us and a builder we liked and trusted, so we decided to go for it. First we applied for planning permission, aware that Monuments Historiques was bound to want to approve our plans and would take some time. Then, emboldened by the negotiations for the termite loan, I enquired about a bigger mortgage. The negotiations were long-winded, *naturellement*, the bureaucracy was considerable, *bien sûr*, but it was perfectly possible. French bureaucracy and Southern *laissez-faire* combined miraculously, typified by the occasion when the charming and sympathetic manager dropped in one day, when she was passing, with papers for us to sign. It turned out she was in a local choir and I look forward to the day we can hear our bank manager sing in the chapel.

Then we had to wait for the builder to start, an honourable tradition, and summer embraced us. I became a tourist again, just another foreigner. At the market the stallholders no longer recognized me and they tried to speak to me in English and count my change out for me.

Although there was more traffic on the road, we continued to raise a hand to people we knew when we passed in the car, a subtle collusion which is oddly comforting.

It was August, high holiday time for the French. There were village fêtes, Bastille Day festivities on 14 July with fireworks and dancing, all culminating in the great zenith of summer on 15 August when the population of Mosset swelled to several hundred and everybody danced the night away to terrible local rock bands with names like Bullshit, Lithium and All Mix Cook. France seemed to close down completely for two days; everything shut – supermarkets, banks, the lot – and the whole world partied.

The religious significance of the festival, the Assumption of the Virgin Mary, is all but lost, despite the handful of old ladies who still go to hear mass in the village church. Now it has reverted to its original bacchanale, the civil holiday, *feriae augusti*, proclaimed by Caesar Augustus in 18 BC to celebrate his month of August. It was only later adopted by the church to mark the Assumption.

But increasingly I found myself preferring less frenetic events, a small flute concert in the village church, say, or a group of villagers dancing the *sardana*, the Catalan dance, in a village square to the sound of the traditional *cobla*, the band of wind instruments. 'I can see you dancing the *sardana* in ten years' time,' commented Miles. I did try once, but the steps are very difficult and I am the least co-ordinated of dancers.

Our tottering technology network took a further blow that summer, with the forces of nature proving as great a threat as France Telecom's pathetic attempt at an Internet interface. Towards the end of August there are always thunderstorms. The heat builds and then breaks and the storms roll round and round the valley. One day the light turned a horrible evil yellow, the air was humid, too hot. It was the kind of weather when only weeds would grow. There was a terrifying storm, with lightning and cracking thunder exploding all around us. We were waiting for guests to arrive and knew they were driving over the Col de Jau for the first time. The mountain was thick with cloud and the rain was lashing down. They finally arrived two hours late and fell out of the car, having survived Macbeth conditions on the mountain top, hailstones as big as golf balls, rain, thunder, thick fog and lightning. They had been tempted to stop in the café in the village, so desperate were they for a drink. Meanwhile, to Theo's great delight we had taken a direct lightning hit on the bell tower. He declared it the best day of his life. 'I always wanted to be struck by lightning,' he said.

Fortunately the tower did not visibly suffer, but we resolved to get a lightning conductor nonetheless. Next day I discovered the real damage when I tried to connect to the Internet. I had disconnected the electricity to my computer in the storm but didn't think of the phone connection. My modem had been struck by lightning. The nearest Apple dealer who could fix it turned out to be in Montpellier, so I was obliged to take the entire Powerbook back to London to have a new modem installed. Fortunately the insurance company paid up. They don't have acts of God in French insurance policies. They have no idea what you are talking about. That night Miles made Catalan Celebration Chicken, roasted with garlic and cinnamon and cognac, which we rechristened Consolation Chicken.

I was consoled by my lavender harvest. It grew happily just about anywhere, even popping up between the cracked tiles of the terrace, where seeds had been accidentally scattered the previous year. I simply let the plants grow and they seemed to like the dry, aerated rubble of the terrace even more than solid earth. I left most of it growing throughout the autumn, because it looked so pretty and smelled divine, but I cut enough to renew the sheaves for pots indoors and filled little squares of muslin to tie up and put in with clothes and linen to keep all the moths and bugs away.

I love lavender. I rub it on my skin in the evenings to ward off mosquitoes, and dab it on straight away if I do get bitten. It is far more effective than any insect repellent and even works for wasp stings. I buy it *en vrac*, in big bottles, from the pharmacy and fill my own little bottles, and carry one everywhere in my bag.

Lavender is a strong antiseptic with antibacterial properties, and was always used in the past to treat cuts, bites, stings, burns, as well as coughs and colds, chest infections, rheumatic aches, giddiness and flatulence. Also considered a soothing tonic for nervous and digestive disorders, it was prescribed to relieve tension, insomnia and depression. I like to put a few drops in the bath if I'm feeling tired and sprinkle it on the pillow to aid sleep.

During World War II, when surgical supplies were scarce, herbs, especially lavender, were requisitioned from thousands of English gardens, in response to the urgent pleas of desperate medical authorities, to be used in combating infection and purifying surgical dressings and wards. English lavender was always reputed to produce the strongest oil, though no doubt the French would dispute that. Sadly, the best lavender fields in England, at Mitcham, where the chalky soils of Surrey provided the lavender with perfect alkaline conditions, are now covered in housing estates.

I discovered you could even use lavender in cooking, but Miles demurred at the idea of lavender chicken. I did make one perfect late-summer meal using all our produce, starting with a dark green, lemony sorrel soup. Sorrel seems to grow all year round here, and I learned the word comes from the French for 'sour', and Roman soldiers used to suck it to quench their thirst. It is also sometimes called 'cuckoo's meat', because according to folklore cuckoos eat sorrel to lubricate their vocal chords. The soup was followed by chicken stuffed under the skin with chèvre and tarragon, and after that raspberries and lavender ice cream, decorated with the flowers.

While we waited for the work in the house to start, we made what preparations we could. Plans had been drawn up for rebuilding the west wing, with new kitchen, bath-rooms, bedrooms, a library at last for Miles and a big sitting room in the old monks' kitchen. As it was almost a separate house, there was the great advantage that all the work could be done while we continued to live in the other end.

It seemed wise to design it so that if necessary it could be closed off and function as a separate house. It was an enormous job, effectively to turn the ruined west end of a monastery turned cow byre into a three-bedroomed semi-detached house. Everyone who came and looked at the place then was frankly horrified at the enormity of the task.

Not that it was possible to see very much at all. We still hardly knew what was there, since all the windows were roughly plugged with stones and it was completely dark inside. We still merely peered in with torches and wondered about rats. The best view was with a flash photo, and we knew that the fireplace itself was in good shape. It had a huge recess with a superb stone arch over it and two intact bread ovens each side, where we imag-ined the monks with their fire, with their pots simmering over the flames. We recruited Pascal and his village team to clean out the ruin before Paul started work, and they set to with hoses to remove centuries of dirt floor and animal manure revealing the uneven rough stones of the floors for the first time. They cleared out the remains of wattle-and-daub walls, old farm equipment, rotten wooden doors hanging off their hinges, roof beams hanging perilously down from the ceiling.

Then the one-man Miles preservation team moved in. He was writing about Burroughs and, in between listening to tapes of William's sonorous almost liturgical voice, he spent hours in the ruin carefully, patiently, chipping away the rotten mortar and plaster off the walls, uncovering a bit of a corbel here, some fresco writing there, a window revealed behind a wall of cement, regularly reappearing covered in dust, and coughing to announce a new discovery. I sometimes thought I would go in there and find he had knocked it all down. As he worked he tried to figure out the architecture of the building, a puzzling palimpsest of periods, as generations of monks altered it, moving stones and arches to suit themselves.

It was critical work that would have taken a mason many hours to do. He cleaned out dozens of rats' nests from inside the thick walls, along with hundreds of peach stones they had discarded where they had been cosily nesting. He found bats living in there too, one of which was snoozing in one of the bread ovens.

Miles also examined all the stones that were scattered everywhere and selected the best ones for Paul to use when the time came. Here and there neat piles of stones grew – and woe betide anyone who didn't know the difference between cut stone and unworked stone.

16

Doctor of Stones

Finally, towards the end of October, three and a half years after we moved to Corbiac, Paul's new truck swung into the driveway, pulling the elderly crane whose rusted framework and friendly squeaking was already so familiar. The Captain was back.

After only a few days there was a scene of indescribable devastation, with trucks, crane, cement mixers and wheelbarrows everywhere, mounting piles of rubble, and a fire constantly burning rotten old wood. Paul's dog, a black-and-white collie called Ellie, which he had rescued from the streets of Perpignan, ran around excitedly, pursued by Bamboo, another black-and-white collie, that had taken up residence outside our door. With horses and donkeys instead of vehicles the scene would have looked much the same when the monastery was first built. Giant new pine beams were delivered and laid out alongside the church wall, and there were lots of bulging sacks of sand and lime. There was yet another new language to learn: *chevrons* and *poutres* for rafters and beams, *chaux*, *ciment* and *sable* for lime, cement and sand.

Paul and his team, faithful Tim and new recruit, Luc, threw off all the old roof tiles. Most were broken and despite the lovely mossy patina they had acquired it was hard to see what we could do with them, except perhaps make more paths for the garden. All the rotten roof beams had to be removed. Paul thought they were probably the original beams installed by the monks when that section of the monastery was constructed. 'There were elm boards underneath and the marks showed they were hand cut in a sawpit.' He took his traditional mason's share of the discarded wood and the rest was sawn up to supply our winter fires.

It soon looked as if there was very little of the west wing of the monastery left. The roof was open to the elements and there was a gaping chasm where half the entire north wall had been removed in order to construct two new windows and repair the stonework of the wall. In a howling wind with leaves whirling round them, Miles and Paul had looked at the great crack in the north wall and the bulge of the stones leaning out. It didn't look good, and Paul confessed there was an argument for knocking the whole wall down and starting again. In the end it was decided to stitch the crack together with concrete lintels on each side.

Then we received a letter from the mayor marked 'urgent'. It said we did not have permission for the roof. Astonished, we checked the application made the year before. It was true: although the document gave permission for the new windows and doorway, all of which had been looked at by the Monuments Historiques' architect, it did not specifically mention the roof although it was obvious nothing else could be done without it. So there was a further delay while we put in another application. Fortunately the architect responded rapidly, and

286

decided we ought to have handmade red tiles on the roof, unlike the rest of the new roof which we had replaced in 1995 with standard new terracotta tiles. These would be more expensive and had to be transported from a *tuilerie* an hour's drive away, so it was just as well Paul had not yet bought any tiles.

The Captain swung into action, creaking and squeaking, and the massive new roof beams were hauled up to the roof. Finally the tiling of the roof could begin. It was January by then, the worst time of year to do the roof, with bitterly cold winds that often made it too dangerous to be exposed so high up. Then we received a letter saying the entire building had been classified a *monument historique*, not just the chapel as we had expected. It was in some ways cause for celebration, as now the quality of the building had been recognized and saved from future depredations, and perhaps we would get grants for the chapel. It was the end of 1999 and the last building in the region to be classified in the second millennium.

With the roof finally on, the work team took refuge in the old monks' kitchen, with its wobbly stone floor, which began to resemble a medieval stonemasons' lodge, scattered with tools and drawings. The lodge was where the masons would shelter on a medieval building site, in a wooden building covered in leather skins. There they kept their tools, ate lunch and took siestas, and could work in bad weather. It was like a club for a floating workforce, and it was here the techniques and secrets of the mason's craft were passed on. This was the origin of the stonemasons' guild of the Middle Ages, and ultimately the origin of the stonemasons' secret association today.

It was extraordinary how little had really changed. The building process, and the basic tools – the wheelbarrows, hods, buckets and trowels – were all the same as the monks would have used. I thought it a pity they didn't all wear special headbands to denote their *métier*, as they would have done in the past. In the Middle Ages plans were often drawn on to the ground itself, on a surface of soil, sand or clay, and often someone would simply grab a stick and scrawl a sketch in the sand as had always been done.

In the past all the stone and wood would have been transported from quarry and forest by horses, oxen or donkeys and carts. The size of capitals, the carved stones on top of columns, was effectively decided by the weight a donkey could carry in panniers each side, two blocks of stone of 50 kilograms each. Although Paul now had a truck, it was still not much use in hill villages with narrow winding streets and flights of steps, and often beams still have to be dragged by tractors, and big stones rolled by hand.

Paul was without doubt the master mason. He cut and assembled the stones for the walls or window frames while the workers transported them and prepared the mortar in the correct proportions. He had learnt his stone work from constructing dry-stone walls in Yorkshire. 'I never studied it, never had a *maître*,' he said. What astonished me was the confidence necessary to construct a wall out of huge stones believing it won't fall down. Paul simply laughed as we talked over a beer one day. 'If you have a stone like this, and a stone like that, it can't fall. This end would have to go up and if there's another stone there, it can't move. It doesn't matter if there is a gap underneath. All the stones are held in place by the others. It's all to do with equilibrium.' He demonstrated with the salt and pepper pots on the table. 'It's not going to move of its own accord – if it's stable, and given there's not an earthquake, it will always be steady.' He smiled at me. 'Nothing changes around stones.'

Paul's team varied in size according to need – young Tim always eager for instruction, occasionally hungover from his nights out with the lads; Luc, cheerful, long-haired, recruited by Paul when the *auberge* he was trying to establish fell foul of French bureaucracy and had to close. From time to time the team was augmented by a motley crew of workers, Spanish, French, German and English, most of whom, along with the core team, seemed to have some kind of handicap. Tim had lost the sight of an eye in a fight; Luc was on a government rehabilitation scheme; the German carpenter had a disabled arm and leg; and the French *compagnon* mason who arrived later turned out to be an alcoholic. Even Paul himself had a bad knee, which wasn't helped by clambering about on freezing roof tops. No doubt a medieval building site would have had an equal number of variously disabled workers too, given the dangers and the primitive nature of medical care. Paul was tough with them. There were no radios playing when he was around. When it was freezing cold and I suggested they came inside the house to eat their lunch, he said it was better to stay cold, since otherwise it was too difficult to start again. No doubt dry-stone walling on the Yorkshire moors was a good training ground.

They worked incredibly hard and I enjoyed having them around, especially when they were whistling as they worked, steadily mixing the cement, pushing wheel-barrows and applying mortar to stone. They were cute too. Paul had cut his long hair and on a good day now looked a bit like Harrison Ford. Sometimes I could hear them joshing one another up on the scaffolding in English or French. 'Come on, you can do it. Don't be a wimp. A young man like you!' Paul would say in brusque Yorkshire tones. 'You daft bugger, not like that!' 'Well, why didn't you tell me in the first place?' Tim would respond truculently.

Theo, who loved the workers, would beg to join them for lunch, sometimes sitting out on the grass on sunny days. He insisted on making his own 'worker's sandwich' to eat with them, ham and mayonnaise in a huge chunk of baguette.

Paul took Theo seriously, told him off when he was naughty or got in the way, gave him rides on the crane and the digger, and answered his questions. He showed him how to lay mortar on stones, and explained the difference between lime mortar and cement. Just as if he was the medieval mason handing down his secrets, he explained the right recipe for mortar, the mix of lime, sand and water, which determined the quality and longevity of the building.

Early one morning as I was mooching about the building site of the west wing, planning the new kitchen, how we were going to fit in a modern fridge and dishwasher between all these doors and stone arches that had to be respected, I saw a shaft of sunlight beam briefly through the reopened north window. Now all the parts of the monastery received sun at some point in the day. There was an old doorway outlined between the monks' kitchen with the big fireplace, where we planned to put the sitting room, and the new kitchen about two metres lower down. I begged to open the door like a serving hatch, so there would be a connection between the two rooms, more light in the new kitchen, and a view of the fire. Miles obligingly chipped away for a few days, revealing a cut stone doorway, intact but needing a new wooden lintel. After the rubble infill was knocked out we could see right through the building from north window to south door, to each side of the valley.

Spring came at last, the peaches blossomed pink, and I snatched some time for the garden, weeded brambles from the copse, and cherished the appearance of the daffodils and crocuses, the few bulbs I had planted the year before. I waited anxiously for the lilac and wisteria to flower, and planted out more little seedlings of rosemary. There is great satisfaction in seeing my little namesakes, my little metaphors, take root so prolifically.

Theo's friend Guillaume came to play one day and I took them down to the river. While they were happily floating sticks, building dams and getting their feet wet under the green canopy of trees, I gathered kindling and tried to identify more trees. I suddenly realized that where we go down to the river, a shallow bank where the Castellane meets the Corbiac rivulet, there is a hazel grove. It was as if scales had dropped from my eyes. Among all these indeterminate trees, I could at last see some of them. I picked up two hazelnuts, which confirmed my judgement, and there they were, huge clutches of hazel wands, almost certainly deliberately planted there near the water. They were used in gardens and also to make the wattle of wattle-and-daub – there had been a wall of woven mud and hazel left in the ruin before we tore it out. This was where I should be getting my garden stakes instead of buying them from the garden centre. I was quite shaken, quivering with happiness at the sight. It was odd, like a revelation.

One morning in the garden Paul and Miles were deep in discussion around a pile of stones. Paul was about to start reconstructing two interior arches, adjacent to each other around the central hall, from which a stone staircase led up and turned in a curve over one of the arches. Only the actual arch remained on one doorway, supported by a wooden post, the cut stone sides long ago removed so cattle could pass through. The sides were completely rebuilt by Paul, using different stones but carefully matched to the originals. Now the whole looks as if it's always been there.

Of the other doorway one side had been completely demolished leaving the other side of carefully cut stone, half an arch, and a small niche above that must have once housed a statue. The keystone, the wedge-shaped stone at the centre of the arch, was gone, but Miles had found the other missing stones of the arch among the rubble outside, as well as several of the missing uprights. While Paul was demolishing the infill on the north wall he uncovered a number of cut stones. One was a keystone, with a few fragments of plaster still adhering to it. When he and Tim lifted it into place to see if they could use it as the missing keystone it slipped in perfectly. The plaster fragments fitted like a jigsaw-puzzle piece. After two hundred years the stone had returned to its original position. Paul was beaming when he came into our kitchen to make coffee for the gang that morning. 'We've found the keystone,' he said with satisfaction. They had also found elements from the rest of the building, obviously destroyed during the Revolution, including the smashed remains of the Baron of Mosset's mausoleum. My vision of the peaceful monastery was replaced with images of angry villagers wrecking the building with mallets and hammers.

The stones for Corbiac were probably cut and prepared by itinerant masons and the arches actually constructed by the monks. The stones are well cut but we had already noticed that sometimes the construction was a bit wobbly, a bit amateurish, and some of the stones seemed to be in the wrong place.

A wooden form had to be constructed first and then the stones were positioned over it. The stone barrel vault of the church would have been constructed in the same way, with wooden arches of green or unseasoned wood to support the roof while the stones of the vault were assembled. Paul said it was a technique that went back to the Greeks and Romans. 'There is no other way of doing it.' So many of the techniques he used were effectively the same as the monks or their masons would have used.

If he wanted to break stone he would use the same method as the Romans. Paul explained: 'You drill a hole in it, put in a wooden peg and soak it with water, so the wooden peg expands and splits the stone, just the way a root splits rock. With granite you have to drill a line of holes and drive wooden pegs in; then some poor slave pours water over them for hours. The pyramids were cut like that.'

Many of his stone-cutting tools, chisels and hammers are the same as the masons of the Middle Ages would have carried in their traditional goatskin bag. After he cut the stones with an electric disc cutter, Paul still used a traditional mason's hammer with a face of sharp points, to rough up the cut stone and give the effect of natural stone.

A medieval mason was known as a Doctor of Stones, and was highly respected. Each mason had his own mark, incised in the stone, a distinctive sign so he could be paid and his work checked. The marks were handed down from fathers to sons. In the early days sculptors were not considered to have a different, more artistic vocation than the general mass of stone-cutters. A distinction was made between good work and bad, but a masterpiece was a matter of degree not of kind. The idea of a difference between worker and artist only arrived with the Renaissance, when sculpture came to be considered a work of art first, before it was a work of stone. When Albert, the Dutch painter and sculptor, saw Paul's stone work he said he was an artist.

Doctor of Stones or not, when Yorkshire brusque met Catalan farmer, sparks flew. The new peach farmer was pruning the peaches, hour after patient hour up and down with his tractor, in a grey chilly mist. He had complained once about a pile of rubble that was encroaching from the building site onto his peach field, but Paul had forgotten to move it. When the farmer spoke to him again, Paul said he couldn't or wouldn't move it that minute, and finally the farmer got angry. He stormed in to see me, red-faced and shouting. I was overstressed by work and pre-menstrual at the time, and so I too got angry. Later I complained bitterly about his behaviour, looking up words for 'menacing' and 'threatening', and saying I didn't want another peach farmer yelling at me. There was an enormous crisis. His pride was hurt and he felt no-one respected the work he was doing. I was trying to apply my feminist principles to a proud, macho Catalan farmer, with predictable results.

He declared his intention of quitting the peaches at the end of the year and from then on did not speak to me at all, driving resolutely up and down on his tractor, studiedly looking the other way. I had by this time decided it was all my fault, that I had overreacted, and it was wrong of me to apply my London–New York feminist standards here. I wanted to apologize, but I was given no chance. I saw him one day talking to Hans, who was cutting brambles in the lower field, ready for his donkeys. When I went to greet them the farmer refused to shake my hand. I had insulted him, he said, and I accepted then that he was never going to forgive me.

He was complaining about Hans being on his land.

'But', I said, 'it is my field.'

'No,' said the farmer. 'I pay the insurance, so it is my field.' It was true that he had paid all the *mutualité* charges, the farmers co-operative insurance, because it had been impossible to divide it up.

'But I pay the land tax, and the water rates too,' I replied. I knew this was not at all what we agreed, but it is hard to argue in French. Anyway, since he didn't even want that field, and had by now declared his intention of giving up even the peaches after the next harvest, there did not seem much point in arguing about it.

He should have been consulted, he insisted. 'This land is for the *paysans*,' he said grimly.

At this point, Hans interjected brightly, '*Je suis paysan*

aussi,' pointing at himself, and I recalled him telling me he had gone on some sort of *paysan* training course.

I realized at this point that I was still using the intimate '*tu*' with the farmer, which was hardly suitable for a declared enemy, and mid-sentence I switched to '*vous*'. He actually could not resist a smile. Finally I threw caution to the winds, and started to shout back at him, saying that if the *paysans* wanted the land why did they treat it so badly, why was it all such a mess, covered in brambles and barbed wire and rubbish? '*C'est très sale!*'

Both men looked astonished and for once I did not end up in tears but left the encounter feeling a great sense of power. Later, though, I realized with dismay that I had now squabbled with four different Catalan farmers. It was just as well I was a woman – though no doubt that was the root of the trouble – because otherwise they would undoubtedly have punched me by now. Miles observed all these altercations from a bemused distance, muttering as usual about French farmers living off EEC subsidies. 'How can he have two cars, a motorbike, a huge house, all from growing peaches?' The next morning Miles suggested with undisguised glee that the donkeys might have got into the peach field and eaten the bark off the trees.

Meanwhile, the work progressed slowly and we could begin to envisage how we would use the spaces that were appearing. The church and monastery are built on rock, and the base of some of the wall was constructed around outcrops, so sometimes the rocks had to be chipped away to achieve a smoother surface for walls or floors. Behind the fridge now there is a craggy piece of the original hill-side. Gradually we were able to visualize the site before the church builders began. It was a reasonably flat promontory with a steep drop to the river below, and no doubt the flattest area was chosen for the church itself. All around it, though, the ground was stepped and craggy, and the monks simply adapted their building to the contours. It was not until we started to unveil the old building that we realized it was on an incline, and that five steps would be necessary at different stages to get from the north-side front door to the back. We had acquired a false sense of flatness in the east end, which had only one big step up to the church level. So many steps was very bad for wheelchairs, and I began to think about ramps.

The old kitchen in particular had a distinctly wavy floor of roughly laid cobblestones. We thought of keeping it – 'It'll be like St Mark's in Venice,' offered Miles – but the thought of trying to balance a table on such a surface had us opting to take all the stones up and lay tiles. So Paul went in with his digger, dragging up the stones and clearing the earth. It was very strange to peer in the window and see this monster machine charging up and down our future sitting room.

The next stage was to lay all the floors with concrete and this meant that all the basic plumbing and cables had to be installed first. We really needed an electrician. Our original Catalan electrician had been nice but not brilliant at understanding us – why on earth did Miles need eighteen sockets in his office for a start? How many kitchen appliances did we have?

Then one day Patrick showed up at Corbiac. Tall, lean, with spiky dark hair and tattoos, he wore combat trousers, a studded belt and fashionably untied sneakers. He wasn't Catalan – he came from Paris originally, he explained – but he lived in the village and had two children: Marie-Lou was at school with Theo. I figured having an electrician so close by would be very useful, which proved to be the case. He would rattle down the hill to us in one of a varied selection of vans, cars and motorbikes. One day he drove down, one hand on the steering wheel, the other holding his coffee in his daughter's Barbie mug. He liked to talk, to practise his English, and always listened sympathetically to my French, so we struggled successfully with all our electricity requirements. When I enquired he explained the French language did not use two words for plug and socket, only *prise*, but you could have a female prise and a male prise. Very French. When he labelled all the switches for us in English he wrote 'socked' for socket, which we liked so much we kept.

We installed all the plumbing on the south side of the building to minimize expense and interference with the original structure. For the monks, plumbing consisted of a hole in the wall and a trough for dishwater from the kitchen, plus the lovely stone sink in the cloister for ritual washing. Perhaps there were also channels of water running around the building, where the *arrosage* channels are today, to sluice away dirty water and sewage.

Wooden beams and great iron girders were installed for the upper floors, the beams resting on cement corbels copied from the original wooden corbels in the walls. Once the floorboards were laid we could see the shapes of the rooms. We decided to dispense with ceilings upstairs, which would have made the rooms lower. The slanted roof and wooden beams were pleasing, though tall rooms would be more difficult to heat. We had also put in two windows in the roof and they allowed an amazing amount of light into the upper floor. From an angle of the stairs it was possible to glimpse the red-brick arch of the bell tower through the roof window.

But the work was going excruciatingly slowly. Stress levels, certainly mine, were rising. I was becoming increasingly frustrated as the old wing crumbled round us, looking shabbier and shabbier and further removed from my vision of the perfect house to come. Whenever Paul disappeared for a week or two to work elsewhere we got anxious, only becoming content again when we could hear the usual whistling, cement mixer turning, and scraping of mortar on stone.

The weather then in early summer was terrible. It was unseasonably cold, and we had to put the fires on again after deciding we definitely would not need any more wood. A howling wind kept us awake at night and unable to think straight during the day. After a week or more of very heavy rain the garden was a jungle. Plants appeared that we had never seen before and the grass was as high as my waist. Suddenly all the problems were reversed after the first real sustained rain we had had in three years.

There were five different workers all bashing away at different parts of the building, and vehicles scattered everywhere. Patrick wanted to know exactly where he should install points in the living room. The guidebook I was updating called for last-minute checks on night clubs that didn't even open till 11 p.m. My Lloyds bank manager in England seemed to have gone mad: he had sent me two letters, both signed by him, saying the exact opposite – one that I could have an overdraft and one that I couldn't. I decided I had to change my bank. There was dust everywhere and the vacuum cleaner packed up. Luc had delivered the *coup de grâce* by using it to clean up building mess and when I tried to vacuum the bedroom it pumped out great clouds of plaster dust over everything. Hans brought the donkeys back and I started worrying about them eating the bark off the trees again. I once read of someone's definition of paradise as eating *foie gras* to the sound of trumpets. I swore I would do precisely that if I ever got into my new kitchen.

The plumbing by now needed to be connected to the septic tank. The main sewer pipe from the restored end had either to go through the terrace or in front of it. This latter choice required the terrace to be extended to cover it, which meant digging up the fine row of lavender and rosemary and other herbs I had planted in front of the terrace. Miles helped me transplant the herbs and soon after developed a strange angry rash on his arm. At first it looked like a burn and then we thought perhaps it was poison ivy. It took me over a week to figure out that the culprit was the rue we had transplanted by the roots.

According to the Greek authority Dioscorides, rue was the principal ingredient in mithridate, the legendary antidote for all poisons ever concocted. It is a very good insect repellent and was much used in the Renaissance by sculptors and painters, including Leonardo and Michelangelo, as a strengthener of eyesight. This has been borne out in recent times; its most active ingredient is rutin, which was found during the Second World War to be of value in the treatment of weakened blood vessels and it is this property that makes it so effective as an eye strengthener. However, it can also produce a nasty inflammation when handled by people with sensitive skin.

For Miles it was further proof of the insidious dangers of the countryside. I have treated it with great respect ever since.

It transpired part of the terrace would need digging up as well. Miles and I had a bitter argument over when to do it. I was anxious that the whole garden was not full of stones and rubble in the middle of summer. When the pipe was installed the steps to the garden were summarily shifted aside so we could no longer get to the garden without jumping over the pipe.

Miles always took the long view, I the short. It usually worked well but just occasionally we clashed horribly.

Me: 'But where will we have dinner? If there are no steps from the terrace we can't get to the shady table. We must have shade!'

Miles: 'Well, the weather has been so terrible it hasn't really mattered.'

I made such a fuss over the steps that Miles laboured to rebuild them, carrying and rolling huge stones. He made

299

a good job of it but did his back in in the process and had to lie down for three weeks.

It was almost summer and guests were due to arrive in less than a month. I had fondly hoped all would be ready. In fact nothing was ready and we tried to negotiate to get a minimum done before they appeared. My pressure, exacerbated by Miles's neatly typed and intimidatingly detailed list of the enormous number of things still to be done, precipitated a crisis and Paul told us he could not do any more of the work. It had all taken far longer than he had allowed for and he was overcommitted to other projects. We would need to find somebody else. We begged and pleaded and finally he agreed to continue. It cleared the air and we set about finding help from other quarters.

The sewer pipe remained adorning the side of the terrace, though thankfully we could at least now step over it quite easily. It figured prominently in the video of Audrey and Theo doing their Lonnie Donegan karaoke performance of 'My old man's a dustman'. While we watched from the table under the tree, we had a good dinner of fresh red tuna from the Mediterranean grilled with a crust of peppercorns and coriander and served with samphire, another of Theo's peculiar passions. And clever Peter raised the tone with his learned discussion of the role of samphire in *King Lear*, corrected by his equally clever wife, Leslie. Because often it grows in perilous places by the sea, it is famous for leading people – and a Shakespearean king – to destruction. It is dedicated to St Peter, the patron saint of fishermen, and thus named the herb of St Pierre, or samphire.

When the children made too much noise we explained that the monks had to be silent at meal times and evolved a complex system of signs to communicate without speaking. On occasions when speaking was permitted, the monks were not supposed to ask for anything directly, but to ask their neighbour if they needed something.

'Would you like some bread, brother?'

'No, but would *you* like some bread, brother?'

'Yes, please.'

Leslie says they still do this at Roedean, one of England's poshest girls' schools.

That summer I began to get up earlier. Dawn is the best part of the day, as the farmers and peasants have long known. The air is cool and fresh; it is quiet. The monks knew it well. By now they had already sung their morning praises, hymned the sun into light again, and were well onto the next office of the day. Sometimes I did yoga as the sun rose. I could feel it rise as the warmth hit my back. I had missed the big mirror I was used to in London, but now with the sun behind me I could see my movements as shadows.

I was also discovering the benefits of taking siestas in the manner of the South. When it was hot it was pleasant to retire to the tree-shaded hammock or a cool dim bedroom after lunch and sleep or doze for half an hour. At first I simply felt sleepy afterwards but then slowly I began to wake refreshed, renewed, as if I had two days in one.

In August the work slowed down again for *les vacances*, as it does everywhere in France. Mosset always seemed to have an event to celebrate. In 2000 it was the Millennium, marked by the French by the planting of a line of trees down the entire length of the French *méridien*, an imaginary line dividing France in two, north–south, from Dunkirk to Prats de Mollo in the Pyrenees. 'What's wrong with the Greenwich Meridian?' muttered Miles. 'Trust the French to want one of their own.' But I liked the idea of planting trees instead of buildings. Mosset was right on the *méridien* line, so lots of people pitched up to join the Incredible Picnic (L'Incroyable Picnic) on 14 July, a

600-mile-long picnic the length of the *méridien* that was celebrated all over France. That same year the artists in Mosset opened a shop to sell paintings, pottery and crafts, and staged an impressive exhibition of their work.

The following year we got the Tour de France through Mosset. Finally a programme of road widening and improvements that had been promised for years, especially outside Corbiac where there were two dangerous bends, was embarked on. For months we had trucks and diggers and rollers outside, in order to have the work completed by the time the cyclists whizzed through, in about five minutes flat, before tackling the gruelling climb up the Col de Jau. Helicopters came flying up the valley like something out of *Apocalypse Now* and an extraordinary cavalcade of promotional vehicles sailed by, hooting and tooting and tossing gifts out to the children waving from the road side. Mosset offered coffee to all, and Gerard rang the church bells for half an hour as the bikes passed.

We went to the beach, spent days at Leucate, swimming and eating seafood, visited the Costa Brava, and wandered round the magnificent Greek and Roman ruins of Ampurias, admiring the mosaics, and gazing on blue sea glittering through rows of umbrella pines and ruined marble columns, that must have reminded the Greeks themselves of their own land. We swam in cool clear water, and eyed up the comfortable *pension* hotel there where I promise we will stay one day. We took the chance to sample more Catalan food in all its sublime simplicity: *pa amb tomaquet*, tomato bread; good Spanish white bread, which seems to have more density and flavour than French *baguette*, rubbed with garlic, then with tomato and olive oil; and monkfish perfectly cooked and served with just olive oil to drizzle over and plain boiled potatoes.

Late that summer I sat for a while alone in the shade of the pine tree in the garden. The house was quiet, there was no wind – there never did seem to be wind in my memory of summers here. My eye followed the new wall we had built, the rosemary and herbs growing along it creating a private space. One day I will build my sweet-pea meditation arbour here perhaps. There were blue and yellow butterflies alighting on the lavender, swallows overhead, a buzzard soaring high above. I was wearing much the same clothes as when we first came eleven years ago: my blue Balinese batik sarong, thinner and more faded now, an old much laundered white cotton camisole. I sank myself back into the memory of the first time, the pleasure potential then. I had learnt a little patience. This was enough. The house was not yet ready, but it was already looking wonderful. It had progressed from being like a new baby I couldn't possibly leave for a moment to being an elderly relative, in need of constant loving care. Miles has succeeded in preserving the spirit of the building, the integrity of the architecture. I have made it functional and we have both made it beautiful.

My cup was half full, not half empty. The farmer was not ploughing madly opposite. Our guests had left. Canigou was visible, putting all in perspective as ever. All was well; the dream was not yet realized but it was possible. I sat on Theo's swing for a few minutes, the breeze I made gently swinging cooling me off. I remembered loving a story my Russian friend Ilona told me about discovering a swing on a mountain top on the coast of Turkey, and swinging there, on top of the world. My swing was not on the mountain top, but it was close.

Then it was the school *rentrée* again. Theo had a new teacher, a young woman in her first post. He came home the first day and said she was very severe and had a fat bottom, so I was unprepared for the extremely pretty young woman she turned out to be. She was disappointingly conventional in her teaching methods, however, and we soon discovered the worst we had heard about French education was true. We had, it transpired, been lucky to avoid it so far. Despite his uncommunicative nature the *maître* had been better at inspiring genuine interest and creativity in the children and Theo had really respected him. The new *maîtresse* was so disgusted with the standard of the children's handwriting she tore up all their work on the first day. Learning by rote became the norm; this was fine for poetry, for times tables and spelling, but Theo also had to memorize facts such as history dates, lengths of rivers and heights of mountains, and was clearly very bored.

A comparison between Theo's work and that of a friend at the same level in Britain revealed considerable differences. While Theo was learning poetry by heart, the English child was analysing texts and writing poems, letters and dialogues. Such discipline did have its benefits, and the new teacher insisted on regular homework for the first time, but it seemed a pity the two approaches could not be combined. Theo remained irrepressible anyway. He had, said one school friend's mother, '*beaucoup de punch*'! His French by now was almost perfect, certainly with no trace of an accent, though I sometimes wondered quite what kind of French he spoke, since he had learnt it mainly from school friends and it was often peppered with *gros mots* (rude words). His English had been learned mainly from adults and he had a good vocabulary though his spelling was poor. I suspect he is a different person in French.

Theo is so engaged by language, by the power it gives him. He loves it when people think he is French and then he can slyly announce later that he is English. He even imitates the French accents of other people: the Belgians, the Parisians and, worst of all, the English. He is beginning to appreciate how speaking different languages enriches you. It is as if he has understood what George Steiner said, that just as you need two eyes you need more than one language to be able to focus properly.

He savours new words in English, sometimes struggles to find equivalents, sometimes finds he simply doesn't know a word in French or in English. He didn't know the word for comb in French. He called his pyjamas 'night trousers'. Once I found tiny baby squid at the fishmonger's and fried them with garlic and parsley. They were delicious, piquant with their own ink; Theo loved them. 'I felicitate you,' he said, meaning 'congratulate', from *félicitations* in French. It is after all a word in English, if somewhat archaic usage, and a charming translation.

He moves happily from one language, and from one culture, to another. He once said he felt English in France, and French in England. And then he added recently, 'I feel I have an English heart,' which is such a very un-English thing to say. On Bastille Day, 14 July, there was the usual village procession to the cenotaph, which is engraved with the names of Mosset's war dead. The mayor laid a wreath in their honour and we all stood in silence in the shade of the *tilleul* tree, symbol of liberty. The children carried the flags, both French and Catalan, and no-one saw any incongruity in Theo marching along with the blue-and-white French flag over his shoulder.

By the end of summer Corbiac was a hive of activity again. Paul had increased his team for a final push and the crew was more motley than ever. A handsome young Spanish guy was helping Tim to paint ceilings white, and Xavier, a professional stonemason, was cutting stones needed to complete the stone stairs. Xavier could have walked out of a cartoon, with his Vercingetorix moustache, curly red hair under a dusty black hat, and a T-shirt emblazoned *Je suis allergique au travail* ('I am allergic to work'). He stopped with hammer in hand to expound on the formal rhetoric of architectural construction, the ideal relation between floor areas and heights.

It was Xavier who discovered the silver coin. As he stood in the stone arch of the north door, expounding the ancient traditions of the stone masons, he explained that in the past the masons had always secreted a coin under the stones of the doorway once they had finished their work. As he talked he bent down and prised up the original stone doorstep, fishing about with his fingers underneath. Then he proudly held aloft a small battered coin, a Louis XIV silver farthing dated 1658. Now we knew when that door was built. The treasure, I realized, was already there, if one had the wisdom to find it.

Help with the plumbing appeared in the form of Ludo, who turned out to be a qualified plumber as well as a potter, and had helped Gerard for many years doing up all the houses in Mosset he had loved and lost. We had admired the shower he had made for their house, especially when Lettie said she had finished the adobe walls herself, using earth she had dug up and sieved, then mixed with water, smoothing it on like icing on a cake. I was reminded of the adobe houses of New Mexico, where it was always the women's task to finish the interior. Here was a more feminine style of building to my taste. Lettie had pressed pottery and tiny shells into her walls, and I thought of decorating a bathroom like that. 'Then we used *fromage blanc* as a sealant,' she told me. I thought this must be the name of a paint of some sort but they assured me they really meant *fromage blanc*. 'You have to be sure to buy it without fat, but then just thin it with water and paint it on with a brush,' Lettie explained. 'It dries very quickly.' She said she would take me one day to dig the right kind of earth for adobe. I went and bought a large pot of fat-free *fromage blanc* from the supermarket, though I had to throw it out before I got round to using it.

Ludo connected pipes and taps, and tiled the bathrooms. But he said he found life in Mosset too busy and stressful and needed the ruminations of their guru, for which they had installed a satellite dish, to keep him cool. One day he arrived with a sorry tale. He was still trying to create the perfect teapot. That day he had finished a load of teapots and fired up the kiln they had installed in their terrace garden, but it had exploded and all the teapots had fused together in one mass. 'Something exploded in my head too,' he said, shaking his silver locks mournfully and rolling another cigarette.

Christian, the *carreleur*, who came to lay the terracotta tiles we bought in Spain in the big old kitchen and the hallway, added to the atmosphere. He and his mate settled down to lunch outside like medieval jouurneymen, making a temporary fireplace of stone and building a fire to grill meat over. They worked long, twelve-hour days and the tiles were magnificent, so varied in colour and texture that they already looked as if the monks had laid them.

The monks' kitchen was emerging as the star of the show. The walls were ochre mortar, with here and there a feature left exposed – in one wall, an arch of red brick; in another, two of the original wooden corbels. The mortar was of a colour and texture that was so handsome we decided not to paint any of it. So often our decisions have been to do less, which often has not only proved cheaper but has also made the finished building simpler, more functional, more true to itself somehow. Two huge slabs of stones had been returned to the back of the fire-place, and the base had been tiled in large slices of slate. The great stone arch over it had been sandblasted, revealing the shapes and colours of each stone, from soft grey speckled granite to pinky marble. It was like a stone necklace. Miles and I had cleaned out the bread ovens each side, shovelling out buckets of earth and rubble and dust so that Paul could lay a cement base. Patrick had lit them from within, illuminating the thin red bricks and stones that lined the curved interior space.

Finally we could break through the arched doorway with the Augustinian symbol above it and open up the connection between the two sections of the cloister. From our temporary, crumbling accommodation we could see two stone arches and part of a third, an elegant geometry of shapes, the glorious colours of the tiles, the gentle pale tones of the mortared walls, and it looked so beautiful.

Despite the breakthrough nothing was quite complete. The marathon had become a mirage now that we could wander through to it at any time. Not one room was finished yet, which was very frustrating. The hot water was not connected up; we had few light fittings so there were lots of bare bulbs; the tiles all needed cleaning yet again after the last onslaught of dust. Bamboo the dog was currently living in my proposed closet.

I experimented with *laque* on the new pine doors, testing and then painting two coats. *Laque* sounded quite glamorous and exotic and it was not until halfway through I concluded I was actually applying a kind of nasty brown varnish, exactly the stuff we were always so anxious to get rid of in the stripped-pine days of yore. It was a bit like the time I got halfway through a recipe for *crème anglaise* and then discovered I was actually making English custard.

By November we slowly began moving into the restored west end, selecting furniture from our motley collection. It had to be spread thinly, since we couldn't afford to buy any more, but fortunately we liked the spare effect. Conversely, it became difficult to maintain the disguise of the current ruin as we moved things out. We put the leather sofa and chairs in to the monks' kitchen and laid the kelims on the floor tiles. I put favourite pots in niches round the fireplace recess. We stacked wood, gathered kindling and lit the wood stove. Miles began to hang pictures. Patrick, a French carpenter living in the village, reconstructed a huge *armoire* Martha had given us. 'Is it a table?' asked Theo, puzzled as he looked at all the dozens of pieces scattered on the floor.

In the bedroom I hung white linen sheets for curtains, each one carefully embroidered with two initials as part of a trousseau. The light filtered through them is soft, as flattering as the muslin over the photographer's lens. Suddenly we had so much more space. Not just one but three spare bedrooms, and a library each, at the farthest reaches of the building. Somehow, though both were huge, they had filled up with books. While at one end I worked in the old library-sitting room, listened to Gregorian chant and wrote about monks and celibacy, Miles at the other played Little Richard and wrote about the sexual liberation of the Sixties. It worked fine.

I ferried pots and pans and bowls and cutlery into the kitchen and, just like everybody else who has ever installed a kitchen, I discovered there was not enough storage space. On the slate shelf by the window I lined up Lettie's elegant earthenware goblets, which have fluted sides and a glaze shading from blue to brown. They are perfect for *tisanes*, which now I can make from the vervain, mint, sage and thyme growing in the garden. We're still waiting for the teapot. I gathered walnuts again and put a big bowl of them on the kitchen counter. First fruits offered up. We moved in on Christmas Eve, with guests arriving the next day, and feasted on *foie gras*, capon and champagne. In the end I forgot the trumpets.

17

Les amis du pot au lait:
Friends of the milk bottle

The village was in crisis. In early 2001 as foot-and-mouth disease was ravaging Britain and *vache folle* suspected in France too, one of the dairy cows belonging to Nenes and Isabelle was suspected of having brucellosis.

No milk was delivered for a few weeks, and eventually the news came that the entire herd had to be destroyed: thirty cows, which had been lovingly cared for and milked twice daily by hand. People collected it from Isabelle's little dairy in the village, or she would deliver it, arriving in her pale-blue car reassuringly and unusually clean for Mosset, always cheerful and smiling. She worked long hours, rising at 5.30 a.m., delivering three times a week around the valley, and presiding over a market stall twice a week in Prades, and in Mosset on Sunday mornings.

Their cows were big black-and-white dairy cattle that come from the Vosges in the north of France, as Nenes did. In the summer months the cows stayed on the high mountain pastures and he still spent most of his time there with them. In the winter sometimes they were pastured in the field across the river opposite Corbiac, and I liked being able to see from my window the cows that have given my muesli milk every day. They had to be fed hay in the winter and sometimes I met Nenes on the road, with great bales of hay each end of the tractor, rattling along way over the speed limit, with a slightly manic grin on his face.

They were devastated by the fate of their beloved cows. It was not just their livelihood – a new cow costs about 9,000 francs – they were fond of the cows and knew them all by name: Lucette, Hirondelle, Jacinthe, Jolie, and all the rest. Due to the subsidy deal they had they were not entitled to compensation. They were *totalement ruiné*, as everyone put it, shaking their heads sadly. Worst of all, it transpired a bit later that the authorities had been overzealous and it had not really been necessary to kill them all, they could simply have been quarantined. Nenes and Isabelle left Mosset, returning temporarily to the Vosges with their little daughter Marie, to Nenes' home village. No more fresh milk on the doorstep, no more yoghurt to go with the honey from up the road, no more sights of Nenes careering along in his tractor.

It was a terrible blow. They had built up the herd from almost nothing, after receiving their first cow as a wedding present. The village was disturbed too, for them of course, but also for an enterprise that symbolized the rebirth of the village. As a couple they had united old Mosset and the incomers.

A few weeks later I went to Mosset one Saturday morning, bought my bread from the new *boulangerie*, extracting almost a smile from Yvette, posted some letters and chatted to the postmistress. Theo and I went into the library, which had now expanded through from its back-street entrance and opened directly onto the square.

Several people were browsing the shelves, children were reading comic books on the new benches, and one farmer was scratching his head in front of the computer with its new Internet connection. Then I saw Lettie in the art shop, and went to say hello, trying to resist all the ravishing pots and bowls I craved whenever I went in. Lettie gave me her big shining smile and handed me a little card inscribed *Les amis du pot au lait*. ('Friends of the milk bottle', basically).

Kind-hearted Lettie could not bear the destruction of all Nenes' and Isabelle's hopes, the waste of all their hard work. 'Nenes' sister, Monique, was nearly in tears talking about their problems,' Lettie explained. 'I just thought: "I give money to charity for people I don't even know, so why not give it to people I do know?"' So she and Monique decided to organize a benefit to raise money for the couple and express sympathy and support. There had been a similar outpouring of sympathy when Thomas, one of the foster children of José and his wife Eileen, had drowned at the hotel in the Alps where he had started work, and his friends in the village had organized a collection in his memory. Later still, a two-year-old child had drowned in the river one cold winter day, and the sense of collective grief was palpable.

About a dozen people pledged support, including Isabelle's parents, Monsieur and Madame Mestres, Nenes' sister Monique, her ex-husband Patrick, the carpenter, and Carole, now his girlfriend. Plans rapidly evolved for an evening event with a tombola and prizes. Alain the chef and his wife, Marie-Christine, offered to cook a paella for 50 francs per person and donate the proceeds. There were a few doomsayers, who grumbled that there were other farmers with problems and no-one had ever done anything for them. 'And what will you do next time a farmer has to kill his cows?' demanded Yvette of the *épicerie*, who can always be relied on to take the gloomiest view. There was a buzz of preparation but everything was kept secret, waiting on the return of Isabelle and her family from the Vosges.

My Martha Stewart leanings emerged as I thought of the severe white walls and harsh lighting of the new *salle polyvalente* (the village hall) where the event was to be held. So Lettie and I decided to decorate it with branches of spring blossom. For the first time I too felt involved. Until then I had contributed little to village events, other than donating a few books to the library, patronizing all the local food producers and assiduously buying tombola tickets. (And of course restoring their *patrimoine* for them.)

That spring morning dawned sweet, warm, with blue skies and birdsong as, armed with saws and secateurs, we set out to pick blossom. The mimosa was in full bloom, its clusters of tiny yellow bobbles scenting the air with that oddly exotic fragrance and dotting the landscape with bright splashes of yellow. Françoise, a farmer's widow with a young daughter, who had a farm just below Corbiac, said we could help ourselves from her huge mimosa trees. The previous year we had dug up a dozen small saplings there to plant at Corbiac, two of which seemed to have taken on the windy hill below the house. We stuffed the car with a tangle of huge sweet-smelling blossoms. 'We need more colours,' Lettie exclaimed, as if she were mixing a glaze for her pots, and so we clipped silvery olive branches, and white apple blossom too, and added a few tall branches of bamboo from a huge plantation behind the house.

We saw Monique and Karla digging in their new *potager* on the adjoining property and asked them for blossom too. In Monique I had finally found a Catalan farmer I could get on with. When I was told there were two women about to plant an olive grove down the road (much to the disgust of the local farmers) one of them

313

Dutch, and one who had been a journalist in Paris, I had somehow expected Gertrude Stein and Alice Toklas.

Monique instead was small, tough, tanned, with sharp brown eyes and an Eton crop of silver curly hair. Despite her years in Paris, she talked like a Catalan, fiercely expressive, gesturing to punctuate everything she said. 'I'm not afraid of anything,' she said, waving her long cheroot contemptuously, when I confessed my problems with the farmers. She was *costaude*, that word meaning 'tough, sturdy' that seems to require a clenched fist to give it proper emphasis. Karla, with her cap of glossy red hair and slow, considered Dutch way of speaking, was as chic and well-groomed as Monique, even in khaki shorts and wellington boots.

Monique, leaning on a spade and wiping sweat from her brow, was very excited to hear from Lettie about an old tractor Gerard might have available. (It was, inevitably, Gerard who had found their property for them. He was like an *éminence gris*, selecting a choice, if eccentric, population for the valley. I found myself wishing he had chosen me.) Monique and Karla had already planted eighty-six olive trees and another two hundred were planned. They were determined to keep them *biologique* (organic) and had attended a government course on olive growing to learn all about it. The property was an old barn and they were still negotiating planning permission to convert it. In the meantime they lived in Monique's house in nearby Eus, where they painted, read, played the flute and looked after their cats. Karla showed me their present provisional arrangements: the washing-up neatly stacked in a drainer on a stone outside the barn, and, inside, a rudimentary kitchen with gas tank and burners, a cupboard hanging from a rope to escape rats and mice, the walls hung with neat rows of tools, and a table with a pretty cloth, already set with Monique's lunch-time *pastis* aperitif. Karla did all

314

the cooking. 'I am married to a Frenchwoman,' she said with a rueful smile, 'so I have to cook twice a day.'

She showed us the land they had been restoring, treating it with as much loving care as we had treated our building. Fields had been tidily cut and fenced, and all were properly irrigated by streams and canals diverted for watering. Under the shadow of a large rock was a *borie*, an old shepherd's hut, which we peered inside, and next to it, shaded by a giant tree, their pride and joy: a huge, round, magical stone, with a cut encircling the circumference like the beginning of a millstone. 'This is where we must dance by moonlight,' said Karla, twinkling. 'I used to be a witch, you know . . .' She had already re-christened me Romarin, which is 'rosemary' in French. I liked the idea of a new secret name. It was like a tribal rite of passage.

Monique and Karla were not the only women who had moved in to farm the valley. There was also Sophie, who had bought a field next-door-but-one to us and was planning to plant herbs there. The farmers were very sceptical about her too, and watched as she struggled alone to put up her fences, prune trees and plant her seedlings.

When we unloaded all the branches of blossom at the *salle polyvalente* there was already a bustle of activity. Gerard was watering the garden he had created from the rubble around the new *mairie* building, already rich with roses, palms, lavender, rosemary and yellow roses, and threaded with paths and little waterfalls. Someone once planted a marijuana plant, which grew quite large before disappearing as mysteriously as it had arrived.

Now Gerard had finished redecorating the church he was planting all of Mosset with flowers and bushes. Eventually he will have beautified the whole village, the heavenly gardener. He sat down on a stone wall and rolled a cigarette with brown fingers, gesturing at the hillside, which was covered in scrubby spring vegetation of green shrubs and dusty grey thyme dotted with bright-yellow broom. 'I found a whole kilo of Californian poppy seeds left over from the Millennium planting,' he confided, 'so I have scattered them over there on the hillside.' He chuckled at the surprise a sudden splash of orange would create. It was as if he was making a painting.

Henri the hunter and Monique were labelling the tombola prizes, there was sound equipment being set up in one corner and Mohammed, another foster son of Eileen and José, arrived with a pile of CDs. We filled every available bucket, milk churn and saucepan with water and stuffed them with flowers, even hanging branches from the walls. Véronique, Guillaume's pretty, dark-haired Belgian mother, placed delicate little sprays of mimosa on the tables. Searching for a broom, I found Hans in the kitchen valiantly scrubbing and scraping mussels for fifty and muttering in wonderment about the community he had found. '*C'est la solidarité!*' he said in his thick Dutch accent, looking as if he would happily scrub several thousand mussels.

José was sweeping outside but happily relinquished the broom so I could clear up the leaves and petals we had dropped; somehow I always seem to end up cleaning. But the room looked pretty, its hard modern lines softened by the bright flowers. '*C'est gentil,*' murmured Madame Mestres, Isabelle's mother. The event was coming as a complete surprise for the couple, and she was fretting about the way they would be dressed. She is always smart, and perfectly coiffed, but she need hardly have worried in Mosset, where dressing down is definitely *à la mode*, though it is true that Nenes in particular might qualify as the very scruffiest resident, normally to be seen in frayed jeans and cut-off T-shirts.

By 6.30 that evening there were at least two hundred people there, drinking *pastis*, *muscat*, wine and juice, munching slices of pizza, salami, tiny tarts, paté and bread, buying tombola tickets and all talking at once. The elderly ladies of the village, who had taken off their flowery pinnies in honour of the occasion, mingled with old hippies down from the Cerdagne, whose ikat shoulder bags, hand-carved flutes and shaggy sheepskin waistcoats made them look as if they had just emerged from smoky tepees. Skall was listening to Louisette tell about her memories of taking the animals up to the old *cortals*; a toothless old man in beret and dungarees was trying to talk to me, in a thick Catalan accent I could barely follow, about going to the village school, how strict the *maître* had been in those days. Yvette, who had turned up anyway, was complaining about the forthcoming euro and the problems for the *épicerie*, which she was threatening to close as a result. She needed a new till, which was so expensive that the *mairie* had offered to pay for it, aware how important it was to keep the village shop open. Yvette's prospects for coping with the euro were not enhanced by her quoting the price of the till in old francs.

There was a commotion when one of the local dogs attacked a visiting poodle, and I almost spilled my wine over the mayor in my haste to escape the bared fangs, but the dogs were bundled summarily out of the door. Poor Nenes and Isabelle arrived, expecting a village event, and were struggling valiantly with a combination of acute embarrassment and gratitude as everyone hugged and kissed them.

The mixture of people, to me, was glorious. All ages and several nationalities: French, Catalan, Spanish, Dutch, Belgian, Algerian, Chilean, English. There were singles, gays, lesbians, divorcees both with different partners, adopted children, foster children, even a few conventional legitimate offspring. Teetotallers and pot-smokers, fascists and feminists, politicians and beekeepers, farmers, gardeners, teachers, potters, donkey-owners, tinkers, tailors, soldiers, sailors, beggarmen and, doubtless, thieves too. Not to mention the writers, artists, nurses, carpenters, builders, librarians and jugglers. There was Marianne's Dutch mother, waving a cigarette, looking cheerfully disreputable with her grey hair coming out of a bun. Marie, the schoolmistress, ready with her piano accordion, André Perpigna, the honeymaker with a Cheshire-cat smile that made him look as if he had just downed a whole potful of his own honey, Casanova, the cow farmer, chatting up a coy-looking girl with a blonde ponytail. Kathy, the mountain recluse with a menagerie, was talking to Monique the social worker, and cackling with laughter. Bar the blacksmith and the ropemaker, it was like the medieval Mosset the Trinitarian monks were sent, unsuccessfully, to tame. They could build a whole world.

There were three mayors in a row at the back of the room, all beaming: M. Mestres, the previous mayor, Alain Siré, the outgoing mayor, and the new incumbent, Olivier Betoin, from La Coume. He usually had a benign, distant smile on his face, but that evening he looked as if he had won the lottery. For Olivier, whose whole philosophy was one of community, it was a remarkable beginning to his tenure.

Olivier told me that the recent census indicated a significant increase in population in the village, compared with others in the region, especially of young people. Alain Siré asked me what we intended to do with the fields around Corbiac, now we had chopped down the peach trees, and I told him about Gerard's plans for trees and horse pasture. He suggested we planted lavender, to make oil in the still they wanted to install for the Tour de Parfum. I groaned inwardly, having suggested this to him more than a year before, and agreed immediately that it was an excellent idea. I am more than happy for my dream to be someone else's idea.

Outside, chef Alain was cooking paella in vast pans on an open fire, and Marie Christine dished it up. M. Mestres was cutting his *langoustines* with a serious-looking traditional pocketknife. Henri with his shining brown pate, in a smart ironed denim shirt with embroidered flowers on the front, was a brilliant master of ceremonies as they drew the tombola. The artists and artisans were generous: there were pictures from Albert, Bob and Gwen, fine pots from Bernard, Ludo and Lettie, local watercolours, and lots of honey, jams, home-made cakes and jars of bottled fruit. As the tombola winners were announced, baskets of fruit were handed over, bemused old ladies received Bob and Albert's abstract art works and Véronique got her boyfriend's photo collage back.

Gerard had drawn a diagram of a large cow that, displayed on an easel in the centre of the stage, was divided into numbered sections and filled in as the tombola prizes were announced and the takings totted up. Gerard laboriously crayoned it all in blue, red and green, and finally it was completed, to cheers all round. They had raised over 20,000 francs. So many people had contributed; even an 82-year-old farmer slipped in early on and put his envelope in the box. Isabelle made a short speech of thanks but soon broke down in tears and was hugged by Nenes' sister, Monique, whereupon we all wept – her mother next to me, Marie-Jo, Eileen. It was a good moment, a necessary carthartic moment. I don't think anybody realized when they embarked on it that the whole event would be as much for the community as it was for Isabelle and Nenes.

The French Algerian artist Michel, who had just bought a small *atelier* in the village, did a long-winded magic act with an old gramophone, top hat and tails, and old 78s, to which people got up and danced. Marie played her accordion, accompanied by Carole on guitar, and Hans attempted to sing French *chansons* but didn't know the

319

words and had to read from a piece of paper. Everybody joined in anyway.

The young DJs couldn't wait any longer and cranked up the music. Margriet bullied shy Pascal into dancing, and he even hopped about a bit. Pascal had designed the village website and Hans had recruited him to design a website for the donkeys, so he is well on the way to becoming the village webmaster. For once, these people who were normally lurking shyly in the background or hugging the bar were centre stage. Fathers danced with daughters and couples jived together with the syncopated familiarity of long practice. Several young boys all did a Village People stage act, dancing in a line and taking off their shirts in unison, to cheers from all. I wondered if they were going to strip completely like the miners from Sheffield. Theo I spotted dancing alone on the stage, doing a John Travolta routine. Miles had of course included *Saturday Night Fever* as essential viewing on the contemporary-culture syllabus.

I danced with a rather proper, white-haired and bespectacled fellow to whom I had only ever said a demure '*Bonjour*' in the *boulangerie*, who picked me up and whirled me around, crying, '*La dame de Corbiac!*'

Theo and I were the only English people there that night. Miles was in London. Rose had gone back to Jamaica, to seek out the people in the township she had photographed twenty years earlier and photograph them again. Bob and Gwen had returned to the UK. The Pyrenees had provided plenty of inspiration for artists but not much opportunity to exhibit or sell their work.

A gang of children reappeared now and again for hugs and kisses, looking like little savages, filthier and more breathless each time. One wondered vaguely what they were doing to get quite so dusty. Theo confided next morning that they had discovered the wood-chips storage bin (an ecological fuel initiative which heats the *mairie*

320

and the school and which we considered for Corbiac until we found it was going to take several decades of the next century to realize the initial investment). Apart from diving into the wood chips, they had been sliding on trays and bottoms down the steep grassy bank below the *mairie*, and melting plastic cups on the paella fire. A small group of *ados* on the steps outside were smoking pot, hardly hidden away, and the unmistakable smell filled the air. '*C'est la droguerie*,' I said to someone, and then felt stupid, remembering that in French of course *droguerie* means 'ironmongery'.

I sat down next to Monique and Karla, and helped myself to another glass of red wine from the carafes, which this evening were mysteriously replenished like the wedding feast at Cana when Jesus turned water into wine. Charles, our soldier neighbour, came over. Tanned, with cropped blond hair, and trim in pressed, faded denims. Sometimes he can be seen at the village bar in his full camouflage uniform, as accepted as everyone else. We exchanged ritual kisses on the cheek, once, twice, and then an unexpected third time. Even he, a Frenchman, complained about never knowing the number of kisses. '*A Montpellier c'est trois, ici c'est deux, à Paris c'est quatre*,' he grumbled. He spent several years in Djibouti followed by a spell in Kosovo, and though he told me recently he never wanted to move again he was already getting itchy feet, it seemed. Most of all he loved the desert, and while I imagined only the horror of shifting corpses in the appalling heat of Djibouti, he was remembering his desert life in Africa with relish. Hélène, his wife, accepted his work and his long absences with resignation. '*Je suis mariée à un soldat*,' she said with a shrug. Charles too was enthusiastic about the village, the community. He had seen so many broken and devastated by war, so he should know.

Everyone danced for hours, and those who didn't dance

sat and gossiped and drank, and had seconds and thirds of paella, which sat in a vast dish on the table. Even the cooks sat down to eat. I asked Alain if he missed the city, the buzz of Marseilles, but not at all. He, too, liked the tranquillity of the mountains, he said, the escape from the freneticism of city life. And he winked and made a mock gesture of meditation swinging up his leg and crossing it over his knee, making mudras with his finger and thumb.

Suddenly, in the middle of all the dancing and merriment there was a hush and the music was turned off. Nenes was sitting on the stage, low down on a stool beneath the coloured-in cow. His shoulders were bowed, his blond hair tangled around his wrinkled face. He held the microphone and just started to speak very quietly. He talked about the loss of his cows, and about going back to the Vosges, to his own village, feeling that that was where his friends were, he must perhaps return there for work. But now, he said, he realized he had friends here too, here in Mosset, a village with a big heart.

I dragged Theo home, protesting, at about 1 a.m., but lots of people stayed till 5 a.m., African dancing, and singing to Carole's guitar.

People sometimes ask me if I feel integrated in the village. I don't think 'integrated' is the right word, since I don't work as part of the village, or even live in it. But I do feel accepted, along with all the other mad foreigners. Recently Albert and Robert wanted to give a party and decided there were so many guests they would have two parties. They gave me the choice of joining the Mossetans (mainly Dutch or French) or the English group. In last year's mayoral elections someone put my name down as a candidate for the village council. A joke, of course, but significant in a way. When Monique, the mother of Olivier, our new mayor, came to see the chapel, she said, 'It is good you are here. We need foreigners.'

Martha had suggested using the chapel for her fiftieth-birthday celebration. She had inherited some money and decided to blow it on a party, inviting a lifetime of friends from all over the world. There was to be a concert in the chapel, and so at last it would be reclaimed. There would be music and singing for the first time in two centuries since the monks left. Corinne Nanette, an opera singer and mother of one of Theo's schoolfriends, was asked to sing and I thought with glee that she would undoubtedly be the first woman ever to sing there.

I wondered what the last moment of song had been like, the last office of the monks. I don't think there is one for leaving a monastery. It must have been so sad. Or perhaps they were hurriedly driven away and there was only time for a prayer, perhaps a psalm of lamentation, before they gathered up what possessions they had, the precious relics and the chalices, and disappeared.

We had made desultory attempts over the years to tidy up the chapel, and the village team of Pascal and Arnaud and Michel had spent a few days clearing out all the ancient dusty bales of straw from the hayloft installed by the farmers. This time the redoubtable Hans had been commissioned to sort it out. Barrowloads of dust and rubble had been wheeled out. The huge oak planks, slices of a single tree, that were built into each side of the chapel to create a manger for the cows had been torn out, so heavy they needed four men to lift them. The oak had hardened like iron, making it impossible to cut, so my bright idea of turning them into a table foundered. Still, they will make wonderful outside benches in our kitchen courtyard.

Once the space was empty Miles started chipping again and almost immediately discovered, painted high on the white plaster covering the stone walls, two more Trinitarian crosses – faded red symbols, crude but still quite distinct. Then he came into the house one day very

323

excited and said he had discovered a new window. 'Look,' he said from the top of the ladder. 'Where the beam has been jammed into the wall? You can see the rounded arch of a Romanesque window.'

A day later he was even more delighted. Further assiduous, patient lifting of chunks of loose plaster revealed a whole wall of fresco, a simple diagonal pattern of faded pinks and yellows featuring what is probably the rose of Roussillon, since it closely resembles the carvings on the tribune at the nearby priory of Serrabone. It is beneath the layer of plaster on which the crosses were painted, which indicate it is the original thirteenth-century church decoration before the Trinitarian monks arrived. The whole church would have been painted and decorated in strong, vibrant patterns and colours. Lit by candles, it would have had a much more rich Byzantine atmosphere than the bone-white plaster and exposed stone austerity to which so many of these chapels are now restored.

I went to Le Moulin for dinner, to discuss the party Martha was planning. I walked down to the mill, the path so familiar from all my previous sojourns, though now it was lit with garden lamps installed by electrician Patrick, so no torch was necessary. I pushed open the big oak Catalan door to the usual cosy welcoming scene. The wood stove was burning, pine smoke scenting the air, and the table was set with glasses and flickering candles. Red curtains framed the windows overlooking the millstream below, flowing fierce and brown after so much rain. Large abstract paintings adorned the walls, in particular a big splash of red and green and yellow by Gwen and a wonderful leafy green and gold canvas by Bob. Martha had asked her artist friends to bring paintings to hang on the walls of the chapel, and Bob and Gwen, Albert and another Swiss friend, Liliane Csuka, were all contributing their work.

Martha gave me a glass of Mas Chichet and told me all

the party developments. She had been trying to find someone to provide a meal for fifty at a reasonable price. 'M.Bénédan, the good butcher in Prades, will supply it all, plus plates and glasses too,' she said triumphantly. 'And we can use the *salle polyvalente* for the party after the concert.' The following day she planned paella for sixty in her garden.

Corinne Nanette arrived to discuss the repertoire of songs she would sing, along with Helen Dixon, an English singer we first met working as an estate agent here. Now, encouraged by Martha, Helen would sing again in public for the first time in five years. Corinne, from Paris, is a black woman whose family come from Guadeloupe. Her husband, Alain, is a blond Northerner, a forester from Normandy. I have always thought their marriage sounded like a fairy tale, or an opera, I suppose: the story of the singer and the woodcutter. Corinne tells us about her love of singing, her upbringing in Paris, where her father took her to Count Basie concerts, and how she was so desperate to sing she answered an ad on the radio and ended up a classical singer, performing regularly at the major festivals in Avignon and Orange.

Like all of us that evening she was dressed in practical trousers and sweater, but I had seen her dressed for the opera, elegant in a black evening gown, distributing roses to the audience when she sang in the church in Molitg a historical medley of opera, which was a wonderful musical introduction to someone as ignorant as I am.

When Corinne saw the interior of the chapel before it was cleaned, she was very dubious about its potential as a performance space, but now it really looked possible. Martha, typically, was undeterred by any problems. A piano was needed, so she asked Olivier, the new mayor, if she could borrow one from La Coume. But since only the concert would take place in the chapel and we would have dinner and dancing in the village hall, the piano would have to be moved in between. 'Oh, it will be no problem,' said Martha airily. I was reminded of the stories of the first piano being brought to La Coume on the back of two donkeys.

'So what language shall we speak?' asked Martha as we sat down to eat the Swiss fondue she had prepared, twirling forkfuls of bread into the unctuous hot cheese liberally spiked with kirsch. It was a good question. She had just collected her daughter Sarah, aged sixteen, from Andorra – a six-hour round trip on difficult mountain roads – where Sarah and two friends had been snow-boarding, taking advantage of the late snow in mid-April. Tam, an English boy, looked slightly shell-shocked, partly from his first snowboarding and partly perhaps from this gaggle of women speaking a jumble of French and English. Sarah's other friend, Magali, lived in Andorra, and it turned out could speak five languages. Schools in Andorra teach Catalan and Spanish and French, her father is English and her mother is German. She moves easily from one to another, and can read and write in all except German, which, she said modestly, she can only speak.

It is a typical Mosset evening with such a mixture of languages. Martha, of course, speaks Swiss German, French, Italian, Spanish and English. (She reads Freud in German and Proust in French, *naturellement*.) We all spoke some French, except for the English boy. We all spoke English except for Corinne, but she had studied English and could understand. She wants to learn it again and asked if I would teach her.

We talked about the singing class Theo and Corinne's son, Clément, had started to attend. This was an attempt to establish a choir of children singing a variety of classical and operatic themes, though the speciality of the teacher was Gregorian chant. Theo was still unconvinced about this enterprise, and my secret scheme to hear them sing junior Gregorian chant in the chapel was a bit of a long shot. I recalled Clément and Theo on the swing in our garden, hearing Clément belting out operatic arias at the top of his voice as he swung higher and higher, and Theo joining in. Theo likes to sing too, revelling in the acoustics of our new space here. On good days I only know he is back from school when I hear him singing.

I love these evenings, this rainbow of nationalities I have fallen into here, this *mélange* of languages. Sometimes I don't feel as if I have moved to France: I have moved to Europe. I know so many mixed couples now too, French and Dutch, Spanish and German, Swiss and French, English and German, Spanish and English, Belgian and Algerian. I am learning new histories, not just French through Theo, but Dutch and Spanish too. When we went to Collioure with my Spanish friend Clara, she wanted to visit the grave of the Spanish poet Antonio Machado, exiled from Franco's Spain, and when she saw it she wept. I don't know many English people who weep over the fate of poets. I have rarely met a contemporary who has lived through the fear and repression that was Spain in the Franco years, or who speaks with such love of her country. She has lived in Britain with her English husband for a long time, and said, 'England has been good to me.' But we take our liberty so for granted.

Miles and I made a brief trip into Spain last year. Theo spent five days on a school trip to the other end of the Pyrenees and we snatched the chance for a couple of days away. We wanted to visit the Romanesque monasteries of Catalonia, see the sculptured façade of Ripoll and the church of Sant Joan les Abadesses with its lovely slender Gothic-cloister columns. It was confirmation that our monastery was part of the Catalan Romanesque tradition. I liked the idea that our monks were Catalan before they were French, frontier monks. The phenomenon of

Catalonia itself, north and south, part of France and part of Spain but with a distinct identity and common language, further undermined the idea of national boundaries.

But it was the moment when we crossed the border that stayed most clearly in our memory. We took an inland route between Prats-de-Mollo and Camprodon, over the Col d'Ares, through what had once been a heavily guarded border post. But now it was abandoned, the barriers torn down and left lying by the road, the searchlight towers fallen. Graffiti was scrawled over the guardhouses by the Catalan independence movement, 'Free Catalunya', and Franca 90 km one way, 'España' 350 km the other. For a privileged English person who had no experience of the reality of frontiers till I crossed the English channel aged nineteen, and showed my new passport for the first time in a Belgian port, it was salutary and oddly moving.

The image of the frontier became most poignant when we went to see the Walter Benjamin memorial in Portbou, the coastal frontier post between Spain and France. For us there were no border guards and we drove through without even stopping. Walter Benjamin was a German Jewish writer who tried to escape to America from France in 1940. He missed the last boat out of Marseilles, the one that took André Breton and Lévi-Strauss to America, so tried to escape via Spain. He was led secretly over the Albères, the range of hills between France and Spain where the Pyrenees come down to the Mediterranean. It was a gruelling twelve-hour journey over rough mule tracks, sometimes on all fours, with Benjamin determined not to let go of his briefcase, heavy with his final manuscript. But when he and his companions arrived in Portbou they were told by the Spanish authorities that they were no longer allowed into Spain. Benjamin was trapped on the frontier unable to go forward or back, in total despair. He committed suicide that night with a large quantity of morphine.

The memorial sculpture to him outside the cemetery where he is buried in Portbou is remarkable; a rusted metal chute descends from the cliff down to the sea, pink against the blue of the water. In the glass frame at the bottom of the chute you can see white waves pounding threateningly, and as you walk down the steps within the chute it is as if you are plunging to certain death. And yet as you descend, an inexplicable feeling of joy, powerful and uplifting, rises in you, along with an irrepressible sense of hope.

18

Finding the treasure

Late one summer morning I rose before the sun, to benefit from the cool of the morning before the heat intensified. The sun gilded the hills to each side of the monastery. A cock at the *ferme auberge* crowed a reveille. Through the still air the bells of Campôme ringing the hour reached my ears. I liked the idea that these last weeks of summer were traditionally celebrated as the most fruitful time of year. As I did my yoga salutations in the garden the brightness increased behind me, illuminating our magic kingdom. Miles had knocked out the rubble in the little lancet window in the apse so it was open to the light, but I was still waiting for the morning when the sun as it rose would shine directly into the chapel, still wondering where it would strike. Waiting to discover the treasure.

I had a bowl of small white peaches on my desk, just ripened, flushed pink and yellow, sweet and fragrant. Now they are our peaches. We left about a dozen trees when the rest were uprooted last year. We did nothing to them: no chemical-spraying, no watering, not even pruning. At first they seemed to be dying, the leaves shrivelled up. But then they produced fruit, small and unpromising. We didn't select and nurture the best as the farmers would have done. We just left them all. Slowly they grew, and finally ripened. Theo climbed each tree to pick them and handed them down to Miles and we had several basketsful to be made into jam and pickles or given away to friends. I liked these peaches; they were much smaller than they used to be, and they were marked where the leaves had shadowed them from the sun, or where they had rested against a branch. There was a beauty in their imperfections.

One day in the spring Theo and I went to collect kindling from the field where Hans had stacked it after clearing the river bank. Theo strolled along swinging the small axe, which he had been eyeing for some time. I was nervous to see him with it but reasoned that in some societies he would be responsible for wood supplies by his age. He says he wants to stay here for ever and I am glad he loves the place so much. But I hope he will be an adventurer too. He is such a sprite, imaginative and creative, open and loving, but self-sufficient already in so many ways.

I began splitting logs with a big axe. Polly had finally insisted on teaching me to do it myself. I told her about the *t'ai chi* of the axe swing, that I needed to utilize the weight of the axe to do the work, but I still couldn't do it, reluctantly accepting that perhaps I simply was not strong enough, or I needed to do decades of *t'ai chi* before I could put the principle into practice.

She showed me how I must position my body, at arm's length from the log, heft the axe with one hand at the end, the other steadying it in the middle, then swing it half up, slide the other hand down to the end and raise it grasped firmly with both hands, high above my head. She had demonstrated in one graceful movement, coming right down to a crouch as she hit the log and cleaved it in two. I tried again, still fearful of lifting the heavy iron tool aloft.

Then as I raised the axe over my head again, I discovered I did know this movement well. I had been stretching my arms above my head like that for twenty years as part of my yoga salutations. Deep long breath, hands in prayer position in front of my chest, then lift arms up to the sky, stretch with the whole body, feeling the stomach muscles pull and straighten, the back and shoulders stretch, the calves tighten, and then bring arms over and down to touch my toes. I already knew the yoga of the axe swing.

That day with Theo in the field it was warm, sunny, with a slight breeze, the air crystalline, Canigou etched blue against the sky. I sat down cross-legged in the middle of the field and shut my eyes. I could feel the warm wind on my face, hear the branches tossing, the river rushing over stones, the birds singing, the cowbells. I could smell the trees. It was sublime, a single brief moment of paradise.

Dusk was gathering as we climbed back up the hill from the river, carrying baskets of wood. The first evening star had already appeared. Our monks would have been preparing for vespers, the lighting of the lamps, the evening prayers: the word vespers comes from the Greek *Hesperus*, the evening star. Theo and I stopped to make a wish on the star. I wished to be able to stay here, to rebuild the cloisters and restore the frescos, to become Romarin, to dance by moonlight, sing old songs, play the flute, gather wild herbs and learn ancient Greek.

Now I know the treasure has been there all along. You just have to find it, like Xavier and the silver coin, the smell of the walnut tree, the hazel grove by the river, the field full of mushrooms, the original frescos hidden under layers of plaster. There was the first moment of song in the chapel, the sound of the human voice rising again in a space designed for the purpose, designed for the endless reverberation of sound, of praise, of joy. As the soprano began with 'Ave Maria', her voice soared up to the vault, filling the entire space till my skin tingled and the tears flowed. I didn't think of the monks then. This was something new. Giving thanks, meditating on beauty, with music and art instead of religion. And with an audience of so many nationalities, listening to songs in French, German, Spanish and English. The songs followed a seasonal theme and at the mention of swallows the very birds came in on cue, flying through the open windows high in the walls and wheeling round the apse beneath the fresco.

I am often reminded of my brother, the moments he described in his journals, my envy of his ability to seize the moment. One day shortly after we moved into the restored west wing, Miles and I were hanging pictures of family and friends on a wall of sandy-textured mortar and stones. Miles paused over a picture of Simon. I had asked for it many years ago when Simon first told me he was gay, and I had always cherished the eccentric romanticism of it, before he knew he had Aids or before we bought a monastery. It is a picture of him celebrating mass in the ruined stone chapel on the island of Bardsey. He is dressed in a long white robe, over it a white chasuble and scarf edged in red. Behind him is a wall of rough granite stones, and an altar of slate is covered in a white linen cloth, prevented from blowing away in the wind by pebbles neatly placed at each corner. Above it is a single candle and a small vase of red and yellow flowers. 'He looks like one of our monks,' said Miles.

At last I felt Simon's presence at Corbiac, although he never came here. Like the quotation that sustained me as I mourned, 'You only die when you fail to take root in others,' he had taken root in me, and I had begun to take root here.

But even if we leave, the building will endure. And perhaps as Simon came to accept death, prepared himself to give everything up, I too needed to get to a place where the experience itself was of such value that it would always be part of me; that it didn't matter whether or not I was physically here, I could carry it in my heart. Perhaps it is only when you feel ready to relinquish everything, as the monks were, can you fully enter into the moment.

A SELECTED LIST OF FINE WRITING
AVAILABLE FROM TRANSWORLD

THE PRICES SHOWN BELOW WERE CORRECT AT THE TIME OF GOING TO PRESS.
HOWEVER TRANSWORLD PUBLISHERS RESERVE THE RIGHT TO SHOW NEW RETAIL
PRICES ON COVERS WHICH MAY DIFFER FROM THOSE PREVIOUSLY ADVERTISED IN THE
TEXT OR ELSEWHERE.

99600	9	NOTES FROM A SMALL ISLAND	*Bill Bryson*	£7.99
99786	2	NOTES FROM A BIG COUNTRY	*Bill Bryson*	£7.99
99702	1	A WALK IN THE WOODS	*Bill Bryson*	£7.99
99808	7	THE LOST CONTINENT	*Bill Bryson*	£7.99
99805	2	MADE IN AMERICA	*Bill Bryson*	£7.99
99806	0	NEITHER HERE NOR THERE	*Bill Bryson*	£7.99
99703	X	DOWN UNDER	*Bill Bryson*	£7.99
99858	3	PERFUME FROM PROVENCE	*Lady Fortescue*	£7.99
81424	9	KITE STRINGS OF THE SOUTHERN CROSS		
			Laurie Gough	£6.99
14681	1	CASTAWAY	*Lucy Irvine*	£6.99
14680	3	FARAWAY	*Lucy Irvine*	£7.99
14595	5	BETWEEN EXTREMES	*Brian Keenan and*	
			John McCarthy	£7.99
99841	9	NOTES FROM AN ITALIAN GARDEN		
			Joan Marble	£7.99
50667	6	UNDER THE TUSCAN SUN	*Frances Mayes*	£6.99
81250	5	BELLA TUSCANY	*Frances Mayes*	£6.99
81448	6	TAKE ME WITH YOU	*Brad Newsham*	£6.99
99852	4	THE ELUSIVE TRUFFLE:	*Mirabel Osler*	£6.99
		Travels in Search of the Legendary Food of France		

Transworld titles are available by post from:

Bookpost, PO Box 29, Douglas, Isle of Man, IM99 1BQ

Credit cards accepted. Please telephone 01624 836000
fax 01624 837033, Internet http://www.bookpost.co.uk
or e-mail: bookshop@enterprise.net for details

Free postage and packing in the UK. Overseas customers: allow £1 per book
(paperbacks) and £3 per book (hardbacks)